U·X·L Encyclopedia of World Mythology

VOLUME 3: G–L

U·X·L Encyclopedia of World Mythology

VOLUME 3: G–L

U·X·L
A part of Gale, Cengage Learning

GALE
CENGAGE Learning™

Detroit • New York • San Francisco • New Haven, Conn • Waterville, Maine • London

U·X·L Encyclopedia of World Mythology

Product manager: Meggin Condino

Project editor: Rebecca Parks

Editorial: Jennifer Stock, Kim Hunt

Rights Acquisition and Management: Kelly A. Quin, Scott Bragg, Aja Perales

Composition: Evi Abou-El-Seoud

Manufacturing: Rita Wimberley

Imaging: Lezlie Light

Product Design: Jennifer Wahi

© 2009 Gale, Cengage Learning

For product information and technology assistance, contact us at Gale Customer Support, 1-800-877-4253.
For permission to use material from this text or product, submit all requests online at cengage.com/permissions. Further permissions questions can be emailed to permissionrequest@cengage.com.

Cover photographs reproduced by permission of Purestock/Getty Images (picture of Statue of Poseidon); Voon Poh Le/Dreamstime.com (drawing of paper cut dragon); Werner Forman/Art Resource, NY (picture of an incense burner of a sun god); Charles Walker/Topfoto/The Image Works (photo of a papyrus drawing of Anubis weighing the heart); and The Art Archive/Richard Wagner/Museum Bayreuth/Gianni Dagli Orti (photo of a drawing of a valkyrie).

While every effort has been made to ensure the reliability of the information presented in this publication, Gale, a part of Cengage Learning, does not guarantee the accuracy of the data contained herein. Gale accepts no payment for listing; and inclusion in the publication of any organization, agency, institution, publication, service, or individual does not imply endorsement of the editors or publisher. Errors brought to the attention of the publisher and verified to the satisfaction of the publisher will be corrected in future editions.

LIBRARY OF CONGRESS CATALOGING-IN-PUBLICATION DATA

U*X*L encyclopedia of world mythology
    p. cm.
    Includes bibliographical references and index.
    ISBN 978-1-4144-3030-0 (set) -- ISBN 978-1-4144-3036-2 (vol. 1) -- ISBN 978-1-4144-3037-9 (vol. 2) -- ISBN 978-1-4144-3038-6 (vol. 3) -- ISBN 978-1-4144-3039-3 (vol. 4) -- ISBN 978-1-4144-3040-9 (vol. 5)
    1. Mythology—Encyclopedias, Juvenile. I. Title: UXL encyclopedia of world mythology. II. Title: Encyclopedia of world mythology.

BL303.U95 2009
201'.303—dc22   2008012696

Gale
27500 Drake
Farmington Hills, MI 48331-3535

ISBN-13: 978-1-4144-3030-0 (set)   ISBN-10: 1-4144-3030-2 (set)
ISBN-13: 978-1-4144-3036-2 (Vol. 1)   ISBN-10: 1-4144-3036-1 (Vol. 1)
ISBN-13: 978-1-4144-3037-9 (Vol. 2)   ISBN-10: 1-4144-3037-X (Vol. 2)
ISBN-13: 978-1-4144-3038-6 (Vol. 3)   ISBN-10: 1-4144-3038-8 (Vol. 3)
ISBN-13: 978-1-4144-3039-3 (Vol. 4)   ISBN-10: 1-4144-3039-6 (Vol. 4)
ISBN-13: 978-1-4144-3040-9 (Vol. 5)   ISBN-10: 1-4144-3040-X (Vol. 5)

This title is also available as an e-book.
ISBN-13: 978-1-4144-3846-7 ISBN-10: 1-4144-3846-X
Contact your Gale, a part of Cengage Learning sales representative for ordering information.

Printed in the United States of America
1 2 3 4 5 6 7 12 11 10 09 08

Table of Contents

Table of Contents by Culture

Reader's Guide

The *U·X·L Encyclopedia of World Mythology* examines the major characters, stories, and themes of mythologies from cultures around the globe, from African to Zoroastrian. Arranged alphabetically in an A–Z format, each entry provides the reader with an overview of the topic as well as contextual analysis to explain the topic's importance to the culture from which it came. In addition, each entry explains the topic's influence on modern life, and prompts the reader with a discussion question or reading/writing suggestion to inspire further analysis. There are five different types of entries: Character, Deity, Myth, Theme, and Culture. The entry types are designated by icons that are shown in a legend that appears on each page starting a new letter grouping so that you can easily tell which type of entry you are reading.

Types of Entries Found in This Book

Character entries generally focus on a single mythical character, such as a hero. In some cases, character entries deal with groups of similar or related beings—for example, Trolls or Valkyries. Deities (gods) are found in their own unique type of entry.

Deity entries contain information about a god or goddess. An example would be Zeus (pronounced ZOOS), the leader of the ancient Greek gods. Deities are very similar to other mythical characters, except that they often appear in many different myths; each Deity entry provides a summary of the most important myths related to that deity.

Myth entries focus on a specific story as opposed to a certain character. One example is the entry on the Holy Grail, which tells the legend of the vessel's origins as well as the many people who sought to locate it. In some cases, the myth is primarily concerned with a single character; the entry on the Golden Fleece, for example, features Jason as the main character. Like the Holy Grail entry, however, this entry focuses on the legends surrounding the object in question rather than the character involved.

Theme entries examine how one single theme, idea, or motif is addressed in the mythologies of different cultures. An example would be the Reincarnation entry that examines different cultural depictions of this eternal cycle of death and rebirth.

Culture entries contain a survey of the myths and beliefs of a particular culture. Each entry also provides historical and cultural context for understanding how the culture helped to shape, or was shaped by, the beliefs of other cultures.

Types of Rubrics Found in This Book

Each entry type is organized in specific rubrics to allow for ease of comparison across entries. The rubrics that appear in these entries are: *Character/Myth/Theme Overview*; *Core Deities and Characters*; *Major Myths*; *[Subject] in Context*; *Key Themes and Symbols*; *[Subject] in Art, Literature, and Everyday Life*; and *Read, Write, Think, Discuss*. In addition, the character, deity, and myth entries all have key facts sections in the margins that provide basic information about the entry, including the country or culture of origin, a pronunciation guide where necessary, alternate names for the character (when applicable), written or other sources in which the subject appears, and information on the character's family (when applicable).

Character Overview offers detailed information about the character's place within the mythology of its given culture. This may include information about the character's personality, summaries of notable feats, and relationships with other mythological characters. *Myth Overview* includes a summary of the myth being discussed. *Theme Overview* provides a brief description of the theme being discussed, as well as a rundown of the major points common when examining that theme in different mythologies.

Core Deities and Characters includes brief descriptions of the main deities and other characters that figure prominently in the given culture's mythology. This is not a comprehensive list of all the gods or characters mentioned in a particular culture.

Major Myths features a brief summary of all the most important or best-known myths related to the subject of the entry. For example, the entry on Odin (pronounced OH-din), chief god of Norse mythology, includes the tale describing how he gave up one of his eyes in order to be able to see the future.

[Subject] in Context provides additional cultural and historical information that helps you understand the subject by seeing through the eyes of the people who made it part of their culture. The entry on the weaver Arachne (pronounced uh-RAK-nee), for instance, includes information on the importance of weaving as a domestic duty in ancient Greece.

Key Themes and Symbols outlines the most important themes in the tales related to the subject. This section also includes explanations of symbols associated with the subject of the entry, or which appear in myths related to the subject. For example, this section may explain the meaning of certain objects a god is usually shown carrying.

[Subject] in Art, Literature, and Everyday Life includes references to the subject in well-known works of art, literature, film, and other media. This section may also mention other ways in which the subject appears in popular culture. For example, the fact that a leprechaun (pronounced LEP-ruh-kawn) appears as the mascot for Lucky Charms cereal is mentioned in this section of the Leprechauns entry.

Read, Write, Think, Discuss uses the material in the entry as a springboard for further discussion and learning. This section may include suggestions for further reading that are related to the subject of the entry, discussion questions regarding topics touched upon in the entry, writing prompts that explore related issues and themes, or research prompts that encourage you to delve deeper into the topics presented.

Most of the entries end with cross-references that point you to related entries in the encyclopedia. In addition, words that appear in bold within the entry are also related entries, making it easy to find additional information that will enhance your understanding of the topic.

Other Sections in This Book

This encyclopedia also contains other sections that you may find useful when studying world mythology. One of these is a "Timeline of World Mythology," which provides important dates from many cultures that are important to the development of their respective mythologies. A glossary in the front matter supplements the definitions that are included within the entries. Teachers will find the section on "Research and Activity Ideas" helpful in coming up with classroom activities related to the topic of mythology to engage students further in the subject. A section titled "Where to Learn More" provides you with other sources to learn more about the topic of mythology, organized by culture. You will also encounter sidebars in many of the entries; these sections offer interesting information that is related to, but not essential to, your understanding of the subject of the entry.

Comments and Suggestions

We welcome your comments on the *U·X·L Encyclopedia of World Mythology* and suggestions for other topics to consider. Please write to Editors, *U·X·L Encyclopedia of World Mythology,* Gale, 27500 Drake Rd., Farmington Hills, Michigan, 48331-3535.

Introduction

On the surface, myths are stories of gods, heroes, and monsters that can include fanciful tales about the creation and destruction of worlds, or awe-inspiring adventures of brave explorers in exotic or supernatural places. However, myths are not just random imaginings; they are cultivated and shaped by the cultures in which they arise. For this reason, a myth can function as a mirror for the culture that created it, reflecting the values, geographic location, natural resources, technological state, and social organization of the people who believe in it.

Values

The values of a culture are often revealed through that culture's myths and legends. For example, a myth common in Micronesian culture tells of a porpoise girl who married a human and had children; after living many years as a human, she decided to return to the sea. Before she left, she warned her children against eating porpoise, since they might unknowingly eat some of their own family members by doing so. Myths such as these are often used to provide colorful reasons for taboos, or rules against certain behaviors. In this case, the myth explains a taboo among the Micronesian peoples against hunting and eating porpoises.

Geography

Myths often reflect a culture's geographic circumstances. For example, the people of the Norse culture live in a region that has harsh, icy winters. It is no coincidence that, according to their myths, the being whose death led to the creation of the world was a giant made of frost. By contrast, the people of ancient Egypt lived in an dry, sunny land; their most important gods, such as Ra, were closely associated with the sun. Geographic features are also often part of a culture's myths, or used as inspiration for mythological tales. Spider Rock, a tall peak located at Canyon de Chelly National Monument in Arizona, is said by the Hopi people to be the home of the creation goddess Spider Woman. The Atlas mountains in northern Africa took their name from the myth that the Titan Atlas (pronounced AT-luhs) had once stood there holding up the heavens, but had been transformed to stone in order to make his task easier.

Natural Resources

Myths can also reflect the natural resources available to a culture, or the resources most prized by a certain group. In Mesoamerican and American Indian myths, maize (commonly referred to as corn) often appears as a food offered directly from gods or goddesses, or grown from the body of a deity. This reflects not only the importance of maize in the diets of early North and Central American cultures, but also the ready availability of maize, which does not appear as a native plant anywhere else in the world. Similarly, the olive tree, which is native to the coastal areas along the Mediterranean Sea, is one of the most important trees in ancient Greek myth. The city of Athens, it is said, was named for the goddess Athena (pronounced uh-THEE-nuh) after she gave its citizens the very first domesticated olive tree.

Sometimes, myths can reflect the importance of natural resources to an outside culture. For example, the Muisca people of what is now Colombia engaged in a ceremony in which their king covered himself in gold dust and took a raft out to the middle of a local lake; there he threw gold trinkets into the water as offerings to the gods. Gold was not commonly available, and was prized for its ceremonial significance; however, when Spanish explorers arrived in the New World and heard of this practice, they interpreted this to mean that gold must be commonplace in the area. This led to the myth of El Dorado, an entire city made of gold that many Spanish explorers believed to exist and spent decades trying to locate.

Technology

A culture's state of technological development can also be reflected in its myths. The earliest ancient Greek myths of Uranus (pronounced

YOOR-uh-nuhs) state that his son Cronus (pronounced KROH-nuhs) attacked him with a sickle made of obsidian. Obsidian is a stone that can be chipped to create a sharp edge, and was used by cultures older than the ancient Greeks, who relied on metals such as bronze and steel for their weapons. This might suggest that the myth arose from an earlier age; at the very least, it reflects the idea that, from the perspective of the Greeks, the myth took place in the distant past.

Social Order

Myths can also offer a snapshot of a culture's social organization. The Old Testament tale of the Tower of Babel offers an explanation for the many tribes found in the ancient Near East: they had once been united, and sought to build a tower that would reach all the way to heaven. In order to stop this act of self-importance, God caused the people to speak in different languages. Unable to understand each other, they abandoned the ambitious project and scattered into groups across the region.

Besides offering social order, myths can reinforce cultural views on the roles different types of individuals should assume in a society. The myth of Arachne (pronounced uh-RAK-nee) illustrates a fact known from other historical sources: weaving and fabric-making was the domestic duty of wives and daughters, and it was a skill highly prized in the homes of ancient Greece. Tales of characters such as Danaë (pronounced DAN-uh-ee), who was imprisoned in a tower by her father in order to prevent her from having a child, indicate the relative powerlessness of many women in ancient Greek society.

Different Cultures, Different Perspectives

To see how cultures reflect their own unique characteristics through myth, one can examine how a single theme—such as fertility—is treated in a variety of different cultures. Fertility is the ability to produce life, growth, or offspring, and is therefore common in most, if not all, mythologies. For many cultures, fertility is a key element in the creation of the world. The egg, one of the most common symbols of fertility, appears in Chinese mythology as the first object to form from the disorder that previously existed in place of the world. In many cultures, including ancient Greece, the main gods are born from a single mother;

in the case of the Greeks, the mother is Gaia (pronounced GAY-uh), also known as Earth.

For cultures that relied upon agriculture, fertility was an important element of the changing seasons and the growth of crops. In these cases, fertility was seen as a gift from nature that could be revoked by cruel weather or the actions of the gods. Such is the case in the ancient Greek myth of Persephone (pronounced per-SEF-uh-nee); when the goddess is taken to the underworld by Hades (pronounced HAY-deez), her mother—the fertility goddess Demeter (pronounced di-MEE-ter)—became sad, which caused all vegetation to wither and die.

For the ancient Egyptians, fertility represented not just crop growth and human birth, but also rebirth into the afterlife through death. This explains why Hathor (pronounced HATH-or), the mother goddess of fertility who supported all life, was also the maintainer of the dead. It was believed that Hathor provided food for the dead to help them make the long journey to the realm of the afterlife.

For early Semitic cultures, the notion of fertility was not always positive. In the story of Lilith, the little-known first wife of Adam (the first man), the independent-minded woman left her husband and went to live by the Red Sea, where she gave birth to many demons each day. The myth seems to suggest that fertility is a power that can be used for good or evil, and that the key to using this power positively is for wives to dutifully respect the wishes of their husbands. This same theme is found in the earlier Babylonian myth of Tiamat (pronounced TYAH-maht), who gave birth to not only the gods but also to an army of monsters that fought to defend her from her son, the hero Marduk (pronounced MAHR-dook).

These are just a few of the many ways in which different cultures can take a single idea and interpret it through their own tales. Rest assured that the myths discussed in this book are wondrous legends that capture the imagination of the reader. They are also mirrors in which we can see not only ourselves, but the reflections of cultures old and new, far and near—allowing us to celebrate their unique differences, and at the same time recognize those common elements that make these enchanting stories universally beloved and appreciated by readers and students around the world.

Timeline of World Mythology

c. 3400 BCE Early Sumerian writing is first developed.

c. 3100 BCE Egyptian writing, commonly known as hieroglyphics, is first developed.

c. 2852–2205 BCE During this time period, China is supposedly ruled by the Three Sovereigns and Five Emperors, mythical figures that may have been based on actual historical leaders.

c. 2100 BCE Earliest known version of the *Epic of Gilgamesh* is recorded in Sumerian.

c. 1553–1536 BCE Egyptian pharaoh Akhenaten establishes official worship of Aten, a single supreme god, instead of the usual group of gods recognized by ancient Egyptians.

c. 1250 BCE The Trojan War supposedly occurs around this time period. Despite the war's importance to Greek and Roman mythology, modern scholars are not sure whether the war was an actual historical event or just a myth.

c. 1100 BCE The Babylonian creation epic *Enuma Elish* is documented on clay tablets discovered nearly three thousand years later in the ruined library of Ashurbanipal, located in modern-day Iraq.

c. 800 BCE The Greek alphabet is invented, leading to a flowering of Greek literature based on myth.

c. 750 BCE The Greek epics known as the *Iliad* and the *Odyssey* are written by the poet Homer. Based on the events surrounding the

Trojan War, these two stories are the source of many myths and characters in Greek and Roman mythology.

c. 750 BCE The Greek poet Hesiod writes his *Theogony*, which details the origins of the Greek gods.

c. 563–480 BCE According to tradition, Gautama Buddha, the founder of Buddhism, is believed to have lived in ancient India and Nepal during this time.

525–456 BCE The Greek dramatist Aeschylus writes tragedies detailing the lives of mythical characters, including *Seven Against Thebes*, *Agamemnon*, and *The Eumenides*.

c. 500–100 BCE The oldest version of the *Ramayana*, the Hindu epic about the incarnation of the god Vishnu named Rama, is written.

c. 496–406 BCE Ancient Greek playwright Sophocles creates classic plays such as *Antigone* and *Oedipus the King*.

c. 450 BCE The Book of Genesis, containing stories fundamental to early Christianity, Judaism, and Islam, is collected and organized into its modern form.

c. 431 BCE Greek builders complete work on the temple of Athena known as the Parthenon, one of the few ancient Greek structures to survive to modern times.

c. 150–50 BCE The Gundestrup cauldron, a silver bowl depicting various Celtic deities and rituals, is created. The bowl is later recovered from a peat bog in Denmark in 1891.

c. 29–19 BCE Roman poet Virgil creates his mythical epic, the *Aeneid*, detailing the founding of Rome.

c. 4 BCE–33 CE Jesus, believed by Christians to be the son of God, supposedly lives during this time period.

c. 8 CE Roman poet Ovid completes his epic work *Metamorphoses*. It is one of the best existing sources for tales of ancient Greek and Roman mythology.

c. 100 CE The *Mahabharata*, a massive epic recognized as one of the most important pieces of literature in Hinduism, is organized into its modern form from source material dating back as far as the ninth century BCE.

c. 570–632 CE The prophet Muhammad, founder of Islam, supposedly lives during this time.

c. 800–840 CE The oldest surviving remnants of *The Book of One Thousand and One Nights*, a collection of Near Eastern folktales and legends, are written in Syrian.

c. 1000 CE The Ramsund carving, a stone artifact bearing an illustration of the tale of Sigurd, is created in Sweden. The tale is documented in the *Volsunga* saga.

c. 1010 CE The oldest surviving manuscript of the Old English epic *Beowulf* is written. It is recognized as the first significant work of English literature.

c. 1100 Monks at the Clonmacnoise monastery compile the *Book of the Dun Cow*, the earliest written collection of Irish myths and legends still in existence.

c. 1138 Geoffrey of Monmouth's *History of the Kings of Britain* is published, featuring the first well-known tales of the legendary King Arthur.

c. 1180–1210 The *Nibelungenlied*, a German epic based largely on earlier German and Norse legends such as the *Volsunga* saga, is written by an unknown poet.

c. 1220 Icelandic scholar Snorri Sturluson writes the Prose Edda, a comprehensive collection of Norse myths and legends gathered from older sources.

c. 1350 The *White Book of Rhydderch*, containing most of the Welsh myths and legends later gathered in the *Mabinogion*, first appears.

1485 Thomas Malory publishes *Le Morte D'Arthur*, widely considered to be the most authoritative version of the legend of King Arthur.

c. 1489 *A Lytell Geste of Robin Hode*, one of the most comprehensive versions of the life of the legendary British character of Robin Hood, is published.

c. 1550 The *Popol Vuh*, a codex containing Mayan creation myths and legends, is written. The book, written in the Quiché language but using Latin characters, was likely based on an older book written in Mayan hieroglyphics that has since been lost.

1835 Elias Lonnrot publishes the *Kalevala*, an epic made up of Finnish songs and oral myths gathered during years of field research.

1849 Archeologist Henry Layard discovers clay tablets containing the Babylonian creation epic *Enuma Elish* in Iraq. The epic, lost for centuries, is unknown to modern scholars before this discovery.

1880 Journalist Joel Chandler Harris publishes *Uncle Remus, His Songs and Sayings: the Folk-Lore of the Old Plantation*, a collection of myths and folktales gathered from African American slaves working in the South. Many of the tales are derived from older stories from African myth. Although the book is successful and spawns three sequels, Harris is accused by some of taking cultural myths and passing them off as his own works.

Words to Know

benevolent: Helpful or well-meaning.

caste: A social level in India's complex social class system.

cauldron: Kettle.

chaos: Disorder.

chivalry: A moral code popularized in Europe in the Middle Ages that stressed such traits as generosity, bravery, courtesy, and respect toward women.

constellation: Group of stars.

cosmogony: The study of, or a theory about, the origin of the universe.

deity: God or goddess.

demigod: Person with one parent who was human and one parent who was a god.

destiny: Predetermined future.

divination: Predicting the future.

dualistic: Having two sides or a double nature.

epic: A long, grand-scale poem.

fertility: The ability to reproduce; can refer to human ability to produce children or the ability of the earth to sustain plant life.

hierarchy: Ranked order of importance.

hubris: Too much self-confidence.

immortal: Living forever.

imperial: Royal, or related to an empire.

indigenous: Native to a given area.

Judeo-Christian: Related to the religious tradition shared by Judaism and Christianity. The faiths share a holy book, many fundamental principles, and a belief in a single, all-powerful god.

matriarchal: Female-dominated. Often refers to societies in which a family's name and property are passed down through the mother's side of the family.

mediator: A go-between.

monotheism: The belief in a single god as opposed to many gods.

mummification: The drying and preserving of a body to keep it from rotting after death.

nymph: A female nature deity.

omen: A mystical sign of an event to come.

oracle: Person through whom the gods communicated with humans.

pagan: Someone who worships pre-Christian gods.

pantheon: The entire collection of gods recognized by a group of people.

patriarchal: Male-dominated. Often refers to societies in which the family name and wealth are passed through the father.

patron: A protector or supporter.

pharaoh: A king of ancient Egypt.

polytheism: Belief in many gods.

primal: Fundamental; existing since the beginning.

prophet: A person able to see the plans of the gods or foretell future events.

pyre: A large pile of burning wood used in some cultures to cremate a dead body.

resurrected: Brought back to life.

revelation: The communication of divine truth or divine will to human beings.

rune: A character from an ancient and magical alphabet.

seer: A person who can see the future.

shaman: A person who uses magic to heal or look after the members of his tribe.

sorcerer: Wizard.

syncretism: The blending or fusion of different religions or belief systems.

tradition: A time-honored practice, or set of such practices.

underworld: Land of the dead.

utopia: A place of social, economic and political perfection.

Research and Activity Ideas

Teachers wishing to enrich their students' understanding of world mythologies might try some of the following group activities. Each uses art, music, drama, speech, research, or scientific experimentation to put the students in closer contact with the cultures, myths, and figures they are studying.

Greek Mythology: A Pageant of Gods

In this activity, students get to be gods and goddesses for a day during the classroom "Pageant of the Gods," an event modeled after a beauty pageant. Each student selects (with teacher approval) a deity from Greek mythology. Students then research their deity, write a 250-word description of the deity, and create costumes so they can dress as their deity. On the day of the pageant, the teacher collects the students' descriptions and reads them aloud as each student models his or her costume for the class.

Materials required for the students:

Common household materials for costume

Materials required for the teacher:

None

Optional extension: The class throws a post-pageant potluck of Greek food.

Anglo-Saxon Mythology: Old English Translation

Students are often surprised to learn that *Beowulf* is written in English. The original Old English text looks almost unrecognizable to them. In this activity (which students may work on in the classroom, in the library, or at home), the teacher begins by discussing the history of the English language and its evolution over the past one thousand years (since the writing of *Beowulf*). The teacher then models how a linguist would go about translating something written in Old English or Middle English (using an accessible text such as *The Canterbury Tales* as an example), and makes various resources for translation available to the students (see below). The class as a whole works on translating the first two lines of *Beowulf*. The teacher then assigns small groups of students a couple lines each of the opening section of *Beowulf* to translate and gloss. When each group is ready with their translations, the students assemble the modern English version of the opening of *Beowulf* and discuss what they learned about the various Old English words they studied.

Materials required for the students:

None

Materials required for the teacher:

Copies of an Old English version of the first part of *Beowulf* for distribution to students.

There are multiple Old English dictionaries available online, so student groups could work on this activity in the classroom if a sufficient number of computer workstations with Internet access are available. There are also many Old English dictionaries in print form. If none is available in the school library, some can be checked out from the public library.

Egyptian Mythology: Mummify a Chicken

The ancient Egyptians believed preserving a person's body ensured their safe passage into the afterlife. The process of Egyptian mummification was a secret for many centuries until ancient Greek historian Herodotus recorded some information about the process in the fifth century BCE. Archaeologists have recently refined their understanding of Egyptian mummification practices. In this activity, students conduct their own mummification experiment on chickens.

The teacher contextualizes the activity by showing students a video on mummies and asking them to read both Herodotus's account of mummification and more recent articles about mummification that center on the research of Egyptologist Bob Brier.

Once students understand the basics of mummification, groups of five or six students can begin their science experiment, outlined below. The teacher should preface the experiment with safety guidelines for handling raw chicken.

Materials required for students:

Scale

One fresh chicken per group (bone-in chicken breast or leg may substitute)

Disposable plastic gloves (available at drugstores)

Carton of salt per group per week

Spice mixture (any strong powdered spices will do; powdered cloves, cinnamon, and ginger are good choices)

Extra-large (gallon size) air-tight freezer bags

Roll of gauze per group (available at drugstore)

Disposable aluminum trays for holding chickens

Cooking oil

Notebook for each group

Materials required for the teacher:

Video on mummies. A good option is: *Mummies: Secrets of the Pharaohs* (2007), available on DVD.

Reading material on mummies, including Herodotus's account. See: http://discovermagazine.com/2007/oct/mummification-is-back-from-the-dead; http://www.nationalgeographic.com/tv/mummy/; http://www.mummytombs.com/egypt/herodotus.htm

Plenty of paper towels and hand soap.

Procedure

1. All students put on plastic gloves.

2. Weigh each chicken (unnecessary if weight printed on packaging) and record the weight in a notebook. Record details of the chicken's appearance in the notebook.

3. Remove chicken organs and dispose of them. Rinse the chicken thoroughly in a sink.

4. Pat the chicken dry with paper towels. Make sure the chicken is completely dry, or the mummification process might not work.

5. Rub the spices all over the chicken, both inside and outside, then salt the entire chicken and fill the chicken cavity with salt.

6. Seal the chicken in the air-tight bag and place it in the aluminum tray.

7. Remove gloves and wash hands thoroughly with soap and water.

8. Once a week, put on plastic gloves, remove the chicken from the bag, dispose of the bag and accumulated liquid, and weigh the chicken. Record the weight in a notebook and make notes on changes in the chicken's appearance. Respice and resalt the chicken, fill the chicken cavity with salt, and seal it in a new bag. Remove gloves and wash hands. Repeat this step until no more liquid drains from the chicken.

9. When liquid no longer drains from the chicken, the mummy is done! Wipe off all the salt and rub a light coat of cooking oil on the mummy. Wrap it tightly in gauze.

Optional extension: Students can decorate their mummies using hieroglyphics and build shoebox sarcophagi for them.

Near Eastern Mythology: Gilgamesh and the Cedar Forest

The story of Gilgamesh's heroics against the demon Humbaba of the Cedar Forest is one of the most exciting parts of the *Epic of Gilgamesh*. In this activity, students write, stage, and perform a three-act play based on this part of the epic. Necessary tasks will include writing, costume design, set design, and acting. The teacher can divide tasks among students as necessary.

Materials required for the students:

Household items for costumes

Cardboard, paint, tape, and other materials for sets

Copy of the *Epic of Gilgamesh*

Materials required for the teacher:

None

Hindu Mythology: Salute the Sun

The practice of yoga, an ancient mental and physical discipline designed to promote spiritual perfection, is mentioned in most of the Hindu holy texts. Today, the physical aspects of yoga have become a widely popular form of exercise around the world. In this activity, the students and teacher will make yoga poses part of their own daily routine.

The teacher introduces the activity by discussing the history of yoga from ancient to modern times, by showing a video on the history of yoga, and by distributing readings from ancient Hindu texts dealing with the practice of yoga. After a class discussion on the video and texts, the teacher leads students through a basic "sun salutation" series of poses with the aid of an instructional yoga video (students may wish to bring a towel or mat from home, as some parts of the sun salutation involve getting on the floor). Students and the teacher will perform the sun salutation every day, preferably at the beginning of class, either for the duration of the semester or for another set period of time. Students will conclude the activity by writing a summary of their feelings about their yoga "experiment."

Materials required for the students:

Towel or mat to put on floor during sun salutations.

Materials required for teacher:

A DVD on the history of yoga. Recommended: *Yoga Unveiled* (2004), an excellent documentary series on the history of yoga.

An instructional yoga video that includes the "sun salutation" sequence (many available).

Handouts of ancient Indian writings on yoga. See *The Shambhala Encyclopedia of Yoga* (2000) and *The Yoga and the Bhagavad Gita* (2007).

African Mythology: Storytelling

Anansi the Spider was a trickster god of West African origin who was known as a master storyteller. In this activity, students work on their own storytelling skills while learning about the spread of Anansi stories from Africa to the Americas.

The teacher begins this activity by discussing the ways that oral traditions have helped the African American community preserve some part of their West African cultural heritage. The spread of stories about Anansi around Caribbean and American slave communities is an example, with the Uncle Remus stories of Joel Chandler Harris being a good demonstration of how the Anansi tales have evolved. The class then conducts a preliminary discussion about what the elements of a good spoken story might be, then watches or listens to models of storytelling. After listening to the stories, the class discusses common elements in the stories and techniques the storytellers used to keep the audience's attention and build interest.

Students then read a variety of Anansi and Uncle Remus stories on their own. With teacher approval, they select one story and prepare it for oral presentation in class (several students may select the same story). After the presentations, students can discuss their reactions to the various oral presentations, pointing out what was effective and ineffective.

Materials required for the students:

Optional: props for story presentation

Materials required for the teacher:

Background reading on West African oral traditions.

Recordings or videos of skilled storytellers. See *The American Storyteller Series* or the CD recording *Tell Me a Story: Timeless Folktales from Around the World* (which includes an Anansi story).

Optional extension: The teacher may arrange for students with especially strong oral presentations to share their stories at a school assembly or as visiting speakers in another classroom.

Micronesian and Melanesian Mythology: Island Hopping

The many islands that make up Micronesia and Melanesia are largely unfamiliar to most students. In this activity, students learn more about these faraway places.

The teacher introduces this activity by hanging up a large map of the South Pacific, with detail of Micronesian and Melanesian islands. The teacher explains that, during every class session, the class will learn the location of and key facts about a particular island. Each day, one student is given the name of an island. It is that student's homework assignment that night to learn the location of the island, its population, and its key industries. The student must also learn two interesting facts about the island. The next day, the student places a push pin (or other marker) on the map showing the location of his or her island. The student presents the information to the class, writes it down on an index card, and files the index card in the class "island" box. In this way, the students learn about a new Micronesian or Melanesian island every day and build a ready resource of information about the islands.

Materials required for the students:

None

Materials required for the teacher:

Large wall map with sufficient detail of Micronesia and Melanesia

Index cards

Box for island index cards

Push pins, stickers, or other markers for islands

Northern European Mythology: The Scroll of the Nibelungen

The *Nibelungenlied* is an epic poem set in pre-Christian Germany. The tale contains many adventures, fights, and triumphs. In this activity, students prepare a graphic-novel version of the *Nibelungenlied*.

To introduce this activity, the teacher gives students a synopsis of the *Nibelungenlied* and describes the various interpretations of the saga (including Richard Wagner's opera and J. R. R. Tolkien's *Lord of the Rings* triology). The teacher then explains that the class will create a graphic novel of the *Nibelungenlied* on a continuous scroll of paper. The teacher shows models of various graphic novels and discusses the conventions of graphic novel representations.

Students are divided into groups of three or four, and each group receives one chapter or section of the *Nibelungenlied* as its assignment.

After reading their sections, the groups meet to discuss possible graphical representations of the action in their chapters and present their ideas to the teacher for approval. After gaining approval, student groups work, one group at a time, to draw and color their chapters on the scroll. When the scroll is finished, each group makes a short presentation explaining what happens in their chapter and how they chose to represent the action. The final scroll can be displayed around the classroom walls or along a school hallway.

Materials required by the students:

None

Materials required by the teacher:

Easel paper roll (200 feet)

Markers, colored pencils, and crayons

Copies of *Nibelungenlied* chapters for students (or refer students to http://omacl.org/Nibelungenlied/)

Inca Mythology: Make a Siku

A siku is an Andean pan pipe. Pipes such as these were important in Inca culture, and remain a prominent feature in Andean music. In this activity, students will make their own sikus.

The teacher begins this activity by playing some Andean pan pipe music, showing students the Andes on a map, and discussing the ways in which Inca culture remains part of the lives of Native Americans in countries like Peru. The teacher shows a picture of a pan pipe (or, ideally, an actual pan pipe) to the students and explains they will build their own.

Students need ten drinking straws each (they can bring them from home, or the teacher can provide them) and a pair of scissors. To make the pipe:

1. Set aside two of the straws. Cut the remaining straws so that each is one-half inch shorter than the next. The first straw is uncut. The second straw is one-half inch shorter than the first. The third is one inch shorter than the first, and so on.

2. Cut the remaining straws into equal pieces. These pieces will be used as spacers between pipe pieces.

3. Arrange the straws from longest to shortest (left to right) with the tops of the straws lined up.

4. Put spacer pieces between each part of the pipe so they are an equal distance apart.

5. Tape the pipe in position, making sure the tops of the straws stay in alignment.

6. The pipe is finished. Cover in paper and decorate if desired. Blow across the tops of straws to play.

Materials required by the students:

Ten drinking straws

Scissors

Tape

Materials required by the teacher:

Andean pipe music

Pictures of a pan pipe or an actual pan pipe

Picture of the Andes on a map

U·X·L Encyclopedia
of World Mythology

VOLUME 3: G–L

G

 Character

Deity

Myth

 Theme

Culture

Nationality/Culture
Greek

Pronunciation
GAY-uh

Alternate Names
Terra, Tellus (Roman)

Appears In
Hesiod's *Theogony*, Ovid's *Metamorphoses*

Lineage
None

Gaia

Character Overview

Also called Gaea or Ge by the Greeks and Terra or Tellus by the Romans, she was a maternal figure who gave birth to many other creatures and deities. Gaia arose from Chaos (pronounced KAY-oss), the period of emptiness and disorder that came before the gods. Her body was the Earth itself. She gave birth to **Uranus** (pronounced YOOR-uh-nuhs), who represented the sky; Pontus (pronounced PON-tus), the sea; and Oure (pronounced OO-ray), the mountains. Gaia was also the mother of **Aphrodite** (pronounced af-ro-DYE-tee), **Echo** (pronounced EK-oh), the **Furies**, and the serpent that guarded the **Golden Fleece**.

Major Myths

Gaia appears in many myths about the early creation of the world and the gods. Her son and husband Uranus was not happy with the children she bore him, including the **Cyclopes** (pronounced sigh-KLOH-peez) and the **Titans**, so he forced them into the deep recesses of the Earth, which were also Gaia's bowels. Gaia convinced the youngest Titan, **Cronus** (pronounced KROH-nuhs), to overthrow Uranus and free her children from within her bowels. When Cronus had children, Gaia and Uranus warned him that one of his offspring would challenge and defeat him. Cronus therefore swallowed each child at birth to prevent their betrayal. However, his wife, Rhea (pronounced REE-uh), managed to trick him and save the youngest one, **Zeus** (pronounced ZOOS). Zeus later overthrew Cronus with the help of Gaia.

Gaia in Context

The myth of Gaia illustrates the places men and women held in ancient Greek and Roman society. Gaia, the female goddess, is the ultimate beginning to all things; this reflects the woman's place as the one who gives birth. However, after giving birth to the sky, ocean, and other gods, the male god of the sky takes control of the heavens. This reflects the fact that men ruled nearly all matters of formal society in ancient Greece and Rome. It is important to note that, despite her lack of ruling power after the time of creation, Gaia is a driving force behind the overthrow of the male gods Uranus and Cronus.

Gaia was widely worshipped at temples in Greece, including the shrine of the oracle at **Delphi**. The Greeks also took oaths in Gaia's name and believed that she would punish them if they failed to keep their word.

Key Themes and Symbols

In **Greek mythology**, the goddess Gaia represented the earth, and she is often associated with plants and the soil. She was one of the most fundamental symbols of creation, and is sometimes pictured with a large, rounded belly symbolizing fertility. An important theme found in myths about Gaia is rebellion. Gaia convinces Cronus to rebel against Uranus in order to help her. Later, Gaia is instrumental in Zeus's rebellion against and overthrow of Cronus. In recent times, Gaia has endured as a symbol for Earth.

Gaia in Art, Literature, and Everyday Life

Gaia is mentioned in Virgil's *Aeneid*, Hesiod's *Theogony*, and many other ancient works. In art, she was usually depicted as a woman half-risen from the ground. The name Gaia has been used in many science fiction works as the name of an Earth-like planet, and she has also appeared as a character in Marvel comic books. The goddess Gaia has also inspired an idea known as the Gaia hypothesis, which theorizes that all parts of the Earth, both living and nonliving, function together as if the entire planet were a single giant organism. This idea has been embraced by many environmentalists looking to maintain a balance between nature and human development.

Read, Write, Think, Discuss

Using your library, the Internet, or other resources, research the Gaia hypothesis. What are the main points of the hypothesis? What changes do supporters suggest that humans make in order to maintain balance on the planet? What elements of the ancient Greek myth of Gaia can be found in this modern view?

SEE ALSO *Aeneid, The*; Cyclopes; Delphi; Echo; Furies; Golden Fleece; Titans; Uranus; Zeus

Galahad

Character Overview

According to Arthurian legend, Galahad was the purest and noblest knight in King **Arthur**'s court at **Camelot**, and the only one ever to see the **Holy Grail**—the cup which Jesus Christ was believed to have used during the Last Supper before he was crucified. The son of **Lancelot**—another celebrated knight—and Elaine, Galahad was raised by nuns and arrived at the court as a young man.

When the knights took their seats at the Round Table, Galahad sat in a special seat known as the Siege Perilous. It was said that only the knight destined to find the Holy Grail could occupy this seat safely. All others who had sat in it had instantly perished. When Galahad remained unharmed, it became clear that he would accomplish great deeds. In some stories, the knight also proved his worth by drawing a special sword from a stone. An inscription on the stone stated that only the best knight in the land could withdraw the sword.

After Galahad's arrival at Arthur's court, the knights began their search for the Holy Grail. Galahad set off alone but later joined forces with two other knights, Perceval and Bors. Their travels took them to the

Nationality/Culture
Romano-British/Celtic

Pronunciation
GAL-uh-had

Alternate Names
None

Appears In
Tales of King Arthur and the Knights of the Round Table

Lineage
Son of Lancelot and Elaine

city of Sarras, where they were imprisoned by a cruel king. However, when the king was dying, he released the knights, and the people of the city chose Galahad to be their next king.

After ruling Sarras for a year, Galahad had a vision in which the Holy Grail was revealed to him. Content with having achieved his life's goal, he prayed to be allowed to die then. According to the legend, his request was granted and "a great multitude of **angels** bore his soul up to **heaven**."

Galahad in Context

Galahad can be seen as a symbolic recreation of Jesus Christ within Anglo-Saxon mythology. As the population of Western Europe moved toward Christianity and away from other local mythologies during the early Middle Ages, church leaders sometimes incorporated Christian elements into existing myths as a way to preserve the traditional tales of the people while still encouraging them to accept Christian beliefs. Including elements of Christian myth, such as the Holy Grail, was also a way to personalize Christianity for the Anglo-Saxon people, most of whom were not familiar with the places mentioned throughout the Bible.

Key Themes and Symbols

In the tales of the knights of the Round Table, Galahad represents purity of heart and spirit. This is reflected in his claim of the Siege Perilous, as well as his ability to see the Holy Grail when no one else can. An important theme of the tale of Galahad is that dedication and perseverance are necessary in order to achieve important goals.

Galahad in Art, Literature, and Everyday Life

Galahad was an important part of Arthurian literature, especially the French Post-Vulgate Cycle of stories. These were used as the basis for Sir Thomas Malory's *Le Morte d'Arthur* in the fifteenth century, considered by many to be the definitive work on Arthurian legend. While many modern tales of King Arthur ignore Galahad and his quest, T. H. White's *The Once and Future King* (1958) includes the myth, as does the 1975 comedy *Monty Python and the Holy Grail*, in which Michael Palin plays the role of Galahad. In the 1989 adventure film *Indiana Jones and the Last Crusade*, archaeologist Jones (played by Harrison Ford) finds himself following in Galahad's footsteps as he sets off to find the Holy Grail.

Read, Write, Think, Discuss

The location of the Holy Grail has been sought by scholars and archaeologists since the early centuries following the spread of Christianity throughout the Western world. Even in modern times, archaeologists continue to search for the Holy Grail even though there is little reliable proof of its existence. Multiple books of fiction and nonfiction have been written on the topic. Richard Barber's 2005 book *The Holy Grail:*

Imagination and Belief is a highly acclaimed overview of the many myths and interpretations of the legend of the Holy Grail.

SEE ALSO Arthurian Legends; Holy Grail; Lancelot

Galatea
See **Pygmalion and Galatea.**

Ganesha

Nationality/Culture
Hindu

Pronunciation
guh-NAYSH

Alternate Names
Ganapati, Vinayaka

Appears In
The Vedas

Lineage
Son of Parvati and Shiva

Character Overview

Ganesha, the god of good fortune and wisdom, is one of the most popular Hindu gods. People call upon him at the beginning of any task because his blessing is believed to ensure success. Ganesha is portrayed as a short man with a pot belly, four hands, and an elephant's head with a single tusk. He is the son of **Shiva** (pronounced SHEE-vuh), the Hindu god of destruction, and his wife, Parvati (pronounced PAR-vuh-tee).

Major Myths

Several legends tell how Ganesha came to have an elephant's head. One says that Parvati was so proud of her son that she asked all the gods to look at him, even the god Shani (pronounced SHAH-nee). Shani's gaze burned to ashes everything he saw, including Ganesha's head. **Brahma** (pronounced BRAH-muh), the god of creation, instructed Parvati to give her son the first head she found, which turned out to be that of an elephant. According to another account, Shiva struck off Ganesha's head and later attached an elephant's head to his son's body.

Ganesha's single tusk is also the subject of various stories. In one tale, he lost his second tusk in a fight with Parasurama (pronounced pah-ruh-soo-RAH-muh), a form of the god **Vishnu** (pronounced VISH-

noo). Another myth claims that Ganesha lost the tusk after using it to write the Hindu epic called the ***Mahabharata***.

Ganesha in Context

Elephants have long been used in areas of India as working animals prized for their intelligence and massive strength. Although they are not domesticated in the same way that horses or other draft animals are, their immense strength and power has been used for hauling loads and uprooting trees. Though wild by nature, elephants have rarely been viewed as a threat despite their size. This may explain why Hindus incorporated a god with the head of an elephant into their pantheon, or collection of recognized and worshipped gods.

Key Themes and Symbols

In Hindu mythology, Ganesha is a symbol of the arts and sciences, as well as representing the beginnings of things. Ganesha is also commonly associated with obstacles; he removes obstacles from deserving followers who are trying to accomplish a goal, while placing obstacles in the paths of those who need to learn strength or dedication. In all these roles, Ganesha functions as a teacher, mentor, or guardian. Like the elephant he resembles, Ganesha is widely regarded as a symbol of intelligence and wisdom. Ganesha is also a symbol of luck.

Ganesha in Art, Literature, and Everyday Life

Ganesha is generally depicted with a human body, a large belly, four arms, and the head of an elephant. He is often shown to be dancing, and sometimes has a serpent wrapped around his neck or waist. He is sometimes shown holding a goad, which is normally used to spur an animal—such as an ox or elephant—to move forward. His distinctive appearance makes him one of the most easily recognized of the Hindu gods, and one of the most popularly depicted. His image appears on many different products in India, including food and incense. Ganesha figurines are features of millions of homes around the world. In addition to his many temples in India, Ganesha is a popular god among many Buddhists throughout Indonesia, and even decorates one denomination of Indonesian currency.

Read, Write, Think, Discuss

The three living species of elephants—the African bush elephant, the African forest elephant, and the Asian (Indian) elephant—are protected worldwide by laws that aim to keep their populations stable and growing. Using your library, the Internet, or other available resources, find out the population status of elephants in Africa and Asia. Would you expect elephants to be in less danger in areas where Ganesha, the elephant-headed god, is worshipped? Is this supported by the population numbers?

The 2006 story collection *The Broken Tusk: Stories of the Hindu God Ganesha* by Uma Krishnaswami offers an enjoyable introduction to the myths surrounding Ganesha.

SEE ALSO Hinduism and Mythology

Geb

See **Nut.**

Genies

Nationality/Culture
Arabic/Islamic

Pronunciation
JEE-neez

Alternate Names
Jinn, Ifrit

Appears In
The Qur'an, *The Book of One Thousand and One Nights*

Lineage
None

Character Overview

Genies (also called jinn or genii) are spirits in cultures of the Middle East and Africa. The term *genie* comes from the Arabic word *jinni*, which refers to an evil spirit that could take the shape of an animal or person. It could be found in every kind of nonliving thing, even air and **fire**. Jinn (the plural of jinni) were said to have magical powers.

In the Qur'an, jinn were created by Allah (pronounced ah-LAH), Islam's single supreme god, from smokeless fire. In perhaps the most well-known tale of jinn found in the Qur'an, Iblis (pronounced IB-liss), a jinni who refused to bow to Allah's creation Adam, was banished to Jahannam (pronounced JAH-hah-nahm; hell). Iblis is similar to the Christian idea of the devil.

In *The Book of One Thousand and One Nights* (a collection of stories of Persian, Indian, and Arabian origin dating from the Middle Ages), two tales centered on genies are included. The first and most famous is the tale of **Aladdin**, a poor boy who was tricked by a sorcerer into taking a magic lamp from a cave. The sorcerer trapped Aladdin in the cave, but Aladdin managed to keep the lamp and escaped the cave thanks to a magic ring that contained a genie. Back home, Aladdin's mother tried to clean the lamp by rubbing it, and accidentally summoned an even more powerful genie that lived within it. The genie of the lamp granted Aladdin great wealth and a palace, and he married the daughter of the emperor. However, the sorcerer managed to find Aladdin and trick his wife into giving up the lamp. Aladdin then had to rely on the lesser genie from his magic ring to help find the sorcerer and reclaim the lamp.

The other tale of genies in *The Book of One Thousand and One Nights* concerns a fisherman who netted a jar while casting for fish. He opened the jar and released a genie that had been imprisoned for

Roman Genius

In ancient Rome, the term *genii*, the plural form of the Latin word *genius*, referred to the spirits that watched over every man. The genius was responsible for forming a man's character and caused all actions. Believed to be present at birth, genius came to be thought of as great inborn ability. Women had a similar spirit known as a *juno*. Some Romans also believed in a spirit, called an evil genius, that fought the good genius for control of a man's fate. In later Roman mythology, genii were spirits who guarded a household or community.

hundreds of years. The genie, angry from being trapped for centuries in the jar, did not offer to fulfill the fisherman's wishes, but instead offered him his choice of death. The fisherman tricked the genie back into the jar by saying that he did not see how the genie could have possibly fit into such a tiny jar. The fisherman resealed the jar until the genie agreed to provide a favor. After being released, the genie led the fisherman to a pond where he caught four magical fish to present to the sultan. The fisherman gave the sultan the fish, and his children became prosperous members of the sultan's court.

Genies in Context

In early Islamic belief, jinn made up a world that existed parallel to humans: although they were invisible to humans, they existed in much the same types of communities and tribes. Just as people were defined by their relation to Islam, there were jinn that accepted Islam and jinn that did not. Jinn were essentially a reflection of the same beliefs and concerns that humans dealt with, but on a grander, more supernatural scale. They also provided an explanation for the temptations and frustrations people faced on a daily basis, which were seen as the work of unholy jinn.

Key Themes and Symbols

Jinn often represent great power that can be devastating if not properly controlled. The vessel that contains a jinni, whether it is a ring, lamp, jar, or some other object, is usually seen as a symbol of imprisonment. One of the main themes of many stories about jinn is wish fulfillment, as shown in the tales of both Aladdin and the fisherman. In many such tales, justice

also plays an important role: those who are undeserving may get their wishes granted, but these wishes often have unforeseen consequences.

Genies in Art, Literature, and Everyday Life

Although genies appear prominently in the Qur'an, they are most popularly known from their appearances in folk tales and *The Book of*

One Thousand and One Nights. This collection of tales has appeared in many translations and versions over the centuries. The story of Aladdin is especially well known, and has been used as the basis for many films—most notably *The Thief of Baghdad* (1940) and the 1992 Disney animated tale *Aladdin.*

Other modern depictions of genies can be found in the novel *Declare* by Tim Powers (2001), and the *Bartimaeus Trilogy* by Jonathan Stroud (2003). Popular depictions of genies in television and film include the 1965 series *I Dream of Jeannie* starring Barbara Eden, and the 1996 Shaquille O'Neal film *Kazaam.*

Read, Write, Think, Discuss

The *Children of the Lamp* series by P. B. Kerr is a series of fantasy novels about twelve-year-old **twins** named John and Philippa who discover they are actually descended from a line of jinn and must find a way to adjust to their new supernatural lives. The first book, *The Akhenaten Adventure* (2005), follows the pair from New York to England to Egypt in pursuit of the ghost of Akhenaten, all while being pursued by an evil jinn named Iblis.

SEE ALSO African Mythology; Roman Mythology; Semitic Mythology

George, St.

Nationality/Culture
Christian

Pronunciation
saynt JORJ

Alternate Names
None

Appears In
Voragine's *The Golden Legend*, Christian myths

Lineage
Unknown

Character Overview

St. George was a Christian who is said to have lived in Anatolia, the area now known as Turkey, in the third century. No historical record of the man is known to exist. Over the centuries, legendary tales about his courage and dedication to God grew in popularity, and he was granted the status of sainthood by the Catholic Church.

The most popular tale about St. George describes how he killed a terrifying dragon. The dragon was threatening the citizens of a local town. The people decided to cast lots each day to choose one person for the dragon to eat, thus sparing the rest of the population. One day the king's daughter was selected to be the dragon's victim. As the dragon prepared to devour her, St. George arrived. He charged forward, made the sign of the cross, and killed the dragon. Impressed with both his faith and his strength, the people of the city decided to convert to Christianity.

Other tales concern St. George's martyrdom, or death for his Christian beliefs, which took place in Palestine. The Roman government there was punishing Christians for their beliefs, and St. George openly opposed their policies. The Romans tortured him for his resistance and beheaded him in 303 CE.

St. George in Context

St. George was an important character in early Christianity because he offered something most Christian figures did not: he was a soldier who fought and conquered in the name of Christ. Although most early Christian figures were described as steadfast in their beliefs, very few actively fought to further those beliefs. For this reason, St. George became especially important during the Crusades, the period from the eleventh through the thirteenth centuries in which European Christians were called by the pope to conquer non-Christians in order to "reclaim" the holy lands in and around Jerusalem in the Middle East.

The legends about St. George spread to Europe during the Crusades, when armies of Europeans traveled to the Middle East. In the 1300s, George became the patron, or protector, saint of England. He is often pictured in Christian art carrying a sword and shield, mounted on a white horse, and wearing armor decorated with a red cross on a white background—a look mimicked by the Crusaders, who took the red cross on a white background as their uniform. The image of St. George slaying the dragon is also shown on the official coat of arms of the city of Moscow, as well as many other locations throughout Eastern Europe.

Today, St. George's position as England's patron saint is touched by controversy. His traditional banner, the red cross on the white background, now associated with the Crusaders' invasion of the Middle East hundreds of years ago, can be seen as insulting to England's growing Muslim population. Many see England's decision to support U.S. military action in Iraq as a type of new Crusade against Islam, and St. George as a symbol of Christian aggression against non-Christians.

A Famous Rallying Cry

William Shakespeare used St. George in one of the most famous military rallying speeches in English literature. In his historical play *Henry V*, King Henry besieges the French city of Harfleur in 1415 and meets stiff resistance. Shakespeare's Henry, nicknamed Harry, urges his soldiers onward:

> Once more unto the breach, dear friends, once more;
> Or close the wall up with our English dead.
> In peace there's nothing so becomes a man
> As modest stillness and humility:
> But when the blast of war blows in our ears,
> Then imitate the action of the tiger; . . .
> For there is none of you so mean and base,
> That hath not noble lustre in your eyes.
> I see you stand like greyhounds in the slips,
> Straining upon the start. The game's afoot:
> Follow your spirit, and upon this charge
> Cry "God for Harry, England, and Saint George!"

Key Themes and Symbols

In Christian mythology, St. George is one of the most popular symbols of bravery and religious dedication, an ideal example of a Christian for others to follow. The white horse St. George rides is seen as a symbol of purity and righteousness. The dragon of the myth is sometimes said to symbolize a non-Christian group or deity; this is emphasized by the fact that after St. George slays the beast, the townspeople all convert to Christianity. In this way, St. George represents the power of Christianity to conquer non-Christian belief systems.

St. George in Art, Literature, and Everyday Life

The most notable source of information about St. George is Jacobus de Voragine's *Golden Legend*, a thirteenth-century collection of stories about the lives of various Catholic saints. The story of St. George and the dragon has been retold numerous times throughout the centuries, and has appeared in two famous paintings by Raphael, as well as paintings by Tintoretto, Peter Paul Rubens, and Gustave Moreau. Several elements of the myth were used in the 1981 fantasy film *Dragonslayer*, though St. George does not appear as a character in the film.

Read, Write, Think, Discuss

St. George was an important symbol to Christians in the years of the Crusades. The Crusades, like modern conflicts in the Middle East, were essentially "holy wars" fought by two groups of differing beliefs who both considered a certain region sacred to their religion. Do you think the myth of St. George promotes the idea of using violence as a way to conquer people with different beliefs? Why or why not?

SEE ALSO Dragons

Giants

Character Overview

Giants play many different roles in myth and legend. These mythical beings, much bigger than people, usually have human form, but some are monstrous in appearance. Giants often seem to be cruel and evil, although they may be merely clumsy or stupid. In some myths and legends, however, they are friendly and helpful or at least neutral.

Many different cultures have their own unique myths about giants. The major sources of myths related to giants are **Greek mythology**, **Norse mythology**, and the various myths of the American Indian tribes, though other cultures also have examples of giants that appear in legend from time to time.

Greek Giants The word *giant* comes from the Greek Gigantes (meaning "earthborn"), a race of huge creatures who were the offspring of **Gaia** (pronounced GAY-uh), the earth, and **Uranus** (pronounced YOOR-uh-nuhs), the heavens. These giants were half man, half monster, with serpents' tails instead of legs. After Gaia became angry with **Zeus** (pronounced ZOOS), the father of the Olympian gods, the giants and the Olympians engaged in a war to the death known as the Gigantomachy (pronounced jih-gan-TOH-muh-kee).

Nationality/Culture
Various

Alternate Names
Gigantes (Greek), Cyclopes (Greek), Rom (Ethiopian)

Appears In
Various mythologies around the world

Lineage
Varies

The gods needed the help of a human hero because the giants could not be killed by gods. Zeus therefore fathered a son, the mighty **Heracles** (pronounced HAIR-uh-kleez), whose mother was a human. The two sides met in battle at the home of the giants, a place called Phlegra (pronounced FLEE-gruh; "Burning Lands"). The giants hurled huge rocks and mountaintops and brandished burning oak trees. The gods fought back strongly, and Heracles picked off the giants one by one with his arrows. Many Greek sculptors and artists depicted the Gigantomachy, with the gods' victory over the giants, as the triumph of Greek civilization over barbarism, or of good over evil. The Greeks used this battle to explain features of the natural world. For example, during the struggle in which the Greek gods overcame the giants, several fallen giants became part of the landscape. As the giant Enceladus (pronounced en-SEL-uh-duhs) ran from the battlefield, the goddess **Athena** (pronounced uh-THEE-nuh) smashed him with the island of Sicily. Thereafter, he lay imprisoned under the island, breathing his fiery breath out through the volcano called Etna. Under Vesuvius, a volcano on the Italian mainland, lay another giant, Mimas (pronounced MYE-muhs). **Hephaestus** (pronounced hi-FES-tuhs), the god of metalsmiths, buried him there under a heap of molten metal.

Two special groups of giants, also the children of Gaia, were the **Cyclopes** (pronounced sigh-KLOH-peez) and the hundred-armed giants. The three Cyclopes each had one eye in the middle of the forehead. The three hundred-armed giants each had fifty heads and one hundred arms. Both groups were loyal to Zeus. The hundred-armed giants were the jailors of Tartarus (pronounced TAR-tur-uhs), the place of punishment in the **underworld**, or land of the dead.

Norse Giants Giants appear in numerous myths of northern Europe. The giants' realm was a place called Jotunheim (pronounced YAW-toonheym), located in Midgard (pronounced MID-gard), the center of the three-tiered Norse universe. There they dwelt in a huge castle called Utgard (pronounced OOT-gard).

Norse myths, like Greek myths, say that the gods fought and conquered the race of giants. Yet the gods and the giants were not always enemies. Friendship and even marriage could occur between them. Male deities mated with female giants. The mother of the thunder god **Thor** was a giantess named Jord (pronounced YORD), for example. However, the gods violently resisted all attempts by giants to mate with goddesses.

The giant Hrungnir (pronounced HRUNG-nur) built a wall around Asgard (pronounced AHS-gahrd), the home of the gods, and for payment desired the goddess **Freyja** (pronounced FRAY-uh). But he received only a crushing blow from Thor's hammer.

Many myths concern Thor's conflict with the giants. In one tale, he journeyed to Utgard to challenge the giants. The giants beat Thor and his companions at several tests of strength but only by using trickery. In one contest, Thor lost a wrestling match to an old woman who was in fact Age, which overcomes all. Though the gods were not always good and the giants were not always bad, the struggle between the two groups constitutes one of the underlying themes of Norse mythology and often symbolizes the struggle of good against evil.

American Indian Giants Most giants in American Indian mythology are evil and dangerous. Some start fights among humans so that in the confusion they can steal the men's wives. Others steal children, sometimes to eat them. Many Native American giants have monstrous or inhuman features. Tall Man, a giant of the Seminole people, smells bad, while giants in Lakota stories look like oxen. In the mythology of the Native American Lakota people, Waziya (pronounced wah-ZEE-uh) is a northern giant who blows the winter wind.

The Shoshone Indians of the American West tell stories of Dzoavits (pronounced ZOH-uh-vits), an ogre or hideous giant who stole two children from Dove. Eagle helped Dove recover her children. When the angry Dzoavits chased Dove, other animals protected her. Crane made a bridge from his leg so she could cross a river. Weasel dug an escape tunnel for her, and Badger made a hole where Dove and her children could hide. After tricking Dzoavits into entering the wrong hole, Badger sealed him in with a boulder.

Ancestral Giants The myths of various cultures associate giants with primal, or primitive, times. Sometimes giants figure in the creation of the world. Norse mythology says that the first thing to appear out of chaos was the frost giant **Ymir** (pronounced EE-mir), father of both giants and people, who had to die so that the earth could be formed from his body. The giant Pan Gu (pronounced PAN GOO) fills a similar role in **Chinese mythology**. Aboriginal people in northwestern Australia have stories about the two Bagadjimbiri brothers, both giants and creator gods, who made the landscape and people. When they died, their bodies

Giants in Native American mythology—such as the one represented by this mask—are evil and often try to steal children. WERNER FORMAN/ ART RESOURCE, NY.

became water snakes and their spirits became clouds. According to the Akamba people of Kenya, a giant hunter named Mwooka created the mountains and rivers.

Myths from many parts of the world say that in some remote time human ancestors were giants and that they have shrunk down to their present size over a very long period. Other stories tell of giants living among people at an earlier time in history. Gog and Magog (MAY-gog) are two giants of British myth. Brutus, the legendary founder of Britain, is said to have conquered them. In Jewish myth, a race of giants lived in the world along with people before the great flood that wiped out most living things. One giant, Og, survived the flood by hitching a ride on **Noah**'s Ark. Later, however, he came into conflict with Noah's descendants, and the prophet Moses (pronounced MOH-ziss) had to kill him.

Other Giants One of the most famous giants from the Judeo-Christian tradition is Goliath (pronounced guh-LYE-uth), a huge Philistine warrior who fought the young Israelite hero David. The Philistine and Israelite armies had agreed to let their battle be decided by their two best warriors, but no one on the Israelite side wanted to fight the mighty Goliath except for David, who felt himself assured of victory despite being at a significant disadvantage in armor, weaponry, and size. In a victory of wit over brute strength, David used a stone from his slingshot to knock Goliath unconscious, and then cut off his head with his own sword. The English folktale of Jack the Giant-Killer tells a similar story as Jack kills the giant Blunderbore (pronounced BLUN-dur-bor).

Occasionally, cruel and kind giants appear in the same myth. The Mensa people of Ethiopia tell a story about a man who tries to steal cattle from one of the Rom, a tribe of giants. Enraged, the giant tries to kill the man. As the man flees, another giant befriends him and hides him in his cloak. Unfortunately, the man is crushed when the two giants come to blows.

Giants in Context

The peoples of the ancient world both relied on and feared the natural forces of the world in which they lived. While needing the **sun** and rain to grow their crops, they were also at the mercy of storms, droughts, and other natural events beyond their control. The stories of giants in various cultures reflect both the good and the bad of the natural world as primal, uncontrollable forces that sometimes help and sometimes destroy. They appear in creation myths as necessary for life, but in other stories they are predators that eat men and cause trouble. The strength of giants prevented most humans from matching them in a physical battle, but humans often defeated giants by acting in clever ways. In the same way, ancient peoples could not hope to control the weather and climate of the natural world, but they could use their intelligence to respond to nature in a way that worked to their benefit and helped them escape harm.

Giants are sometimes described as beings that are from a more ancient time period, a time before the establishment of gods and order, which connects them more closely with an uncivilized world. Through the stories of giants, ancient peoples attempted to explain natural phenomena. Even more recent cultures used giants to explain phenomena they did not understand; the writers of European folklore thought that construction projects from Roman times were the work of giants because they did not believe that mere men could have completed such huge works.

Key Themes and Symbols

Giants represent both the good and bad side of powerful natural forces. In some traditions, a giant appears as a symbol of chaos or disorder, threatening to disrupt the orderly natural world or social community. Their size makes them able to cause significant damage. But there are other giants that protect humans, such as Talos, the guardian of the island of Crete. Many stories have giants as key figures in the creation of the world.

The evil giants of myth generally need to be defeated, either by humans or by supernatural beings such as gods. Their conflict with the gods, in particular, is a key theme in world mythology, representing the clash between the old world and the new, good and evil. Although immensely powerful, these creatures fall when faced with bravery and cleverness because they generally act on instinct, using brute force. Many myths describe giants as being stupid and ugly.

Giants in Art, Literature, and Everyday Life

Giants have remained popular figures in art and literature even through modern times. Jonathan Swift's classic humorous novel *Gulliver's Travels* (1726) features a race of giants called the Brobdingnagians, and John Bunyan's well-known Christian allegory *The Pilgrim's Progress* (1678) depicts Despair as a giant. More recent books such as the *Harry Potter* series by J. K. Rowling and the *Spiderwick Chronicles* by Holly Black also feature giants as important characters.

Read, Write, Think, Discuss

The tall tale of Paul Bunyan and his giant blue ox is a relatively recent addition to myths about giants. Use your library and the Internet to find out more about Paul Bunyan and his place in American culture. How is his story different from the giant myths of much older cultures? How is it the same?

SEE ALSO Cyclopes

Gilgamesh

Character Overview

The best-known and most popular hero in the mythology of the ancient Near East, Gilgamesh (pronounced GIL-guh-mesh) was a Sumerian (pronounced soo-MER-ee-un) king who wished to live forever. Endowed with superhuman strength, courage, and power, he appeared in numerous legends and myths, including the *Epic of Gilgamesh*. This long, grand-scale poem, written more than three thousand years ago, may be the earliest work of written literature. It is an adventure story that explores human nature, dealing with values and concerns that are still relevant today.

The *Epic of Gilgamesh* begins with a brief account of Gilgamesh's ancestry, his youth, and his accomplishments as king. Although acknowledged to be a wise man and a courageous warrior, Gilgamesh is criticized as a cruel ruler who mistreats the people of Uruk (pronounced OO-rook). The nobles of the city complain bitterly of Gilgamesh's behavior. Their complaints attract the attention of the gods, who decide to do something about it.

Enkidu The gods create a rival for Gilgamesh—a man named Enkidu (pronounced EN-kee-doo) who is as strong as the king and who lives in the forest with the wild animals. Their plan is for Enkidu to fight Gilgamesh and teach him a lesson, leading the king to end his harsh behavior toward his people. When Gilgamesh hears about Enkidu, he sends a woman from the temple to civilize the wild man by showing him how to live among people.

After learning the ways of city life, Enkidu goes to Uruk. There he meets the king at a marketplace and challenges him to a wrestling match. The king and the wild man struggle, and Gilgamesh is so impressed by Enkidu's strength, skill, and courage that he embraces his rival, and the two men become close friends. Because of this loving friendship, Gilgamesh softens his behavior toward the people of Uruk and becomes a just and honorable ruler.

One day Gilgamesh and Enkidu decide to travel to a distant cedar forest to battle the fierce giant Humbaba (pronounced hum-BAB-uh)

Nationality/Culture
Sumerian

Pronunciation
GIL-guh-mesh

Alternate Names
None

Appears In
The *Epic of Gilgamesh*

Lineage
Son of Lugalbanda

who guards the forest. Knowing that he cannot live forever like the gods, Gilgamesh hopes that he will gain the next best thing—lasting fame—by slaying the monster. Together the two **heroes** kill Humbaba, and Enkidu cuts off the monster's head.

The Insulted Goddess Impressed with Gilgamesh's courage and daring, the goddess **Ishtar** (pronounced ISH-tahr) offers to marry him. He refuses, however, and insults the goddess by reminding her of her cruelty toward previous lovers. Enraged by his refusal and insults, Ishtar persuades her father, the god Anu (pronounced AH-noo), to send the sacred Bull of Heaven to kill Gilgamesh. Anu sends the bull, but Gilgamesh and Enkidu kill the bull. Enkidu further insults Ishtar by throwing a piece of the dead bull in her face.

That night, Enkidu dreams that the gods have decided that he must die for his role in killing the Bull of Heaven. His death will also be the punishment for his dear friend Gilgamesh. Enkidu falls ill and has other dreams of his death and descent to the **underworld**, or land of the dead. He grows weaker and weaker and finally dies after twelve days of suffering. Gilgamesh is overwhelmed with grief. He also fears his own death and decides that he must find a way to gain immortality, or the ability to live forever.

Search for Utnapishtim After Enkidu's funeral and burial, Gilgamesh sets out on a long and hazardous journey to seek a man named Utnapishtim (pronounced oot-nuh-PISH-tim). Utnapishtim had survived a great flood and was granted immortality by the gods. Gilgamesh travels through various strange lands and meets people who tell him to end his search and accept his fate as a mortal. Refusing to give up, Gilgamesh finally reaches the sea and persuades a boatman to take him across the waters to the home of Utnapishtim.

Utnapishtim tells Gilgamesh the story of the Great Flood and of the boat that he constructed to save his family and various animals. He then offers the hero a challenge: if Gilgamesh can stay awake for seven days, he will be given the immortality he desperately desires. Gilgamesh accepts the challenge but soon falls asleep. When he awakes seven days later, he realizes that immortality is beyond his reach, and with sorrow, he accepts his fate. Utnapishtim tells him not to despair because the gods have granted him other great gifts, such as courage, skill in battle, and wisdom.

In appreciation of Gilgamesh's courageous efforts to find him, Utnapishtim tells the hero where to find a plant that can restore youth. Gilgamesh finds the plant and continues on his journey. Along the way, while he bathes in a pool, a snake steals the plant. This explains the snake's ability to slough off its old skin and start afresh with a new one. Disappointed and tired, but also wiser and more at peace with himself, Gilgamesh returns to Uruk to await his death.

The last part of the *Epic of Gilgamesh*, thought to be a later addition, tells how the spirit of Enkidu returns from the underworld and helps Gilgamesh find some lost objects he received from Ishtar. Enkidu also tells his close friend about the **afterlife** and describes the grim conditions of the underworld.

Gilgamesh in Context

Although most tales about Gilgamesh are obviously myths, they may be based on an actual historical figure. Ancient lists of Sumerian kings identify Gilgamesh as an early ruler of the city of Uruk around 2600 BCE. These same texts, however, also say that Gilgamesh was half-man and half-god, and reigned for 126 years.

According to legendary accounts, Gilgamesh was the son of the goddess Ninsun (pronounced nin-SOON) and of either Lugalbanda, a king of Uruk, or of a high priest of the district of Kullab. Gilgamesh's greatest accomplishment as king was the construction of massive city walls around Uruk, an achievement mentioned in both myths and historical texts.

Gilgamesh first appeared in five short poems written in the Sumerian language sometime between 2000 and 1500 BCE. The poems— "Gilgamesh and Huwawa," "Gilgamesh and the Bull of Heaven," "Gilgamesh and Agga of Kish,"

Statue of the Assyrian hero Gilgamesh. ERICH LESSING/ ART RESOURCE, NY.

"Gilgamesh, Enkidu, and the Nether World," and "The Death of Gilgamesh"—relate various incidents and adventures in his life.

However, the most famous and complete account of Gilgamesh's adventures is found in the *Epic of Gilgamesh*. Originally written between 1500 and 1000 BCE, the epic weaves various tales of Gilgamesh together into a single story. Its basic theme is the king's quest for fame, glory, and immortality through heroic deeds. One of the best-known parts of the epic is the tale of a great flood, which may have inspired the story of **Noah** (pronounced NOH-uh) and the flood in the Bible.

The epic appears on twelve clay tablets found at the site of the ancient city of Nineveh (pronounced NIN-uh-vuh). The tablets came from the library of King Ashurbanipal (pronounced ah-shoor-BAH-nee-pahl), the last great king of Assyria (pronounced uh-SEER-ee-uh), who reigned in the 600s BCE.

Key Themes and Symbols

One of the key themes in the story of Gilgamesh is mortality, or the knowledge that one will eventually die. This knowledge is what drives Gilgamesh to search the world for a way to live forever. This certainty of death is emphasized when his best friend and companion, Enkidu, dies in his company. Gilgamesh's fear of his own death is overcome when he finally realizes that all men must die, and that the gods have already given him many other great gifts.

Another important theme in the epic of Gilgamesh is the power of friendship. Enkidu is originally sent by the gods to harm Gilgamesh for his cruel ways. Instead, the two men find respect in each other's abilities, and become great friends. This ultimately accomplishes the same goal the gods set out to do: it helps Gilgamesh learn to become a better person. When Gilgamesh loses his friend, he is devastated.

Gilgamesh in Art, Literature, and Everyday Life

As the first known work of literature, the *Epic of Gilgamesh* has inspired countless re-tellings and adaptations over thousands of years. These adaptations have taken the form of stage plays, operas and choral works, radio dramas, films, novels, and comic books. Some notable versions of the tale include Robert Silverberg's 1984 novel *Gilgamesh the King*, the three-act opera *Gilgamesh* created by Rudolf Brucci in 1986, and *Never Grow Old: The Novel of Gilgamesh* (2007) by Brian Trent. Many other works have been loosely inspired by the Gilgamesh myth, including the Japanese animated science fiction series *Gilgamesh* (2003) and the surreal 1985 Quay Brothers animated short *This Unnameable Little Broom*. Gilgamesh is also mentioned in the song "The Mesopotamians" on the 2007 album *The Else* by They Might Be Giants.

Read, Write, Think, Discuss

The epic of Gilgamesh is largely the story of two best friends experiencing a grand adventure together. This same formula has been used countless times in literature, television, and film; in fact, a subgenre known as the "buddy movie" is built upon this very foundation. Can you think of a modern example of a similar tale that you have seen or read? How is it similar to the story of Gilgamesh? How is it different?

SEE ALSO Floods; Ishtar; Noah

Gluskabe

See **Gluskap.**

Gluskap

Character Overview

Gluskap is a culture hero of the Algonquian-speaking people of North America, usually known as the Wabanaki (pronounced wah-buh-NAH-kee). Tabaldak, the creator god, made Gluskap and his brother Malsum from the dust that had built up on his hands. According to the mythology of several tribes in the Northeastern United States and Canada, Gluskap was responsible for making all the good things in the universe—the air, the earth, the animals, and the people—from his mother's body. His evil brother Malsum created the mountains and valleys and all the things that are a bother to humans, such as snakes and stinging insects. Malsum is sometimes described as a wolf.

Nationality/Culture
American Indian/
Wabanaki

Pronunciation
GLOOS-kahb

Alternate Names
Gluskabe, Glooscap

Appears In
Northeastern American
Indian creation mythology

Lineage
Formed out of the dust
from Tabaldak's hands

There are many tales about Gluskap's adventures and how he served his people, teaching them to hunt, fish, weave, and do many other useful things. In one story, a giant monster stole all the water and would not share it with anyone else. Gluskap fought the monster and turned it into a bullfrog. In another myth, Gluskap freed all the rabbits in the world, which were being held prisoner by the Great White Hare. The rabbits then became food for his people.

Gluskap in Context

To the Wabanaki people, Gluskap reflected the importance of treating the land and nature with respect. He was often tasked with correcting imbalances in nature, such as returning water to the world or limiting a giant bird's ability to create storms with its wings. After the Wabanaki people came into contact with white settlers, their differing views on the treatment of the natural world were reflected in their myths: Gluskap, it was said, was unhappy with the way the white people acted toward the land and creatures of the earth.

Key Themes and Symbols

One of the main themes in the myths of Gluskap is the idea of protecting the order of the natural world. Gluskap is associated with order, in contrast to his brother Malsum, who is seen as an agent of disorder and difficulty. It is Malsum who disrupts the natural state of things and makes circumstances difficult for both humans and animals.

Gluskap in Art, Literature, and Everyday Life

As with many characters from American Indian myth, Gluskap was given little opportunity to become part of mainstream American culture. In recent years, however, as the significance of these belief systems has been recognized, Gluskap has experienced more popularity than ever before. Statues of the hero have been erected in Parrsboro and Truro, both in the Canadian province of Nova Scotia. Gluskap is the featured character of the children's book *Gluskabe and the Four Wishes* (1995) by Joseph Bruchac, and is mentioned in the Newbery Honor book *The Sign of the Beaver* (1984) by Elizabeth George Speare.

Read, Write, Think, Discuss

To the Wabanaki people, Gluskap worked hard to maintain harmony between the different parts of the natural world. Some modern critics of the environmentalist movement suggest that nature itself—not humans—is the best regulator for keeping balance in the natural world. They point to examples where human interference with nature, such as the prevention of small-scale forest fires, has unintentionally led to bigger problems (massive forest fires that could have been prevented by natural, small-scale burns). Do you think human attempts to regulate nature are helpful, or do you think the unintended consequences of these actions are more damaging to nature? What about human attempts to "clean up" damage that has resulted from human activity?

SEE ALSO Animals in Mythology; Native American Mythology

Golden Bough

Myth Overview

In **Roman mythology**, the Golden Bough was a tree branch with golden leaves that enabled the Trojan hero **Aeneas** (pronounced i-NEE-uhs) to travel through the **underworld**, or land of the dead, safely. The bough was said to be sacred to Proserpina (pronounced prah-sur-PEE-nuh; the Roman version of Greek goddess **Persephone**, pronounced per-SEF-uh-nee), the queen of the underworld, and was associated with the goddess Diana (the Roman version of the Greek goddess **Artemis**, pronounced AHR-tuh-miss).

The story of Aeneas and the Golden Bough is found in the *Aeneid*, the epic poem by the Roman poet Virgil (pronounced VUR-juhl). According to this tale, the spirit of Anchises (pronounced an-KY-seez), Aeneas's dead father, appears and tells Aeneas to visit the underworld, where he will learn what the future holds in store for people. First, however, Aeneas must find the oracle known as the Sibyl of Cumae (pronounced KYOO-mee), who will lead him to the land of the dead.

Aeneas locates the oracle, who informs him that he cannot pass through the underworld safely without the Golden Bough. When Aeneas

Nationality/Culture
Roman

Alternate Names
None

Appears In
Virgil's *Aeneid*

enters the forest to look for the sacred branch, two doves lead him to an oak tree that shelters the bough of shimmering golden leaves. Aeneas gets the Golden Bough and returns to the Sibyl of Cumae.

Together Aeneas and the Sibyl enter the underworld. With the Golden Bough in his possession, the hero is able to pass safely through the various dangers and obstacles there. At the deadly and magical river Acheron (pronounced AK-uh-ron), the boatman Charon (pronounced KAIR-uhn) sees the sacred bough and takes Aeneas and the Sibyl across the water to the kingdom of **Hades** (pronounced HAY-deez). There Aeneas finds the spirit of his father.

The Golden Bough also appears in other legends, particularly in connection with the goddess Diana. According to some accounts, it was a custom among worshippers of Diana for a slave to cut a branch from a sacred tree and then kill the priest responsible for guarding the tree. The slave took the priest's place and was later killed himself in the same way.

The Golden Bough in Context

Some scholars, such as James Frazer, have suggested that the Golden Bough was actually mistletoe. Virgil describes the Golden Bough as being sheltered by an oak, much as mistletoe grows as a parasite on many trees, including oaks. In addition, mistletoe has a long history of supernatural associations in different cultures. Ancient Romans may have believed that mistletoe was dropped from the heavens and landed in the trees where it grew, which suggested that it would contain divine powers.

Key Themes and Symbols

In the tale of Aeneas and the Golden Bough, the magic branch represents both light and life. In this way it protects Aeneas from darkness and death while in the underworld. In the legend of the priest of Diana, the Golden Bough represents the sacred duty of the order that watches over it. It also represents the endless cycle of death and rebirth, as the priest who guards it is killed and replaced by a new priest, who will eventually meet the same fate.

The Golden Bough in Art, Literature, and Everyday Life

Although mentioned as part of a minor story in the *Aeneid*, the Golden Bough has become especially well known among modern scholars. The legends of the Golden Bough inspired Scottish scholar Sir James Frazer to write *The Golden Bough: A Study in Magic and Religion*, a multivolume study of religion and mythology published in 1890. This landmark work has in turn inspired many works of both fiction and nonfiction, and is the main source of the Golden Bough myth for modern readers. *The Assassin Tree*, an opera based on the myth of the slaves and the priest guarding the Golden Bough, was created by Stuart MacRae and Simon Armitage and premiered in 2006.

Read, Write, Think, Discuss

Why do you think death and **sacrifice** are so often connected with fertility goddesses like Prosperina?

SEE ALSO Aeneas; *Aeneid, The*; Artemis; Balder; Persephone; Roman Mythology; Underworld

Golden Fleece

Myth Overview

One of the best-known stories in **Greek mythology** concerns the hero **Jason** and his quest for the Golden Fleece. The fleece, which came from a magic ram, hung in a sacred grove of trees in the distant land of Colchis (pronounced KOL-kis). Jason's adventure, however, was only one part of the story of the Golden Fleece, which began years earlier.

According to legend, King Athamas (pronounced ATH-uh-mas) of Boeotia (pronounced bee-OH-shuh) in Greece had two children by his wife Nephele (pronounced NEF-uh-lee): a son, Phrixus (pronounced FRIK-suhs), and a daughter, Helle (pronounced HEL-ee). After a time, Athamas grew tired of Nephele and took a new wife, Ino (pronounced EYE-noh), with whom he had two sons. Jealous of Phrixus and Helle, Ino plotted against them. First, she cunningly had seeds destroyed so that crops would not grow, resulting in a famine. She then arranged to have blame for the famine placed on her stepchildren and convinced Athamas that he must **sacrifice** Phrixus to

Nationality/Culture
Greek

Alternate Names
None

Appears In
Pindar's *Pythian Ode*, Apollonius Rhodius's *Argonautica*, Euripides' *Medea*

Zeus (pronounced ZOOS), the king of the gods, to restore the kingdom's prosperity.

Fearful for her children's lives, Nephele sought help from the god **Hermes** (pronounced HUR-meez), and he sent a winged ram with a fleece of gold to carry Phrixus and Helle to safety. While flying over the water on the ram, Helle fell off and drowned. But Phrixus reached the land of Colchis and was welcomed by its ruler, King Aeëtes (pronounced ye-EE-teez). Phrixus sacrificed the ram to Zeus and gave the Golden Fleece to the king, who placed it in an oak tree in a sacred grove. It was guarded by a dragon that never slept.

The story of the Golden Fleece resumes some time later when Jason and the **Argonauts** (pronounced AHR-guh-nawts), a band of Greek **heroes**, set out in search of the fleece aboard a ship called the *Argo*. Jason undertook this quest in order to gain his rightful place as king of Iolcus (pronounced ee-AHL-kuhs) in Thessaly (THESS-uh-lee). The country had been ruled for a number of years by his uncle Pelias (pronounced PEEL-ee-uhs).

After many adventures, Jason and the Argonauts finally reached Colchis. However, King Aeëtes refused to give up the Golden Fleece unless Jason could harness two fire-breathing bulls to a plow, plant **dragons**' teeth in the ground, and defeat the warriors that sprang up from the teeth. Aeëtes had a daughter, **Medea** (pronounced me-DEE-uh), who was a sorceress. She fell in love with Jason and helped him accomplish these tasks. Medea also helped Jason steal the Golden Fleece by charming the serpent that guarded it and putting the creature to sleep. Jason, Medea, and the Argonauts then set sail for Iolcus with the fleece. Although Jason returned with the fleece, he did not become king and was punished by the gods for betraying Medea's love; however, Jason's son, Thessalus (pronounced THESS-uh-luhs), did eventually become king.

The Golden Fleece in Context

The myths of the Golden Fleece center on the passing of royal power from one generation to the next. These myths pre-date government rule by elected officials, and represent an older system of rule still common in many regions during the height of the Greek empire. Historical records suggest that plots and overthrows of rulers were all too common in ancient Greece and Rome. The myths of the Golden Fleece help to encourage the traditional passing of power from a king to his son; this is done by casting both Phrixus and Jason in sympathetic and heroic roles, prompting the audience to root for their success.

Key Themes and Symbols

In the myth of Jason and the Argonauts, the Golden Fleece is a symbol of that which is unattainable or cannot be possessed. Pelias only gives Jason the task because he believes it cannot be completed. Even after arriving in Colchis, the fleece seems impossible to take. And once Jason returns to Iolcus with the fleece, he is still unable to attain his rightful place as king. The Golden Fleece can also be seen as a symbol of rightful heirs to royal power, as both Phrixus and Jason possessed the fleece and both were rightful heirs to their fathers' thrones.

The Golden Fleece in Art, Literature, and Everyday Life

Many writers have been inspired by the subject of Jason's quest for the Golden Fleece. Among the ancient Greek works concerning the subject are Pindar's *Pythian Ode,* Apollonius Rhodius's *Argonautica,* and Euripides' play *Medea.* In the Middle Ages, Chaucer retold the story in the *Legend of Good Women,* and in the 1800s, William Morris wrote the long narrative poem *Life and Death of Jason* which centered on the quest. Robert Graves's novel about Jason, *The Golden Fleece,* was published in 1944, and John Gardner's *Jason and Medeia* was published in 1973. The story of the search for the Golden Fleece has also been adapted to film, most notably the 1963 movie *Jason and the Argonauts.*

Read, Write, Think, Discuss

The notion of a "rightful heir" to a throne is common in modern fantasy, as it is in ancient myth. However, in most modern societies, people are not born into power but are chosen by the public to govern, and even then they may only rule for a short time instead of ruling for life. Why do you think so many modern works of fantasy focus on kings and their successive heirs instead of including types of government more common in modern times?

SEE ALSO Animals in Mythology; Argonauts; Jason; Medea

Golems

Nationality/Culture
Jewish

Pronunciation
GOH-luhmz

Alternate Names
None

Appears In
The Talmud, Jewish folk tales

Lineage
None

Character Overview

According to Jewish legend, a golem was a human-shaped object brought to life by a magic word. Usually the golem functioned like a robot and could perform simple tasks. However, in some tales, the golem became a violent monster that could not be controlled, even by its creator.

Although the idea of a golem goes back to biblical times, most legends about the creature appeared during the Middle Ages. A golem was created from mud or clay. Typically, the golem came to life when a special word such as "truth" or one of the names of God was written on a piece of paper and placed on the golem's forehead or in its mouth. At any point, the creator of the golem might end its life by removing the paper with the sacred word. If the word *emet* ("truth") was used to activate the golem, the golem could be made still by erasing the first letter so that it read *met* ("death").

In a famous story from the 1500s, Rabbi Judah Low ben Bezulel of Prague created a golem from clay in order to defend the city's Jews from attack after the Emperor ordered the Jews to leave. The Emperor, seeing the power and destruction the golem was capable of, agreed to let the Jews stay. According to legend, the deactivated golem remains in the attic of a Prague synagogue just in case the Jews need protecting again in the future. In another legend, set in Poland, a golem made by Rabbi Eliyahu of Chelm became so powerful and dangerous that the rabbi hurriedly changed it back into a lifeless heap. Unfortunately, when the golem collapsed to the ground, it crushed its creator.

Golems in Context

The Jewish people that settled throughout Europe had a long history of being persecuted by others, especially European Christians. They were often blamed for the death of Jesus—citing an old legend surrounding the Crucifixion—and were commonly thought to be selfish and unclean. Because of this, Jewish communities in many European cities were fairly self-contained and separate from other districts. The idea of a creature that could protect the Jews from being attacked or driven out of their homes was a welcome and, in some ways, inevitable development in Jewish folklore.

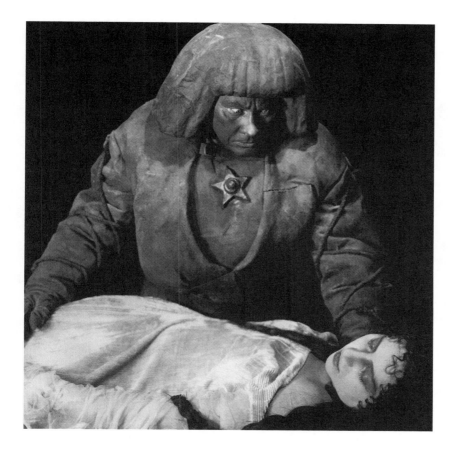

Key Themes and Symbols

Golems are symbols of pure, mindless power and strength. They are also symbols of protection for the Jewish people, though their power can prove dangerous as well. The tale of Rabbi Eliyahu is centered on the theme of hubris, or overconfidence in one's abilities. The rabbi creates a golem thinking he will be able to control it, but is eventually destroyed by his creation.

Golems in Art, Literature, and Everyday Life

The idea of the golem was influential outside traditional Jewish folklore. The creature in Mary Shelley's 1818 novel *Frankenstein* bears some resemblance to the classic description of a golem, though the book makes no mention of the Jewish myth. The 1915 silent film *The Golem*, co-written and directed by Paul Wegener (who also starred as the golem), was the first and most well-known cinematic adaptation of the traditional golem myth. Karel Capek's 1921 play *Rossum's Universal Robots*, in which the author invented the term "robot," was a science fiction version of the golem legend. A golem also features prominently in the 2000 Pulitzer Prize–winning novel *The Amazing Adventures of Kavalier and Clay* by Michael Chabon.

Read, Write, Think, Discuss

Compare myths about the golem in Jewish folklore with modern myths about robots. Do the stories in movies like *The Matrix* and *The Terminator* resemble traditional tales of the golem? How are they different?

SEE ALSO Semitic Mythology

Gorgons

Character Overview

The Gorgons, three terrifying creatures in **Greek mythology**, were sisters named Stheno (pronounced STHEE-noh; "strength"), Euryale (pronounced yoo-RYE-uh-lee; "wide-leaping"), and **Medusa** (pronounced meh-DOO-suh; "ruler" or "queen"). Daughters of the sea god Phorcys (pronounced FOR-sis) and his sister and wife, Ceto (pronounced SEE-toh), they lived in the west near the setting **sun**.

According to legend, the Gorgons were ugly monsters with huge wings, sharp fangs and claws, and bodies covered with dragonlike scales. They had horrible grins, staring eyes, and writhing snakes for hair. Their gaze was so terrifying that anyone who looked upon them immediately turned to stone. It was said that blood taken from the right side of one of the Gorgons had the power to revive the dead, while blood taken from the left would instantly kill any living thing. Two of the Gorgons, Stheno and Euryale, were immortal (able to live forever), but Medusa was not. In one of the more famous Greek myths, the hero **Perseus** (pronounced PUR-see-uhs) killed and beheaded her with help from **Athena** (pronounced uh-THEE-nuh). When Medusa was beheaded, the

Nationality/Culture
Greek/Roman

Pronunciation
GOR-guhnz

Alternate Names
None

Appears In
Hesiod's *Theogony*, Ovid's *Metamorphoses*

Lineage
Daughters of Phorcys and Ceto

winged horse **Pegasus** (pronounced PEG-uh-suhs) sprang from her headless neck. Athena later placed an image of Medusa's head on her armor.

The Gorgons had three sisters known as the Graeae (pronounced GREE-ee; "the gray ones"). These old women—Enyo (pronounced eh-NYE-oh), Pemphredo (pronounced pem-FREE-doh), and Deino (pronounced DAY-noh)—shared one eye and one tooth, and they took turns using them. The Graeae guarded the route that led to their sisters, the Gorgons. Perseus, however, stole their eye and tooth, forcing them to help in his quest to find and kill Medusa.

Gorgons in Context

In ancient Greece and Rome, Gorgon images were common household decorations; their hideous faces were thought to ward off evil. They often adorned entrances to buildings as a way to protect those inside, and commonly appeared on household items like water jugs. This type of magic—where evil is kept away, usually by an unappealing word or image—is known as apotropaic (pronounced ap-uh-troh-PAY-ik) magic. Although the Gorgons are described as hideous, awful creatures, they also served as protectors against outside forces.

Key Themes and Symbols

Gorgons, as with their sisters the Graeae, usually symbolize ugliness and solitude. They have few interactions with outsiders. The Gorgons and Graeae also represent the bonds of sisterhood, since they remain together and care for one another apart from the rest of the world.

Gorgons in Art, Literature, and Everyday Life

Medusa is the most popular of the Gorgons. She has appeared in art by Rubens, Pablo Picasso, and Leonardo da Vinci (the two paintings of Medusa by da Vinci have not survived). Perhaps the most famous images of Medusa are the headless portrait painted by Caravaggio in 1597, and the 16th century bronze statue of Perseus holding Medusa's head sculpted by Benvenuto Cellini. The story of Perseus and Medusa is retold in the 1981 film *Clash of the Titans*, with Medusa depicted as a grotesque woman with the lower body of a snake. Medusa also appears in Rick Riordan's 2005 novel *The Lightning Thief*, a modern retelling of several ancient Greek myths.

Read, Write, Think, Discuss

The ancient Greeks often associated physical ugliness, especially in a woman, with evil and an undesirable personality. What details can you find in the myths of the Gorgons that emphasize their ugly appearance? Are your culture's ideas about ugliness similar to those of the ancient Greeks? How are unattractive people treated in your society?

SEE ALSO Greek Mythology; Medusa; Perseus

Graces

Nationality/Culture
Greek

Pronunciation
GRAY-siz

Alternate Names
Charites, Gratiae (Roman)

Appears In
Hesiod's *Theogony*, ancient Greek hymns and odes

Lineage
Daughters of Zeus and Eurynome

Character Overview

In Greek and **Roman mythology**, the Graces were minor goddesses who symbolized beauty, charm, and goodness. The number of Graces varied, though most myths included three sisters: Aglaia (pronounced uh-GLAY-uh; "brightness" or "splendor"), Thalia (pronounced thuh-LYE-uh; "good cheer" or "blossoming one"), and Euphrosyne (pronounced yoo-FROS-uh-nee; "mirth" or "joyfulness"). Other Graces sometimes mentioned were Cleta (pronounced KLEE-tuh; "sound"), Pasithea (pronounced puh-SITH-ee-uh; "shining"), and Peitho (pronounced PYE-tho; "persuasion").

Major Myths

According to most stories, the Graces were the children of **Zeus** (pronounced ZOOS) and Eurynome (pronounced yoo-RIN-uh-mee), a daughter of the **Titans** Oceanus (pronounced oh-SEE-uh-nuhs) and Tethys (pronounced TEE-this). In some myths, however, the Graces' parents were Zeus and **Hera** (pronounced HAIR-uh). The Graces always appeared as a group rather than as separate individuals. They were also frequently linked with the **Muses** (pronounced MYOO-siz), another group of female goddesses.

The main role of the Graces was to bestow beauty, charm, and goodness on young women and to give joy to people in general. They were usually associated with **Aphrodite** (pronounced af-ro-DYE-tee), the goddess of love, and appeared among the attendants of the gods **Apollo** (pronounced uh-POL-oh), **Dionysus** (pronounced dye-uh-NYE-suhs), and **Hermes** (pronounced HUR-meez). They entertained the gods by dancing to the music of Apollo's lyre, an ancient stringed musical instrument. At times, the Graces were considered the official goddesses of music, dance, and poetry.

The Graces in Context

The Graces were meant to embody the characteristics that ancient Greeks considered attractive in young women. The ideal young woman was not only beautiful, but also a source of good cheer and brightness of spirit. Girls were expected to never show an ill mood, because it was considered an ugly quality that would repel any possible suitors.

Key Themes and Symbols

The Graces represent beauty, joy, and the arts. They also symbolize the way in which beauty and happiness were considered to be fundamentally connected by the ancient Greeks, as the Graces are always shown together and usually holding hands. They are also seen as symbols of youth, creativity, and fertility.

The Graces in Art, Literature, and Everyday Life

The Graces provided inspiration to artists throughout the centuries. Most works of art portray them with their hands entwined and their bodies either nude or partially draped with flowing robes. The Graces have been painted by Raphael, Rubens, and Paul Cezanne among others, and appear in a well-known sculpture by Antonio Canova. One of the most famous paintings of the Graces is *Primavera* by Sandro Botticelli, an Italian artist of the late 1400s.

Detail of Sandro Botticelli's painting **Primavera**, *showing the three Graces.* DAVID LEES/ TIME & LIFE PICTURES/GETTY IMAGES.

Read, Write, Think, Discuss

In ancient Greece, the Graces functioned as role models for young women, offering an example of ideal behaviors and qualities. What qualities do you think the most popular modern role models for young women exhibit? How do they compare to the qualities of the Graces? Which do you think provides a better example to follow, and why?

SEE ALSO Apollo; Greek Mythology; Muses; Roman Mythology

Greek Mythology

Greek Mythology in Context

The mythology of the ancient Greeks included a dazzling array of gods, demigods (half-human, half-god), monsters, and **heroes**. These figures inhabited a realm that stretched beyond the Greek landscape to the palaces of the gods on snow-capped Mount Olympus (pronounced oh-LIM-puhs), as well as to the dismal **underworld** or land of the dead. In time, Greek mythology became part of European culture, and many of its stories became known throughout the world.

Despite their awesome powers, the Greek gods and goddesses were much like people. Their actions stemmed from recognizable passions, such as pride, jealousy, love, and the thirst for revenge. The deities (gods) often left Mount Olympus to become involved in the affairs of mortals, interacting with men and women as protectors, enemies, and sometimes lovers. They were not above using tricks and disguises to influence events, and their schemes and plots often entangled people.

Heroes and ordinary humans in Greek myths frequently discovered that things were not what they appeared to be. The underlying moral principle, though, was that the gods rewarded honorable behavior and obedience, and people who dishonored themselves or defied the gods usually paid a high price.

Geography helped shape Greek mythology. Greece is a peninsula surrounded by sea and islands. Rugged mountains and the jagged coastline break the land into many small, separate areas. Ancient Greece never became a unified empire. Instead, it consisted of small kingdoms that after

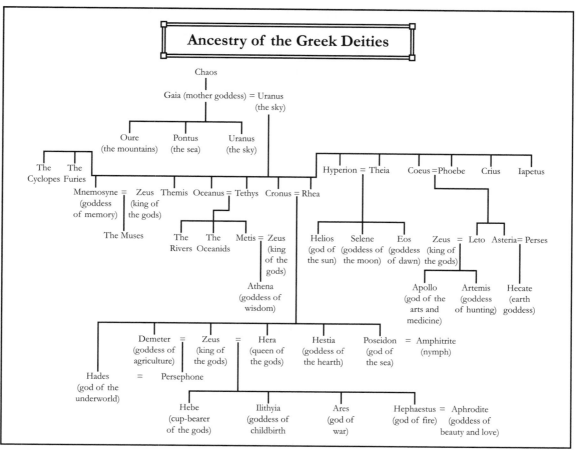

Ancestry of the Greek Deities

Chaos

Gaia (mother goddess) = Uranus (the sky)

Oure (the mountains) — Pontus (the sea) — Uranus (the sky)

The Cyclopes — The Furies

Mnemosyne (goddess of memory) = Zeus (king of the gods)

The Muses

Themis — Oceanus = Tethys — Cronus = Rhea

The Rivers — The Oceanids — Metis = Zeus (king of the gods)

Athena (goddess of wisdom)

Hyperion = Theia — Coeus = Phoebe — Crius — Iapetus

Helios (god of the sun) — Selene (goddess of the moon) — Eos (goddess of dawn) — Zeus (king of the gods) = Leto — Asteria = Perses

Apollo (god of the arts and medicine) — Artemis (goddess of hunting) — Hecate (earth goddess)

Demeter (goddess of agriculture) = Zeus (king of the gods) = Hera (queen of the gods) — Hestia (goddess of the hearth) — Poseidon (god of the sea) = Amphitrite (nymph)

Hades (god of the underworld) = Persephone

Hebe (cup-bearer of the gods) — Ilithyia (goddess of childbirth) — Ares (god of war) — Hephaestus (god of fire) = Aphrodite (goddess of beauty and love)

ILLUSTRATION BY ANAXOS, INC./CENGAGE LEARNING, GALE.

about 800 BCE became city-states. Because travel was easier by sea than by land, the Greeks became a nation of seafarers, and they traded and established colonies all over the Mediterranean and the Near East.

Greek mythology is a patchwork of stories, some conflicting with one another. Many have been passed down from ancient times in more than one version. The roots of this mythology reach back to two civilizations that flourished before 1100 BCE: the Mycenaean (pronounced mye-suh-NEE-uhn), on the Greek mainland, and the Minoan (pronounced mi-NOH-uhn), on the nearby island of Crete (pronounced KREET). The ancient beliefs merged with legends from Greek kingdoms and city-states and myths borrowed from other peoples to form a body of lore shared by most Greeks.

For hundreds of years, these myths passed from generation to generation in spoken form. Then, around the time the classical Greek culture of the city-states arose, people began writing them down. The works of Hesiod and Homer, which date from the 700s BCE, are key sources for the mythology of ancient Greece. Hesiod's *Theogony* tells of creation and of the gods' origins and relationships. The ***Iliad*** and the ***Odyssey***, epic poems said to have been written by Homer, show the gods influencing human fortunes. In addition, Pindar, a poet of around 600 BCE, wrote poems called odes that contain much myth and legend.

Non-Greek sources also exist. The Romans dominated the Mediterranean world after the Greeks and adopted elements of Greek mythology. The Roman poet Ovid's poem the *Metamorphoses* retells many Greek myths.

Core Deities and Characters

The word *pantheon*, which refers to all the gods of a particular culture, comes from the Greek *pan* (all) and *theoi* (gods). The pantheon of the ancient Greeks consisted of the Olympian gods and other major deities, along with many minor deities and demigods.

Olympian Gods The principal deities, six gods and six goddesses, lived on Mount Olympus, the highest peak in Greece. **Zeus** (pronounced ZOOS; called Jupiter by the Romans) was the king of the gods and reigned over all the other deities and their realms. He was the protector of justice, kingship, authority, and the social order. His personal life was rather disorderly, however. Many myths tell of his love affairs with various goddesses, **Titans**, and human women—and their effects.

Hera (pronounced HAIR-uh; Roman Juno), queen of the gods, was Zeus's sister and wife. She could cause all kinds of trouble when her husband pursued other women. Although the patron of brides, wives, and mothers in childbirth, Hera could be cruel and vengeful toward Zeus's mistresses and their children.

Poseidon (pronounced poh-SYE-dun; Roman Neptune), Zeus's brother, was god of the sea and of earthquakes. He was married to Amphitrite (pronounced am-fi-TRY-tee), a sea nymph or female nature deity, but like Zeus, he fathered many children outside his marriage. Among his descendants were **nymphs**, sea gods, and monsters such as the Hydra (pronounced HYE-druh).

Major Greek Deities

Aphrodite: (*Roman name: Venus*) goddess of love and beauty.

Apollo: (*Roman name: Apollo*) god of the sun, arts, and medicine; ideal of male beauty.

Ares: (*Roman name: Mars*) god of war.

Artemis: (*Roman name: Diana*) goddess of hunting and protector of wild animals.

Athena: (*Roman name: Minerva*) goddess of wisdom, warfare, and crafts.

Demeter: (*Roman name: Ceres*) goddess of grain, farming, and soil.

Dionysus: (*Roman name: Bacchus*) god of wine and revelry.

Hades: (*Roman name: Pluto*) king of the underworld.

Hephaestus: (*Roman name: Vulcan*) god of fire, volcanoes, and industry.

Hera: (*Roman name: Juno*) queen of the gods, protector of marriage and childbirth.

Hermes: (*Roman name: Mercury*) messenger of the gods, patron of travelers, merchants, and thieves.

Hestia: (*Roman name: Vesta*) goddess of the hearth.

Persephone: (*Roman name: Proserpina*) queen of the underworld.

Poseidon: (*Roman name: Neptune*) god of the sea.

Prometheus: giver of fire and crafts to humans.

Zeus: (*Roman name: Jupiter*) king of the gods, protector of justice and social order.

Demeter (pronounced di-MEE-ter; Roman Ceres), a sister of Zeus, was the goddess of grain, farming, and soil. She had a daughter, **Persephone** (pronounced per-SEF-uh-nee), by Zeus. Before merging into the Olympian pantheon, Demeter and Hera were aspects of a much older deity called the Great Goddess, an earth goddess worshiped by the agricultural Greeks.

Aphrodite (pronounced af-ro-DYE-tee; Roman Venus), the goddess of love, beauty, and desire, greatly resembled Near Eastern goddesses such as **Ishtar** (pronounced ISH-tahr) and Astarte (a-STAR-tee). Her husband was **Hephaestus** (pronounced hi-FES-tuhs; Roman Vulcan), god of **fire**, volcanoes, and invention. The other gods mocked Hephaestus because he was lame and also because of Aphrodite's adulteries, such as her love affair with the god of war, **Ares** (pronounced AIR-eez; Roman Mars).

Two Olympian goddesses were virgins who resisted sexual advances from gods and men. **Athena** (pronounced uh-THEE-nuh; Roman Minerva), the daughter of Zeus and a female Titan, was the goddess of wisdom, military skill, cities, and crafts. **Artemis** (pronounced AHR-tuh-miss; Roman Diana) was the goddess of hunting and the protector of wild animals. She and her twin brother, the handsome young god **Apollo** (pronounced uh-POL-oh), were the children of Zeus and the Titan Leto (pronounced LEE-toh). Apollo functioned as the patron (official god) of archery, music, the arts, and medicine and was associated with the **sun**, enlightenment, and prophecy or predicting the future. He also served as the ideal of male beauty.

Hermes (pronounced HUR-meez; Roman Mercury) was the son of Zeus and yet another Titan. He served as the gods' messenger and also as the patron of markets, merchants, thieves, and storytelling. Hestia (pronounced HESS-tee-uh; Roman Vesta), another sister of Zeus, was goddess of the hearth, and her identity included associations with stability, domestic well-being, and the ritual of naming children.

Other Major Deities Hades (pronounced HAY-deez; Roman Pluto), the brother of Zeus and Poseidon, was god of the underworld, where the dead could receive either punishment or a blessed **afterlife**. Hades dwelt in his underground kingdom and not on Mount Olympus. He controlled supernatural forces connected with the earth and was also associated with wealth.

Dionysus (pronounced dye-uh-NYE-suhs; Roman Bacchus), born as a demigod, became the god of wine, drunkenness, and altered states of consciousness, such as religious frenzy. Like plants that die each winter only to return in the spring, Dionysus is said to have died and been reborn, a parallel to Cretan and Near Eastern myths about dying-and-returning gods. Dionysus eventually took Hestia's place on Mount Olympus.

Major Myths

Stories about the gods—along with other supernatural beings, demigods, heroes, and ordinary mortals—illustrate the major themes of Greek mythology. They explain how the world came to be and offer examples of how people should and should not live. The myths provided support for the Greeks' idea of community, especially the city-state.

Myth and History

Generations of readers have wondered whether the great Greek myths were based on true stories. One reader who decided to investigate was German archaeologist Heinrich Schliemann. Convinced that the ancient city of Troy mentioned in Homer's *Iliad* had actually existed, he set out to find it. In the early 1870s, Schliemann began digging at a site in northwestern Turkey that matched Homer's description of Troy. He found the buried remains of a city as well as gold, silver, pottery, and household objects. Later excavations by other researchers revealed that a series of different settlements had risen on the same site over thousands of years. One of these may have been Homer's Troy.

Origins of the Gods and Humans The theme of younger generations overcoming their elders runs through the history of the Greek gods. Creation began with Chaos (pronounced KAY-oss), first imagined as the gap between earth and sky but later as formless confusion. The mother goddess, **Gaia** (pronounced GAY-uh), the earth, came into being and gave birth to **Uranus** (pronounced YOOR-uh-nuhs), the sky. Joining with Uranus, she became pregnant with six male and six female Titans. But before these children could be born, Uranus had to be separated from Gaia. **Cronus** (pronounced KROH-nuhs), the youngest Titan, cut off his father's sexual organs and threw them into the sea. Aphrodite was born from the foam where they landed.

The twelve Titans mated with each other and with nymphs. Cronus married his sister Rhea (pronounced REE-uh; Roman Cybele). Perhaps remembering what he had done to his own father, Cronus swallowed his children as they were born. When Rhea gave birth to Zeus, however, she tricked Cronus by substituting a stone wrapped in baby clothes for him to swallow. Later, when Zeus had grown up, a female Titan named Metis (pronounced MEE-tis) gave Cronus a drink that made him vomit up Zeus's brothers and sisters. They helped Zeus defeat the Titans and become the supreme deity. Zeus then married Metis. However, because of a prophecy that her children would be wise and powerful, he swallowed her so that her children could not harm him. Their daughter Athena sprang full-grown from Zeus's head.

The matings of the gods and goddesses produced the rest of the pantheon. As for human beings, one myth says that they arose out of the soil. Another says that Zeus flooded the earth and drowned all human beings because they did not honor the gods. Deucalion (doo-KAY-lee-uhn) and Pyrrha (pronounced PEER-uh), the son and daughter-in-law of Zeus's brother **Prometheus** (pronounced pruh-MEE-thee-uhs), survived the flood in a boat. Afterward they created the present human race from stones, which they threw onto the muddy land.

The Ages of the World According to the poet Hesiod, the world had seen four ages and four races of human beings before this time. The Titans created the people of the golden age, who lived in comfort and peace until they died and became good spirits. The Olympian gods created the silver race, a childish people whom Zeus destroyed for failing to honor the gods. Zeus then created the bronze race, brutal and warlike people who destroyed themselves with constant fighting.

Zeus next created a race of heroes nobler than the men of the bronze age (no metal was associated with this age). The Greeks believed that distant but semihistorical events such as the Trojan War had occurred during this fourth age, the age of heroes. Some heroes died, but Zeus took the survivors to the Isles of the Blessed, where they lived in honor. The fifth age, the age of iron, began when Zeus created the present race of humans. It is an age of toil, greed, and strife. When all honor and justice have vanished, Zeus will destroy this race like those before it.

Heroes Many Greek myths focus on the marvelous achievements of heroes who possessed physical strength, sharp wits, virtue, and a sense of honor. These heroes often had a god for a father and a human for a mother. One cycle of myths concerns the hero **Heracles** (pronounced HAIR-uh-kleez; known as Hercules by the Romans)—Zeus's son by a mortal princess—renowned for his strength and for completing twelve remarkable feats. Unlike other heroes, who died and were buried, Heracles eventually became immortal (able to live forever) and was worshipped as a god by both Greeks and Romans. Other heroes include **Perseus** (pronounced PUR-see-uhs), who killed the serpent-haired monster **Medusa** (pronounced meh-DOO-suh) and rescued a princess from a sea monster; **Theseus** (pronounced THEE-see-uhs), who defeated the man-eating **Minotaur** (pronounced MIN-uh-tawr) of Crete; **Jason**, who led a band of adventurers to capture the **Golden Fleece**; **Achilles** (pronounced uh-KILL-eez), a mighty warrior of the Trojan War; and **Odysseus** (pronounced oh-DIS-ee-uhs), who fought at

Troy and afterward faced many challenges from gods, men, and monsters during his long journey home.

Key Themes and Symbols

The gods were born in strife and struggle, and the theme of war as an inescapable part of existence runs through Greek mythology. Many myths recount episodes in the Olympians' conflict with the Titans. Others are connected to the Trojan War, a long conflict in which both people and deities displayed such qualities as courage, stubbornness, pride, and anger. In addition to the war itself, the travels and adventures of warriors after the war ended are subjects of myth and legend.

Many myths deal with love, especially the loves of Zeus, who sometimes disguised himself in order to enjoy sexual relations with mortal women. Other myths present examples of trust, loyalty, and eternal love—or of the pitfalls and problems of love and desire. The tragic myth of Pyramus (pronounced PEER-uh-muhs) and Thisbe (pronounced THIZ-bee) illustrates a divine reward for lovers who could not live without each other. The story of **Eros** (pronounced AIR-ohs) and **Psyche** (pronounced SYE-kee) revolves around the issue of trust. In another myth, the gods reward the elderly Baucis (pronounced BAW-sis) and Philemon (pronounced fye-LEE-muhn) for their devotion to each other and their kindheartedness toward strangers.

Another recurring theme in Greek myth is death. Characters in Greek myths sometimes enter the underworld, the kingdom of the god Hades. Heroes may go there seeking advice or prophecies from the dead. Persephone, Demeter's daughter, was carried to the underworld by Hades, who fell in love with her. Her myth explains the seasons: plants grow and bear fruit while Persephone is aboveground with her mother but wither and die during the months she spends with Hades. The tale of **Orpheus** (pronounced OR-fee-uhs) and **Eurydice** (pronounced yoo-RID-uh-see) explores the finality of death and the tempting possibility of a reunion with loved ones who have died.

Many Greek myths deal with themes of right and wrong behavior and the consequences of each. The myth of **Baucis and Philemon**, for example, illustrates the importance of hospitality and generosity toward all, for a humble stranger may be a deity in disguise with power to reward or punish. Another story tells how the handsome **Narcissus** (pronounced nar-SIS-us), so vain and heartless that he could love only himself, drowned while gazing at his reflection in a stream. The myth of Icarus (pronounced IK-uh-ruhs), who gains the ability to fly but soars so close to the sun that his wings melt, points out the dangers of tempting fate and rising above one's proper place in life. Such stories often involve unexpected changes or transformations. For example, the myth of King **Midas** (pronounced MY-duhs), whose request for a golden touch turns his own daughter into a golden statue, warns of the perils of greed.

Like Icarus, those who claim godlike qualities, who defy the gods, or who perform outrageous acts suffer swift and severe punishment. **Arachne** (pronounced uh-RAK-nee) was a mortal who boasted that she could weave better cloth than the goddess Athena, inventor of weaving. The goddess turned the boastful girl into a spider weaving its web. The gods devised eternal punishments in the depths of Hades for **Sisyphus** (pronounced SIZ-ee-fuhs), who tried to cheat death, and for Tantalus (pronounced TAN-tuhl-uhs), who killed his own son and fed him to the gods. They also punished **Oedipus** (pronounced ED-uh-puhs), who killed his father and married his mother, even though he did not know their identities when he did so.

Transformation—the act of changing from one form into another—is a common theme in Greek mythology. The gods had the power to change themselves into animals, birds, or humans and often used this power to trick goddesses or women. Zeus, for example, turned himself into a bull for one romantic adventure and into a swan for another. Sometimes the gods and goddesses transformed others, either to save them or to punish them. Daphne (pronounced DAF-nee), for example, was changed into a laurel tree; Narcissus and Hyacinthus (pronounced high-uh-SIN-thuhs) became the flowers that bear their names.

Greek Mythology in Art, Literature, and Everyday Life

Greek mythology has profoundly influenced Western culture. So universally familiar are its stories that many of our common words and sayings refer to them. The myth of Narcissus, for example, produced *narcissism*, or excessive vanity, and something that causes an argument may be called an "apple of discord," after an apple that Eris (pronounced AIR-is), the goddess of discord, used to start a dispute among Athena, Aphrodite, and Hera. Greek myths and legends span the sky in the names of constellations and planets.

The Greek gods made their home on Mt. Olympus as illustrated in this painting by Jan van Kessel, **The Feast of the Gods.**
© MUSEE D'ART ET D'HISTOIRE, SAINT-GERMAIN-EN-LAYE, FRANCE/GIRAUDON/THE BRIDGEMAN ART LIBRARY.

Literature and drama have long drawn upon themes and stories from Greek myth. Besides the works of the ancient Greeks themselves—including the plays of Sophocles and Euripides—writers from ancient times to the present have found inspiration in Greek mythology. Roman authors Virgil (the ***Aeneid***) and Ovid (the *Metamorphoses*) used Greek stories and characters in their poems. References to Greek myths appear in the works of the medieval Italian poets Petrarch and Boccaccio and in those of the English poet Geoffrey Chaucer. William Shakespeare's *A*

Midsummer Night's Dream contains the story of Pyramus and Thisbe as a comic play-within-a-play. Modern writers who have drawn upon Greek mythology include James Joyce (*Ulysses*) and Mary Renault (*The Bull from the Sea*).

Artists from the Renaissance to the present have depicted scenes from Greek mythology. Sandro Botticelli's *Birth of Venus* (c. 1480), Nicolas Poussin's *Apollo and Daphne* (c. 1630), and Pierre-Auguste Renoir's *Diana* (1867) are just a few of many such paintings. The Greeks chanted songs and hymns based on myth at religious festivals, and Greek mythology has continued to inspire composers of the performing arts. Operas based on mythic stories include Claudio Monteverdi's *Ariadne*, Richard Strauss's *Elektra*, and Jacques Offenbach's *Orpheus in the Underworld*. Marcel Camus's film *Black Orpheus* also came from the story of Orpheus and Eurydice. *Apollo* and *Orpheus* by George Balanchine, *Ariadne* by Alvin Ailey, and *Clytemnestra* by Martha Graham are four modern ballets that interpret Greek myths through dance.

Read, Write, Think, Discuss

Percy Jackson and the Olympians by Rick Riordan (2005) is a series of books about a troubled boy named Perseus (Percy for short) who lives in New York and discovers he is the son of Poseidon. Soon he embarks on many adventures along with his best friend—who, he discovers, is actually a satyr (half-human, half-goat)—and encounters an array of characters from ancient Greek myth. In the first book, *The Lightning Thief*, Percy must find Zeus's stolen lightning bolt before the angry god destroys humankind.

SEE ALSO Creation Stories; *Iliad, The*; *Odyssey, The*; Roman Mythology

Griffins

Character Overview

The griffin was a creature that appeared in the mythology of Greece and the ancient Near East. A popular figure in art, it had the body of a lion

Nationality/Culture
Greek and Persian

Pronunciation
GRIF-ins

Alternate Names
Gryphon, Gryps

Appears In
Herodotus's *Histories*, Persian and Scythian myths

Lineage
None

and the head and wings of an eagle or other bird. Sometimes the griffin is shown with the tail of a serpent.

According to **Greek mythology**, griffins pulled the chariots of **Zeus** (pronounced ZOOS), the king of the gods, as well as his son **Apollo** (pronounced uh-POL-oh). They also guarded the gold that lay near the lands of the Hyperboreans (pronounced hye-pur-BOR-ee-uhnz) and the Arimaspians (pronounced air-uh-MAS-pee-uhnz), mythical peoples of the far north, and represented Nemesis (pronounced NEM-uh-sis), the goddess of vengeance.

The griffin appears in Christian art and mythology as well. At first, it symbolized **Satan** and was thought to threaten human souls. But the griffin later became a symbol of the divine and human nature of Jesus Christ. During the Middle Ages, Christian myths often spoke of the magical powers of griffins' claws, which if made into drinking cups were said to change color when they came in contact with poison. The griffin was also thought to prey on those who mistreated Christians.

Griffins in Context

Scythians, who lived in a large region northeast of Greece, popularized myths about griffins, and may have done so to protect their own resources against invaders. It was common legend that griffins guarded the gold that could be found in the area called the Pontic-Caspian steppe. These legends may have dissuaded people who lived in nearby regions from trying to claim this gold. Scythians may have even used dinosaur bones—also commonly found in this area—as evidence that the monstrous griffins really did exist.

Key Themes and Symbols

With its eagle's head and lion's body, the griffin represented mastery of the sky and the earth. It became associated with strength and wisdom, with the head of the eagle—wisdom—leading the way for the strength of the lion's body. To the ancient Hebrews, the griffin symbolized Persia because the creature appeared frequently in Persian art.

Griffins in Art, Literature, and Everyday Life

Griffins have become a common fixture in art and literature, especially in Europe. Griffins appear regularly on coats of arms, and are used as the

heraldic symbol for many European cities. Griffins have appeared as characters in literary works such as Dante's *Divine Comedy* (c. 1320) and Lewis Carroll's *Alice's Adventures in Wonderland* (1865). Sir John Tenniel's illustrations of the Gryphon from Carroll's novel are perhaps the best-known images of griffins today. Griffins also appear in many other fantasy works, including J. K. Rowling's *Harry Potter* series and C. S. Lewis's *Chronicles of Narnia* books.

Read, Write, Think, Discuss

Dark Lord of Derkholm (1998) is a humorous fantasy novel by Diana Wynne-Jones that takes place in a magical world constantly being invaded by tourists looking for supernatural adventure. The main character, Derk, has several children who are griffins. The book won the 1999 Mythopoeic Fantasy Award for Children's Literature. The novel has a sequel, *Year of the Griffin* (2000), which features one of the griffins from *Dark Lord of Derkholm* as its main character.

SEE ALSO Animals in Mythology; Greek Mythology; Persian Mythology; Semitic Mythology

Guinevere

Character Overview

Guinevere was the wife of King **Arthur**, the legendary ruler of Britain. She was a beautiful and noble queen, but her life took a tragic turn when she fell in love with **Lancelot**, one of Arthur's bravest and most loyal knights. The relationship between the queen and Lancelot eventually destroyed the special fellowship of the Knights of the Round Table.

Guinevere was the daughter of King Leodegrance (pronounced lee-oh-duh-GRANTZ) of Scotland. Arthur admired the king's lovely daughter and married her in spite of a warning from his adviser **Merlin** that Guinevere would be unfaithful to him. As a wedding gift, Leodegrance gave Arthur a round table that would play a central role in his court.

After the marriage, Guinevere became acquainted with Lancelot, who performed various deeds to honor and rescue her. At first, Arthur took no notice of the growing attachment between the queen and Lancelot. Later, however, the king accused his wife of being unfaithful, and had to fight her lover. Several violent battles between Arthur and Lancelot followed, with groups of knights joining in on each side. Eventually, Guinevere returned to Arthur.

Another group of legends concerning Guinevere show the queen in a more loyal role. In these tales, King Arthur left his nephew **Mordred** in charge of the kingdom during a military campaign. Mordred began to plot against Arthur, planning to marry Guinevere and take over as ruler of Britain. The queen refused to cooperate with Mordred and locked herself in the Tower of London to avoid marrying him. When Arthur returned to reclaim his throne, the two men fought. Arthur killed Mordred but was fatally wounded.

Following the death of Arthur, Guinevere entered a convent, where she spent the rest of her life praying and helping the poor. Filled with remorse for the trouble she and her lover had caused, she vowed never to see Lancelot again. When Guinevere died, she was buried beside King Arthur.

Nationality/Culture
Romano-British/Celtic

Pronunciation
GWEN-uh-veer

Alternate Names
None

Appears In
Thomas Malory's *Le Morte d'Arthur*, tales of King Arthur

Lineage
Daughter of King Leodegrance of Scotland

Guinevere in Context

The story of Guinevere can be seen as a reflection of medieval European beliefs about adultery. The affair between Guinevere and Lancelot is the root cause of the fall of **Camelot**, since all other events leading to

Arthur's downfall stem from this betrayal. Guinevere is typically portrayed more negatively than Lancelot, suggesting that women—especially married women—were expected to live by a higher moral standard than the men of the time.

Key Themes and Symbols

Throughout the myths of King Arthur and his court, Guinevere represents both loyalty and betrayal. She is seen by the people of Camelot as a devoted supporter of her husband's deeds and ideas. Even after she betrays Arthur by having an affair with Lancelot, Guinevere regrets the betrayal and stays with Arthur, devoting herself to no other man even after his death.

Guinevere in Art, Literature, and Everyday Life

Guinevere appears in nearly every adaptation of the legend of King Arthur, including Sir Thomas Malory's *Le Morte d'Arthur*, T. H. White's *The Once and Future King*, and the *Avalon* series of novels by Marion Zimmer Bradley. On film, she has been played by actresses such as Ava Gardner, Vanessa Redgrave, and Keira Knightley. Guinevere has also appeared as the main character in a number of works, including the *Guinevere Trilogy* novels by Persia Woolley and the television series *Guinevere Jones* (2002).

Read, Write, Think, Discuss

The story of Guinevere can be viewed as a tale that illustrates the dangers of unfaithfulness in a romantic relationship. This theme has appeared many times in books, films, and television shows. Can you think of a modern tale that focuses on this same theme? Describe the story, and compare it to the message found in the myth of Guinevere and Lancelot.

SEE ALSO Arthur, King; Arthurian Legends; Camelot; Lancelot; Merlin

H

Character

Deity

Myth

Theme

Culture

Nationality/Culture
Greek

Pronunciation
HAY-deez

Alternate Names
Pluto (Roman)

Appears In
Hesiod's *Theogony*,
Homer's *Iliad*, Greek and
Roman creation myths

Lineage
Son of Cronus and Rhea

Hades

Character Overview

In **Greek mythology**, Hades was the god of the **underworld**, the kingdom of the dead. Although the name *Hades* is often used to indicate the underworld itself, it rightfully belongs only to the god, whose kingdom was known as the land of Hades or house of Hades.

Hades was the son of **Cronus** (pronounced KROH-nuhs) and Rhea (pronounced REE-uh), two of the **Titans** who once ruled the universe. The Titans had other children as well: the gods **Zeus** (pronounced ZOOS) and **Poseidon** (pronounced poh-SYE-dun) and the goddesses **Demeter** (pronounced di-MEE-ter), **Hera** (pronounced HAIR-uh), and Hestia (pronounced HESS-tee-uh). When Hades was born, Cronus swallowed him as he had swallowed his other children at birth. However, Zeus escaped this fate, and he tricked Cronus into taking a potion that made him vomit out Hades and his siblings.

Together, these gods and goddesses rebelled against the Titans and seized power from them. Each was given a special weapon or magic item by the **Cyclopes** (pronounced sigh-KLOH-peez) to help them win the battle; Hades was given a helmet that would allow him to become invisible. After gaining control of the universe, Hades, Poseidon, and Zeus drew lots to divide it among themselves. Zeus gained control of the sky, Poseidon took the sea, and Hades received the underworld.

The kingdom of the dead was divided into two regions. At the very bottom lay Tartarus (pronounced TAR-tur-uhs), a land of terrible blackness where the wicked suffered eternal torments. Among those imprisoned there were the Titans, who were guarded by **giants** with one hundred arms. The other region of the underworld, Elysium (pronounced eh-LEE-zee-um) or the Elysian Fields, was a place where the souls of good and righteous people went after death.

To reach Hades' kingdom, the dead had to cross the river Styx (pronounced STIKS). A boatman named Charon (pronounced KAIR-uhn) ferried the dead across the river, while the monstrous **Cerberus** (pronounced SUR-ber-uhs), a multiheaded dog with a serpent's tail, guarded the entrance to the underworld to prevent anyone from leaving. Four other rivers flowed through the underworld: Acheron (pronounced AK-uh-ron; river of woe), **Lethe** (pronounced LEE-thee; river of forgetfulness), Cocytus (pronounced koh-SEE-tuhs; river of wailing), and Phlegethon (pronounced FLEG-uh-thon; river of fire).

Hades supervised the judgment and punishment of the dead but did not torture them himself. That task was left to the **Furies** (pronounced FYOO-reez), the female spirits of justice and vengeance. Although portrayed as grim and unyielding, Hades was not considered evil or unjust.

Major Myths

Hades appears in very few myths. The best known myth concerns his kidnapping of **Persephone** (pronounced per-SEF-uh-nee), daughter of Demeter, the goddess of fertility and the earth. Hades saw the beautiful Persephone while he was riding in a chariot on earth and fell in love with her. When Hades asked Zeus for permission to marry Persephone, Zeus told him that Demeter would never agree. However, Zeus did agree to help Hades seize her.

One day while picking flowers, Persephone reached for a fragrant blossom, and the earth opened up before her. Hades emerged in a chariot, grabbed Persephone, and carried her to the underworld. When Demeter discovered that her daughter was missing, her despair distracted her from her duties as a goddess of fertility and growth, and drought and devastation plagued the lands. After finally learning what had happened, she threatened to starve all mortals as punishment to Zeus and the other gods.

Fearing the consequences of Demeter's anger, Zeus sent word to Hades that Persephone must be returned to her mother. Before letting her go, however, Hades gave Persephone a piece of fruit to eat. Persephone ate the fruit, not realizing that anyone who ate food in the kingdom of the dead must remain there.

Zeus intervened again and arranged for Persephone to spend part of every year with her mother and part with Hades. During the growing and harvest season, she lived on earth, but during the barren winter months she had to return to Hades' kingdom and reign there as queen of the underworld.

Hades in Context

In ancient Greece, Hades was generally feared enough that his name was not often spoken out loud. Instead, the name Pluton, meaning "giver of wealth," was used and understood as a more positive substitute. However, fear did not translate to worship; the ancient Greeks built no known temples to honor Hades. The Greeks' treatment of Hades reflects their attitude toward the **afterlife**: they did not view the afterlife as something glamorous, fun, or beautiful, but as something dark and frightening.

Key Themes and Symbols

Unhappiness and isolation are often associated with Hades in ancient Greek myths. Although he is a brother to Zeus and the other Olympian gods, he cannot reside on Mount Olympus as they do. He is separated from the land of the gods and the land of the living, and has no companions other than his part-time queen Persephone.

Hades in Art, Literature, and Everyday Life

In ancient art, Hades was often depicted with his queen Persephone or accompanied by his guardian hound, Cerberus. He was usually shown holding a scepter. Although Hades was not as popular with later artists as many other gods were, depictions of the god were created by Rubens, Annibale Caracci, and the sculptor Bernini. The operetta *Orpheus in the Underworld* by composer Jacques Offenbach (1858) features Hades as a main character. Hades is also memorably voiced by James Woods in the 1997 animated Disney film *Hercules*. Hades lent his Roman name—Pluto—to the pet dog of Walt Disney's signature cartoon character, Mickey Mouse. In the realm of astronomy, Pluto is the name given to what was once referred to as the ninth and most distant planet in our solar system. In 2006, it was reclassified as a dwarf planet.

Read, Write, Think, Discuss

What do you think the myth of Hades suggests about how ancient Greeks and Romans viewed the afterlife? How does this compare with other, more modern views of the afterlife?

SEE ALSO Cerberus; Demeter; Furies; Greek Mythology; Lethe; Persephone; Titans; Underworld

Harpies

Character Overview

Greek mythology contains two accounts of the Harpies. In both cases, the Harpies were female creatures who caused mischief and torment wherever they went. Though most often pictured as grotesque birdlike creatures, they were originally considered to be the embodiment of storm winds.

In the older myth, the Harpies were spirits of the wind who snatched people and caused things to disappear. On one occasion, they seized the daughters of Pandareos (pronounced pan-DAHR-ee-ohs), king of the city of Miletus (pronounced mye-LEE-tuhs), and took them off to be the servants of female spirits known as the **Furies**. Sometimes considered cousins of the **Gorgons** (pronounced GOR-guhnz, female monsters with snakes for hair), the four Harpies were named Aello (pronounced EE-oh, "hurricane"), Celaeno (pronounced suh-LEE-noh, "dark one"), Ocypete (pronounced ah-si-PEE-tee, "swift"), and Podarge (pronounced poh-DAHR-jee, "racer").

The later myth describes the Harpies as hideous birds with the faces of women. In the legend of **Jason** and the **Argonauts** (pronounced AHR-guh-nawts), they terrorized Phineus (pronounced FIN-ee-us), the king of Thrace, by blinding him and stealing his food. Phineus promised to tell the Argonauts their future if they would drive away the Harpies.

In Virgil's epic poem the **Aeneid**, the Harpies torment the hero **Aeneas** (i-NEE-uhs) and his companions, making it impossible for them to eat. Celaeno tells Aeneas that he and his followers will not return home until they become hungry enough to eat their tables.

Harpies in Context

Like the Gorgons, the Harpies of later myth reflect an ancient Greek and Roman view of what are considered the worst characteristics for a woman to display. Aside from their ugly appearance and foul smell, they prevent Phineus and Aeneas from enjoying their meals by stealing the food away. This is in direct contrast to the traditional role of

Nationality/Culture
Greek/Roman

Pronunciation
HAR-peez

Alternate Names
None

Appears In
Hesiod's *Theogony*, Homer's *Odyssey*, Virgil's *Aeneid*

Lineage
Daughters of Thaumas and Electra

women as domestic providers. In addition, the Harpies are shown to be impossible to satisfy; no matter how much food is laid out, they never stop taking it before the men can eat. This is a reversal of the expected behavior of an ancient Greek woman during a meal, who is expected to eat in moderation and only after others have been served.

Key Themes and Symbols

Harpies are often seen as a force of disruption or withholding in ancient myths. As a disruptive or destructive force, they symbolize the dangerous properties of storm winds. In later myths, they are shown to be the tormentors of those who deserve punishment for revealing too much of the gods' plans to humans, specifically Phineus.

Harpies in Art, Literature, and Everyday Life

Early depictions of the Harpies show them as beautiful winged women. It was not until later that Harpies were seen as hideous-faced women with the lower bodies of birds. This grotesque portrayal of the Harpies reached its height during the Middle Ages. Harpies can be found in Dante's *Inferno*, where they torture those who have committed suicide. Harpies also appear in William Shakespeare's play *The Tempest*, as well as Philip Pullman's *His Dark Materials* trilogy of novels. The term "harpy" is often used in modern times to describe a woman who is seen as nagging or controlling. The American Harpy Eagle, one of the largest living species of eagle in the world, takes its name from the mythological creatures.

Read, Write, Think, Discuss

Harpies appear in many video games as enemies the player must fight against. The Sony PlayStation game *Suikoden II* is one example. Find at least two more examples of Harpies appearing in different video games, and compare them. Do all three versions of Harpies have the same characteristics? Why do you think these mythical figures are so popular in this form?

SEE ALSO Aeneas; *Aeneid, The*; Argonauts; Furies; Gorgons; Greek Mythology; Jason

Hathor

Character Overview

Hathor was one of the most important and complex goddesses of ancient Egypt. A mother goddess who created and maintained all life on earth, Hathor was also worshipped as goddess of the sky, fertility, music, and dance and as the symbolic mother of the pharaoh, or ruler of Egypt. She was said to be the mother of **Horus** (pronounced HOHR-uhs), the god of the sky. In some versions of the myth, Hathor is created as the daughter of **Ra**, the **sun** god.

In addition to being a goddess of the sky, Hathor was often linked with the dead. In this role, she provided food to the dead when they arrived in the **underworld**, or land of the dead. Anyone who carried her clothing would have a safe journey through the underworld. Many foreign lands around Egypt were considered to be under her protection, especially those from which the Egyptians obtained important resources, such as timber or minerals. In one inscription, she is called the "mistress of turquoise."

Hathor has also been identified with the warrior goddess of the sun known as Sekhmet (pronounced SEK-met). In addition, she has been linked to the Eye of Horus, a symbol that reflected the mythical battle for the unification of Egypt under Horus. In some versions of the myth, the Eye of Horus was given to him by his mother in place of one of his eyes, which was damaged by his uncle **Osiris** (pronounced oh-SYE-ris) during their battle for control of Egypt.

Major Myths

One myth from **Egyptian mythology**, developed much later than other writings about Hathor, concerns her violent actions as the goddess Sekhmet. Sekhmet served at the order of Ra, the sun god, and may have even been created by him. One day, while Egypt was split in two with each half worshipping a different god, Ra ordered Sekhmet to punish all humans who had rebelled against him and instead worshipped another. Sekhmet destroyed Ra's enemies, but her blood-lust was not yet satisfied, and she continued to kill even after her mission was complete. To stop her from killing all of humanity, Ra turned the Nile River red; Sekhmet,

Nationality/Culture
Egyptian

Pronunciation
HATH-or

Alternate Names
Mehturt

Appears In
Ancient Egyptian creation myths

Lineage
Mother of Horus

thinking the river was blood and crazed with her love of violence, drank it down hungrily. However, Ra had actually transformed the river into alcohol, and when Sekhmet drank it down, she became drunk and stopped her violent rampage.

Hathor in Context

Hathor's role in Egyptian mythology was ever-changing, but she was perhaps most beloved as a goddess of joy, music, love, and happiness. Her festivals included singing, dancing, and drunken ceremonies that undoubtedly helped to cement the popularity of the ruling pharaoh. In addition, Hathor may have emphasized the importance of women satisfying all the various roles they were expected to fulfill, which included caring for their young and loving their husbands. This multifaceted role of Hathor also reflects the ever-changing nature of Egyptian society. Although many gods existed for centuries, as political control of Egypt shifted from region to region, these gods were modified or combined with other gods. Often deities with similar traits were combined, as with Hathor and the cow-goddess Bat. However, gods did not always match up perfectly, and new myths were created to explain the new facet of a deity's nature. This explains how a single god or goddess might have what appear to have several unique personalities or backgrounds.

Hathor's status as a goddess of both birth and death may reflect another aspect of Egyptian culture as well. Egyptians held a strong belief in the **afterlife**, or a world beyond our own that a person enters after death. The Egyptians saw death in our world as birth into the afterlife. For this reason, the two events were intimately connected, and the goddess who brought life into our world was also an important part of the journey into the next world.

Key Themes and Symbols

The Egyptians associated the goddess Hathor with fertility and sexual love. The ancient Greeks identified Hathor with their own goddess of love, **Aphrodite** (pronounced af-ro-DYE-tee). Hathor is also associated with water and the beginnings of life, and the rupturing of the amniotic sac just before childbirth may have been seen as a sign from the goddess. Hathor was also believed to symbolize the Milky Way as it was visible in the ancient Egyptian night sky. Hathor was seen as the ultimate caretaker, providing food for both the living and the dead. She is also associated with a sycamore tree, which the Egyptians believed was her body on earth. Egyptians made coffins out of sycamore trees in the hope that Hathor would guide them back to the womb after death.

Egyptian wall paintings typically show Hathor as a woman bearing the disk of the sun above her head, representing her role as the divine eye of the sun god Ra. Other paintings show her as a cow or a woman with a cow's head or horns. Some statues show her as a cow suckling the pharaoh with the milk of life.

Hathor in Art, Literature, and Everyday Life

Throughout the history of ancient Egypt, Hathor's popularity continued to grow. She was the subject of many paintings and sculptures, and was eventually recognized as the most popular god in the entire Egyptian pantheon, with more festivals held in her honor than any other. In modern times, Hathor has appeared as a character on the science fiction television series *Stargate SG-1* (1997–2007).

Read, Write, Think, Discuss

Cows were an important part of ancient Egyptian agriculture and diet, which explains their association with Hathor, who was seen as a provider and nourisher. Think about the different products that humans get from cows, even today. Do you think the cow could be accurately described as the ultimate nourisher and provider in modern cultures as well? Why or why not?

SEE ALSO Aphrodite; Egyptian Mythology

Heaven

Theme Overview

Heaven is the general name given to an **afterlife** that is considered a place of eternal happiness and peace. It may be an actual physical place, or it may be a plane of existence separate from the known world. Heaven has often been described as a paradise of some kind, located above or beyond the limits of the ordinary world, perhaps high on a mountain peak or floating on a distant island. Over the centuries, traditional ideas have changed, and many people now think of heaven more in terms of a state of spiritual existence or salvation than as a precise though otherworldly place.

Major Myths

Buddhist View A version of Buddhism based on Amida or Amitabha (pronounced uh-mee-TAH-buh), the Buddha of Boundless Light, emerged in Japan in the 1100s. Followers of this sect believed in an eternal afterlife in a realm called the Pure Land or the Western Paradise. Anyone could enter the Pure Land through sincere spiritual devotion to Amida, who taught that the road to salvation lay in saving others from suffering. Other versions of Buddhism described the soul's ideal fate not as arriving in a heaven but as achieving nirvana (pronounced nur-VAH-nuh), a state of being in which individual desires have ceased to exist.

Chinese View Traditional Chinese religion and mythology included multiple concepts of heaven. Tian (pronounced tee-AHN), associated with the sky, was both heaven and a deity—or god—who was the supreme power over gods, men, and nature and the source of order in the universe. The Chinese believed that their rulers' authority came from Tian, and they called their king or emperor Tianzi, Son of Heaven.

The Taoist tradition of **Chinese mythology** spoke of Penglai (pronounced pang-LYE) Shan (Mount Penglai), a mountain with eight peaks. On each was perched the palace of one of eight beings that could live forever. Like many heavens, Penglai was described in terms of precious things: it had trees of coral that bore pearls instead of fruit. No human could enter Penglai because it was surrounded only by air.

Pre-Christian European View Before Christianity became the dominant religion of Europe, earlier cultures had various ideas about the dwelling places of the gods and the destinations of human souls after death. Some of these are comparable to heavens. In **Norse mythology**, for example, the gods lived in Asgard (pronounced AHS-gahrd), the highest realm of existence. Like the human world below, Asgard had farms, orchards, and estates. The souls of **heroes** who had died in battle went to **Valhalla** (pronounced val-HAL-uh), the "hall of the slain," where they spent their afterlife in joyous fighting and feasting.

Myths of the Slavic peoples of eastern Europe mentioned a paradise called Buyan (pronounced BOO-yahn), described as either a silent and peaceful underwater city or an island washed by a river of healing. The Celtic peoples had myths of an island paradise called Avalon (pronounced AV-uh-lahn). Some legends say that King **Arthur** was carried there after he fell in battle. The Greeks imagined their deities as dwelling in a palatial heaven high above the mortal world on Mount

Olympus (pronounced oh-LIM-puhs). The blessed dead, however, went to Elysium (pronounced eh-LEE-zee-um), or the Elysian Fields, a green garden-like afterworld.

Jewish View The ancient Hebrew religion featured an afterlife, but it did not include a heaven or a **hell**. By about 200 BCE, however, the influence of other cultures had introduced the ideas of reward and punishment after death. Heaven came to be seen as a place where the righteous dead would dwell with God. Certain Jewish traditions pictured heaven as a mountain with seven tiers or layers. According to some accounts, King Solomon's throne, which had six steps leading to the throne itself, provided the model for the structure of heaven.

Christian View The Christian idea of heaven is based on the Jewish one. Although modern Christians are more likely to interpret heaven as spiritual union with God, earlier generations of believers placed that union in a physical setting that was often described in great detail. In the early 1300s, Italian poet Dante Alighieri created a vision of heaven in the *Paradiso*, the last section of *The Divine Comedy*, a long symbolic poem about the soul's journey after death. Drawing on both Christian and pre-Christian traditions, Dante portrayed paradise as high above the earthly world. It consisted of nine heavens, one inside the other, rotating around the earth. The tenth heaven, which included all the others, was the destination of blessed souls who were ranked in order of their virtue, the more virtuous being closer to God.

Artists and writers of the Renaissance developed three visions of heaven. The first, the realm beyond the skies, was the source of images of heaven as a place of clouds and winged **angels**. The second, the garden of paradise, was the natural world raised to the level of divine perfection—an image associated with the Garden of **Eden**, the lost paradise that once existed on earth. The third vision was that of the heavenly city, a symbol of perfect organization and harmony.

Islamic View Building on earlier Jewish and Christian traditions, Islamic mythology also envisioned a multilayered paradise. Heaven was a pyramid, cone, or mountain rising from the lowest level to the highest. Some interpretations include eight levels, while others specify seven levels. The phrase "seventh heaven," meaning the highest happiness, comes from this image. The Muslim heavens are garden paradises of shade trees, flowing streams, and abundant pleasure. The various levels are associated with precious substances such as gold, silver, and pearls, but the highest level is made of pure, divine light and is devoted to the ceaseless, joyous praise of God.

Heaven and Immortality

The idea of heaven is bound up with that of eternal life. Descriptions of many heavens make a special point of mentioning immortality, whether of the gods or of human souls. In the Norse Asgard, for example, the gods guard a precious treasure—the golden apples of immortality. The apples of eternal life also grow on the Celtic island of Avalon, a name that means "apple isle." In Penglai, one of the 108 different heavens in the Chinese Taoist tradition, the Dew of Eternal Life flows through streams and fountains, offering immortality to anyone who drinks it—but only insects, birds, and the gods can ever reach Penglai.

Heaven in Context

Heaven, as a sacred place or a state of being, appears in the myths and legends of cultures around the world. It can be the dwelling place of the god or gods, the place where people find their reward after death, or both. It offers a group or culture the comfort of knowing that some form of existence continues after death. In many cases, heaven is seen as a reward for living according to the standards and laws of the culture. Many religions include the idea of heaven as a place where people are rewarded for living a life of virtue or goodness. Some scholars have argued that, without this incentive for living according to established laws, humans would have no reason to keep from doing anything they desired, regardless of how it affected others.

The reward of heaven is a reflection of the culture in which it arises. For the Norse, the best heaven was Valhalla, a place of feasts that was earned by dying a glorious death in battle. Indeed, the ultimate reward for those in Valhalla was to once again fight, this time alongside **Odin** (pronounced OH-din) in the final battle between the gods and the **giants**. By contrast, heaven as found in Christianity and Islam is a place of eternal peace, love, and beauty. It serves as a reward for remaining faithful on earth even when these things were not to be found. For Buddhists, heaven is not an eternal place at all, but an endless sequence of higher levels of consciousness and existence. This reflects the Buddhist ideal of constant improvement and spiritual progress.

Heaven on Earth?

Life has been hard for most humans throughout history. War, disease, natural disasters, and the simple day-to-day struggle to get food all make for a poor quality of life. The suffering of mankind has led many philosophers through the ages to imagine a better world—not after death, but on Earth. The ancient Greek philosopher Plato wrote an influential book called *The Republic* in about 360 BCE that outlined his ideas for a truly just society. In the fifth century, Christian philosopher Saint Augustine wrote *The City of God* explaining in detail his vision for a city filled with devout Christians devoted to piety. Sir Thomas More's *Utopia* is, like *The Republic*, a political work. It describes a sort of communal (in which resources are shared by all) paradise in which money has no practical meaning.

The idea of communal paradise gained popularity among nineteenth-century American thinkers, some of whom tried to put the idea into practice on Brook Farm in Massachusetts. This utopian social experiment lasted from 1841 to 1847, and required all members to live and work together and share the produce of the farm. The Oneida commune, another utopian group, existed in New York from 1848 to 1881. The idea of utopian communes, now called intentional communities, experienced a surge in popularity in the 1960s during the "cultural revolution" in the United States. There are still thousands of such collectives in the United States, most devoted in one way or another to achieving, as far as is possible, a heaven on Earth.

Heaven in Art, Literature, and Everyday Life

The subject of heaven has been a popular theme among artists and writers over the past several centuries. Painters such as Michelangelo and Hieronymus Bosch have painted their versions of heaven, and writers like Dante and John Milton have done the same through their poetry. More recently, Alice Sebold's novel *The Lovely Bones* (2002) featured a main character who resides in heaven. Heaven has also appeared as a place in many films, including *What Dreams May Come* (1998), *Made in Heaven* (1987), and *Down to Earth* (2001).

Read, Write, Think, Discuss

Do you think the idea of heaven is the main reason people follow the rules of a given culture, so that they will be rewarded after death? Why or why not? Be sure to provide reasons and examples to support your opinion.

SEE ALSO Afterlife; Angels; Eden, Garden of; Hell; Valhalla

Hecate

Nationality/Culture
Greek

Pronunciation
HEK-uh-tee

Alternate Names
Selene

Appears In
Ancient myths of Asia Minor, Hesiod's *Theogony*

Lineage
Daughter of Perses and Asteria

Character Overview

Hecate was a complex, ancient goddess known to the Greeks but originally worshipped by people of Asia Minor. She held several different roles, including earth goddess, queen of the **underworld** (land of the dead), and goddess of magic and witchcraft.

According to the Greek writer Hesiod, Hecate was the daughter of Perses (pronounced PUR-seez), a Titan, and Asteria (pronounced as-TEER-ee-uh), a nymph or female nature deity. Hesiod claimed that Hecate was a favorite of **Zeus**, who made her goddess of the earth, sea, and sky. As a triple goddess, she was also identified with the three aspects of the moon and was represented by women of three different ages. In the sky, she took the form of the old woman Selene (pronounced suh-LEE-nee), the moon. On earth, she was linked to **Artemis** (pronounced AHR-tuh-miss), goddess of the hunt and the moon. In the underworld, she was connected with the maiden **Persephone** (pronounced per-SEF-uh-nee), wife of **Hades** (pronounced HAY-deez).

Because of her association with the moon and the land of the dead, Hecate was seen as a goddess of the darkness, magic, and spells. The ancient Greeks believed magic was strongest where roads met, and the Greeks established shrines to her at crossroads, especially where three roads came together.

Major Myths

Although not known for any major myths in which she is the main character, Hecate appears in the tale of Persephone and her abduction by Hades, the lord of the underworld. When Hades kidnapped Persephone, Hecate—who lived in a nearby cave—heard the commotion, though she did not see who took the maiden. Days later, when Persephone's mother

Demeter (pronounced di-MEE-ter) passes by Hecate's cave searching for her daughter, Hecate tells her what she knows and joins in her search. After Demeter is reunited with her daughter, Persephone and Hecate become close companions.

Hecate in Context

Hecate was not originally a part of the Greek pantheon, or collection of recognized gods. This meant that many elements with which she was connected, such as fertility and the moon, were already associated with other goddesses, especially Artemis. Her identity as a goddess of magic fulfilled a function that had not been addressed in the Greek pantheon, and assured that Hecate would not be absorbed into the already existing goddesses.

Hecate's magic was not considered evil by the ancient Greeks. To her worshippers, she could bring both good fortune and bad fortune. Later Christian tradition emphasized the negative side of her nature, portraying Hecate as queen of witches.

Key Themes and Symbols

Hecate represented the power of magic. She also represented watchfulness, as evidenced by her ability to keep watch over all paths at a crossroads. She was usually shown holding two torches, and was often accompanied by a black she-dog or a polecat. The torches symbolized her ability to guide souls through the underworld. In her role as goddess of magic, Hecate was sometimes depicted as a three-headed figure who kept watch over the crossroads where ceremonies were performed in her honor.

Hecate in Art, Literature, and Everyday Life

In William Shakespeare's play *Macbeth*, Hecate appears as the leader of the three witches. She

Hecate was a triple goddess to the Greeks as goddess of the earth, sea, and sky. Statues often show her as a three-headed figure. © MUSEO ARCHEOLOGICO, VENICE, ITALY/THE BRIDGEMAN ART LIBRARY.

appears in several artworks and poems by Romantic writer William Blake. In modern times, Hecate has appeared in the Marvel Comics universe as a powerful humanoid who earns her name when she is mistaken for the goddess Hecate by ancient people after visiting Earth long ago. She is also a character in the 2007 novel *The Alchemyst: The Secrets of the Immortal Nicholas Flamel* by Michael Scott.

Hecate's popularity has surged in recent years along with the Wiccan religion—a modern attempt at recreating the nature-based religious practices of pre-Christian Europe. Among some groups of Wiccans, Hecate has again become a respected goddess.

Read, Write, Think, Discuss

Jennifer, Hecate, Macbeth, William McKinley and Me, Elizabeth is a novel by E. L. Konigsburg about a girl named Elizabeth who arrives in a new town with no friends. Soon she meets a strange girl named Jennifer, who claims she is a witch, and Elizabeth becomes her apprentice as they participate in odd rituals and attempt to create magic potions. Eventually, the two become close friends. This book was selected as a Newbery Honor recipient when it was first published in 1971.

SEE ALSO Greek Mythology; Witches and Wizards

Hector

Nationality/Culture
Greek/Roman

Pronunciation
HEK-tur

Alternate Names
None

Appears In
Homer's *Iliad*, Hyginus's *Fabulae*, other tales of the Trojan War

Lineage
Son of Priam and Hecuba

Character Overview

In **Greek mythology**, Hector was the son of King Priam of Troy and his wife, **Hecuba**. A Trojan hero and warrior, he fought bravely against the Greeks in the Trojan War. In the *Iliad*, Homer's epic poem about the war, Hector is portrayed as a noble and honorable leader. He was a good son, a loving husband to Andromache (pronounced an-DROM-uh-kee) and father to Astyanax (pronounced uh-STEE-uh-naks), and a trusted friend.

Honest and forthright, Hector greatly disapproved of the conduct of his brother Paris, who carried off **Helen**, the wife of the Greek ruler Menelaus (pronounced men-uh-LAY-uhs). These actions set the stage for the Trojan War. Despite his feelings about Paris, Hector stood ready to defend Troy when the Greeks arrived to avenge the seduction of Helen. When the first Greek warrior set foot on Trojan land, it was Hector who killed him. In the long war that followed, Hector fought valiantly and with great vigor against the Greeks. He was the Trojans' greatest champion.

During the first nine years of the war, neither the Greeks nor the Trojans gained a clear advantage. The tide of war favored first one side and then the other. Then in the tenth year of the war, a dispute arose between **Achilles** (pronounced uh-KILL-eez), the greatest of the Greek warriors, and **Agamemnon** (pronounced ag-uh-MEM-non), the leader of the Greek forces. As a result, Achilles left the field of battle and refused to fight. His absence provided Hector and the Trojans with an opportunity to march out from Troy and attack the Greeks.

With Achilles gone, Hector's most formidable opponents were the Greek champions Diomedes (pronounced dye-uh-MEE-deez) and Ajax. When Diomedes faced Hector in battle he saw that **Ares** (pronounced AIR-eez), the god of war, accompanied the Trojans. The sight of Ares caused the Greeks to retreat. But then the goddesses **Hera** (pronounced HAIR-uh) and **Athena** (pronounced uh-THEE-nuh), who favored the Greeks, helped Diomedes wound Ares. When the wounded god left the field of battle, the Greeks attacked and forced the Trojans to turn back.

Faced with this crisis, Hector went back to Troy to consult with his father and to ask the Trojan women to pray to the gods for help. No longer confident of victory and certain that he would soon die, Hector bid a sad farewell to his wife and son.

Returning to battle, Hector met and fought the Greek champion Ajax in one-on-one combat. The duel continued until nightfall, with neither hero gaining victory. They finally stopped and exchanged gifts as a sign of respect for each other.

When fighting between the Greeks and Trojans resumed, Hector and his forces seemed unable to be defeated. Hector killed many Greeks and succeeded in pushing them back to defenses they had built around their ships. Hector was about to burn the Greek ships when the god **Poseidon** (pronounced poh-SYE-dun) appeared, urging the Greeks to pull themselves together and fight back. At the same time, the Greek warrior Patroclus (pronounced pa-TROH-kluhs), the beloved friend of Achilles, entered the battle wearing Achilles' armor.

Believing that Achilles had returned, the Greeks rallied and caused the Trojans to retreat. But then Hector, under the protection of the god **Apollo** (pronounced uh-POL-oh), killed Patroclus and took the armor he was wearing. Hearing of his friend's death, Achilles reentered the battle and aimed his fury at Hector.

Achilles pursued Hector around the walls of Troy three times before catching him. Aware that Hector was fated to die at Achilles' hand, Apollo abandoned him and allowed Achilles to strike a mortal blow. As he lay dying, Hector pleaded with Achilles to return his body to his father, Priam. Achilles refused. Hector predicted that Achilles, too, would die very shortly.

After Hector died, Achilles tied the warrior's body to a chariot and dragged the body around Troy before the grief-stricken eyes of the Trojans. Then he dragged the body around the tomb of his friend Patroclus. When Achilles' fury and vengeance were finally satisfied, he left Hector's body on the ground to be devoured by dogs and birds of prey.

The abuse of the dead Hector angered **Zeus** (pronounced ZOOS), who sent a messenger to order Achilles to release the corpse to Priam. He also sent word to Priam to offer a ransom for the body to Achilles. Priam did so and begged the Greek warrior for his son's body. Moved by Priam's grief, Achilles agreed.

Priam brought Hector's body back to Troy, and an eleven-day truce allowed the Trojans to arrange an elaborate funeral to mourn their great warrior. Hector's funeral marks the conclusion of the *Iliad*, as well as the beginning of the end for the Trojans. They later suffered a devastating defeat at the hands of the Greeks. After the fall of Troy, the Greeks killed Hector's son Astyanax, fearing that he might try to avenge his father's death. Thereafter, the surviving Trojans honored Hector as one of their greatest **heroes**.

Hector in Context

Despite the legendary rivalry between Greece and Troy that leads to the Trojan War, Hector is a clear example of the respect with which many Trojans were regarded by the Greeks. His portrayal in tales of the Trojan War is nearly always sympathetic, and many Greeks related more to him than to the godlike Greek hero Achilles who kills him. This treatment of Hector illustrates how the Greeks understood the complex nature of war and the allegiances of soldiers.

Key Themes and Symbols

For the most part, Hector stands as a symbol of courage and bravery. When he knows he will be killed by Achilles, he does not run away, but faces his fate. Hector also represents reason and sensibility; he warns Paris that his actions endanger all of Troy, but Paris does not listen. Hector also represents the fall of Troy, for as one of its greatest warriors, his defeat foreshadows the eventual destruction of the city.

Hector in Art, Literature, and Everyday Life

Hector has long been a favorite example of courage and heroism for writers and artists. In the fourteenth century, French writer Jacques de Longuyon listed Hector in his work *Voeux du Paon* as one of the nine worthiest figures from history to display the true meaning of chivalry. He was the subject of paintings by Jacques-Louis David, Peter Paul Rubens, and Giorgio di Chirico, among others.

Read, Write, Think, Discuss

When a country is at war, the enemy is often depicted negatively by the mainstream media of the time—which can include songs, oral tales, books, or in recent times, films and television shows. Do you think negative portrayals such as these should be encouraged in times of war? Do you think sympathetic portrayals of those considered enemies would be harmful? Why or why not?

SEE ALSO Achilles; Agamemnon; Hecuba; Heroes; *Iliad, The*

Hecuba

Character Overview

In **Greek mythology**, Hecuba was the second wife of Priam, king of the city of Troy. She bore Priam many children, including **Hector**, Paris, Polydorus (pronounced pol-ee-DOR-uhs), and **Cassandra**. As queen of Troy, she is an important character in the tales of the Trojan War.

Nationality/Culture
Greek/Roman

Pronunciation
HEK-yoo-buh

Alternate Names
Hekabe

Appears In
Homer's *Iliad*, Ovid's *Metamorphoses*, other tales of the Trojan War

Lineage
Daughter of Dymas and Eunoe

While pregnant with Paris, Hecuba had a dream in which she gave birth to a fiery torch that was covered with snakes. This was considered a sign from the gods; the prophets of Troy, who were believed to be able to see the future, told her that if her child lived, he would be responsible for the fall of Troy. When Paris was born, Hecuba ordered two servants to kill the child. Unable to perform such a terrible act, the servants left Paris on a mountain to die, and he was found and raised by a shepherd.

Years later, Paris returned to Troy, and as predicted, he caused the city's destruction. He began the Trojan War by taking away **Helen**, wife of King Menelaus (pronounced men-uh-LAY-uhs) of Sparta. All the rulers of Greece had sworn to defend Helen. To rescue her, they declared war on Troy, sacking and burning it after a long and persistent attack.

Hecuba became a slave to the Greek hero **Odysseus** (pronounced oh-DIS-ee-uhs). On his way back to Greece, Odysseus journeyed through Thrace, which was ruled by King Polymestor (pronounced pol-ee-MES-tor). Before the war, Hecuba had asked Polymestor to protect her son Polydorus. However, upon reaching Thrace, she found that the king had killed the boy. The enraged Hecuba tore out Polymestor's eyes and murdered both of his sons. As Odysseus was trying to control her, she turned into a dog. Her tomb was placed on a rocky outcrop located on a narrow strip of water called the Hellespont (pronounced HEL-uh-spont) between Greece and Turkey.

Hecuba in Context

In ancient times of war, it was common for members of the losing side—particularly family members of the leaders—to be taken as slaves by the victorious soldiers. In tales of the Trojan War, the surviving women of Trojan royalty, Cassandra and Hecuba, are taken as slaves by **Agamemnon** and Odysseus, respectively. This was done as a way to gain slave labor, but, more importantly, it served as a final humiliation to the fallen men of Troy to have their women become the property of their Greek captors.

Key Themes and Symbols

Hecuba's dream of a torch covered in snakes is a symbol of death and doom, and foreshadows the fall of Troy. An important theme in the tale of Hecuba is destiny, or the idea that future events have already been determined by the gods. Although Hecuba tries to have Paris destroyed before he can bring about the destruction of Troy, she fails because this is Paris's destiny. Despite her attempt to have her own son killed, Hecuba also represents the fierceness with which a mother can avenge her child's death, as she does in Thrace. This ferocity is illustrated by her transformation into a dog.

Hecuba in Art, Literature, and Everyday Life

Hecuba is found in the *Iliad* and the *Aeneid*. She also appears in the plays *Hecuba* and *The Trojan Women* by Euripides and is mentioned in Shakespeare's *Hamlet*. Her transformation into a dog is described in Dante's *Inferno*.

Read, Write, Think, Discuss

Throughout history, the victorious side in a war traditionally has been able to take anything of value from the losing side, including land, treasures, or people. Although slaves are no longer considered appropriate spoils of war, many other treasures are often taken from countries in the wake of their defeat. Do you think a country (or group of countries) that wins a war against another country automatically has rights to claim property or land from their defeated foes? What about historical artifacts? Should victorious troops be allowed to take items from citizens of a defeated country who did not participate in battle?

SEE ALSO *Aeneid, The*; Cassandra; Greek Mythology; Hector; Helen of Troy; *Iliad, The*; Odysseus; *Odyssey, The*

Heimdall

Character Overview

In **Norse mythology**, the god Heimdall stood guard over Asgard (pronounced AHS-gahrd), the home of the gods. He lived near Bifrost (pronounced BIV-rost), the rainbow bridge that connected Asgard to the world of humans and from there kept watch for the approach of the

Nationality/Culture
Norse

Pronunciation
HIGHM-dahl

Alternate Names
None

Appears In
The Eddas

Lineage
Son of Odin

giants, who were the enemies of the gods. Heimdall had incredibly sharp senses that allowed him to see great distances even at night and to hear sounds as soft as wool growing on sheep or grass growing in the field. Furthermore, he needed little sleep. He was said to be the son of **Odin** (pronounced OH-din) in some accounts, and born to nine different mothers in other accounts.

Major Myths

According to legend, Heimdall would one day call the other gods to **Ragnarok** (pronounced RAHG-nuh-rok), the final battle that would result in the destruction of gods and humans. When the giants drew near to Asgard, Heimdall would summon the gods by blowing his horn, Gjallarhorn (pronounced YAHL-lahr-horn), which could be heard all over creation. During the battle, Heimdall would kill the evil trickster god **Loki** (pronounced LOH-kee) and then meet his own death.

Sometimes called Rig (meaning king), Heimdall was considered the father of all people on earth. According to legend, he traveled around the earth and stayed three nights with married couples from different social classes. First, he visited some serfs, or forced laborers, then some peasants, and finally a noble couple. Nine months after each visit, a child was born to each couple. The first was an ugly but strong boy named Thrall (pronounced THRAHL), who became the ancestor of all serfs. The second, Karl, was skilled at farmwork and became the ancestor of all peasants. Jarl (pronounced YARL), the last of the children, was intelligent and quick to learn the skills of hunting and combat. He became the ancestor of all warriors and nobles. The words *thrall, karl*, and *jarl* mean serf, farmer, and nobleman in the Norse language.

Heimdall in Context

For the Norse people, hunting horns were an essential part of their way of life. These horns, literally hollowed out and carved from the horns of an animal such as a reindeer, provided communication between members of a hunting party so they could work together to capture prey. Like Heimdall, the Norse people often named their most important pieces of equipment, including weapons and other tools of the hunt.

The story of Heimdall's visit to the three couples reflects the social classes of the Norse people at the time. According to the story, the

One of Heimdall's most important duties will be to blow his horn Gjallarhorn as a signal of the start of Ragnarok, the final battle between good and evil during which all Norse gods and humans will die. © ARNI MAGNUSSON INSTITUTE, REYKJAVIK, ICELAND/THE BRIDGEMAN ART LIBRARY.

establishment of the social classes by a god indicates that those who are born into a particular class belong in that class, and it is appropriate for warriors and nobles to be superior to and live off the labor of the lower classes. In Norse society, there was little movement between social classes, with riches often handed down from one family member to the next. However, not all slaves were born as such: many were taken as war prisoners, and others fell into slavery because they owed debts. It was not uncommon for serfs to earn or buy their freedom after a period of servitude.

Key Themes and Symbols

Heimdall is a symbol of vigilance, always watching over the entrance to Asgard and ready to warn of attacking giants. His vigilance is also illustrated by his keen sense of sight and hearing. Heimdall's horn symbolizes danger, for it is only blown in the event of an attack.

Heimdall in Art, Literature, and Everyday Life

Heimdall may not be as well known as some other Norse gods, even though he holds an important place in Norse mythology. Aside from illustrations in ancient manuscripts, Heimdall has been depicted by the nineteenth-century painter Nils Blommér. Heimdall has also appeared as a superhero in the Marvel Comics universe, along with many other figures from Norse mythology.

Read, Write, Think, Discuss

Heimdall functioned as the vigilant sentry for Asgard. Nowadays, many homes and automobiles have their own automatic sentries: security alarms. More and more suburban communities are gated and fenced and feature private security guards at the entrance. Do you think these modern "sentries" are necessary? Are they effective? Why or why not?

SEE ALSO Loki; Norse Mythology; Ragnarok

Hel

Nationality/Culture
Norse

Pronunciation
HEL

Alternate Names
None

Appears In
The Eddas

Lineage
Daughter of Loki and Angrboda

Character Overview

Hel was the Norse goddess of the dead, daughter of the trickster god **Loki** (pronounced LOH-kee) and the giantess Angrboda (pronounced AHNG-gur-boh-duh). She is recognized as the goddess of all the dead who do not die with glory—in other words, those who die from illness or old age. The realm she presides over is also referred to as Hel, and is a cold, cheerless place.

Shortly after her birth, Hel was cast out of Asgard (pronounced AHS-gahrd), home of the gods, by **Odin** (pronounced OH-din). He sent her to Niflheim (pronounced NIV-uhl-heym), the **underworld** or land of the dead, and made her queen of all who died without glory. Warriors who fell in combat did not become her subjects but went instead to the hall called **Valhalla** to live with Odin.

Sources describe the goddess as a monster who is half flesh-colored and half bluish-black. She lived in a castle called Eljudnir (pronounced el-YOOD-neer) and ate her meals with a dish named Hunger and a knife called Famine. She was attended by two servants, Ganglati and Ganglot, who moved so slowly that they appeared to be standing still.

Major Myths

Hel was the keeper of the soul of the god **Balder** (pronounced BAWL-der) after he was killed by mistletoe through Loki's trickery. When Balder's mother **Frigg** (pronounced FRIG) asked for his soul to be returned, Hel agreed, but only if every living thing in the world cried in mourning over his death. Frigg got all living things to cry except one—a giantess that may have been Loki in disguise. Balder had to remain in the underworld.

Hel in Context

In Norse culture, much emphasis was placed on dying with honor. The most honorable deaths were achieved on battlefields in foreign lands. Those who died in such a way were guaranteed to spend eternity with Odin in the paradise of Valhalla. Those who died defending their homes or local lands were also honored, though not as greatly. To die of old age or illness was considered to be a death without honor, and therefore those who died in this way were destined to spend eternity in the dismal underworld of Hel.

Key Themes and Symbols

To the Norse people, Hel represented death without honor. She symbolized the denial of everything enjoyable in the world, as shown by her plate, Hunger, and her knife, Famine. Hel may also be seen as a victim of circumstance, since she is banished from Asgard simply because her father is Loki. Her refusal to release Odin's son Balder from the underworld may be seen as revenge against Odin.

U•X•L Encyclopedia of World Mythology

Hel in Art, Literature, and Everyday Life

Hel is not as well known or well regarded as many other Norse deities. When depicted, she is often shown accompanied by Garmr (pronounced GARM), her watchdog and guardian of the gates to her realm. Hel appears as a villain in the *Everworld* series of novels by K. A. Applegate, as well as the *Thor* comic series by Marvel and numerous video games. *Hell*, the English word for the underworld reserved for the damned, is taken from the name of the goddess.

Read, Write, Think, Discuss

The idea of what makes a "good death" varies from culture to culture. **Norse mythology** included several different possible fates after death, all of which depended upon the way in which one died. Dying on battlefields in foreign lands led a person to the highest level of the **afterlife**. This seems to suggest foreign conquest was very important to the Norse. By contrast, many modern Americans believe that the best way to die is of old age, in one's bed. What cultural values does such a death represent? How are they different from the cultural values of the ancient Norse society?

SEE ALSO Loki; Norse Mythology; Odin; Underworld; Valhalla

Helen of Troy

Nationality/Culture
Greek/Roman

Pronunciation
HEL-en

Alternate Names
None

Appears In
Homer's *Iliad*, Ovid's *Metamorphoses*, other tales of the Trojan War

Lineage
Daughter of Zeus and Leda

Character Overview

In **Greek mythology**, Helen of Troy was the most beautiful woman in the world. A daughter of the god **Zeus** (pronounced ZOOS), she is best known for the part she played in causing the Trojan War, a story told by Homer in the *Iliad* and the *Odyssey*. Some myths say that Helen's mother was Leda, the wife of King Tyndareus (pronounced tin-DAIR-ee-uhs) of Sparta. Others name Nemesis (pronounced NEM-uh-sis), the goddess of revenge, as her mother. Helen had a sister, Clytemnestra (pronounced klye-tem-NES-truh), who later became the wife of King **Agamemnon** (pronounced ag-uh-MEM-non) of Mycenae (pronounced mye-SEE-nee). She also had twin brothers named **Castor and Pollux** (pronounced PAHL-uhks).

Stories claiming Leda as Helen's mother tell how Zeus disguised himself as a swan and raped the Spartan queen. Leda then produced two eggs. From one came Helen and her brother Pollux. Clytemnestra and Castor emerged from the other. Other versions of the myth say that Zeus seduced Nemesis, and she laid the two eggs. A shepherd discovered them and gave them to Queen Leda, who tended the eggs until they hatched and raised the children as her own. In some variations of this legend, Helen and Pollux were the children of Zeus, but Clytemnestra and Castor were actually the children of Tyndareus.

When Helen was only twelve years old, the Greek hero **Theseus** (pronounced THEE-see-uhs) kidnapped her and planned to make her his wife. He took her to Attica (pronounced AT-i-kuh) in Greece and locked her away under the care of his mother. Helen's brothers Castor and Pollux rescued her while Theseus was away and brought her back to Sparta. According to some stories, before Helen left Attica, she had given birth to a daughter named Iphigenia (pronounced if-uh-juh-NEYE-uh).

Some time after Helen returned to Sparta, King Tyndareus decided that it was time for her to marry. Suitors came from all over Greece, hoping to win the famous beauty. Many were powerful leaders. Tyndareus worried that choosing one suitor might anger the others, who could cause trouble for his kingdom.

Among those seeking to marry Helen was **Odysseus** (pronounced oh-DIS-ee-uhs), the king of Ithaca (ITH-uh-kuh). Odysseus advised Tyndareus to have all the suitors take an oath to accept Helen's choice and promise to support that person whenever the need should arise. The suitors agreed, and Helen chose Menelaus (pronounced men-uh-LAY-uhs), a prince of Mycenae, to be her husband. Helen's sister Clytemnestra was already married to Menelaus's older brother, Agamemnon.

For a while, Helen and Menelaus lived happily together. They had a daughter and son, and Menelaus eventually became the king of Sparta. But their life together came to a sudden end.

Paris, a prince of Troy, traveled to Sparta on the advice of the goddess **Aphrodite** (pronounced af-ro-DYE-tee). She had promised him the most beautiful woman in the world after he proclaimed her the "fairest" goddess. When Paris saw Helen, he knew that Aphrodite had kept her promise. While Menelaus was away in Crete, Paris took Helen back to Troy. Some stories say Helen went willingly, seduced by Paris's charms. Others claim that Paris kidnapped her and took her by force.

When Menelaus returned home and discovered Helen gone, he called on the leaders of Greece, who had sworn to support him if necessary. The Greeks organized a great expedition and set sail for Troy. Their arrival at Troy marked the beginning of the Trojan War. During the war, Helen's sympathies were divided. At times, she helped the Trojans by pointing out Greek leaders. At other times, however, she sympathized with the Greeks and did not betray them when opportunities to do so arose.

Helen had a number of children by Paris, but none survived infancy. Paris died in the Trojan War, and Helen married his brother Deiphobus (pronounced dee-IF-oh-buhs). After the Greeks won the war, she was reunited with Menelaus, and she helped him kill Deiphobus. Then Helen and Menelaus set sail for Sparta.

The couple arrived in Sparta after a journey of several years. Some stories say that the gods, angry at the trouble Helen had caused, sent storms to drive their ships off course to Egypt and other lands bordering the Mediterranean Sea. When they finally arrived in Sparta, the couple lived happily, although by some accounts, Menelaus remained suspicious of Helen's feelings and loyalty.

Many stories say that Helen remained in Sparta until her death. But others say that she went to the island of Rhodes after Menelaus died, perhaps driven from Sparta by their son Nicostratus (pronounced nye-KOS-truh-tuhs). At first she was given refuge on Rhodes by Polyxo (pronounced puh-LIKS-oh), the widow of Tlepolemus (pronounced tlay-POL-ee-muhs), one of the Greek leaders who had died in the Trojan War. Later, however, legend has it that Polyxo had Helen hanged to avenge the death of her husband.

Helen of Troy in Context

The abduction of Helen by Paris reflects the ancient idea of women as trophies that can be taken from an enemy. Victorious soldiers commonly took the women of their fallen enemies as slaves; in the myth, Paris actually provokes a war by taking Helen with him while Menelaus is away. Versions of the story differ on whether or not Helen went with Paris willingly, but this is irrelevant to Menelaus's reaction: he behaves as if Paris has stolen property from him, an attitude typical of the time period.

Helen also reflects Greek ideas about the importance of physical beauty. According to the ancient Greeks, outer beauty was a reflection of the mind and spirit. Therefore, beauty was considered to be a sign of intelligence, health, and a pure heart. Although the Greeks focused on physical beauty, it is because they did not consider beauty to be merely "skin deep."

Although Helen was the daughter of Zeus, she is a mortal woman in the myth of the fall of Troy. Some scholars suggest that Helen was once a very ancient goddess associated with trees and birds, but whose status was reduced to a mere mortal when the Greeks stopped worshipping her.

Key Themes and Symbols

In Greek mythology, Helen is said to represent the ultimate in human beauty. Aphrodite herself identifies Helen as the most beautiful woman in the world. Helen is also seen as a victim of the advances of men; she is abducted against her will at least once, and is plagued by suitors when her father announces she is looking for a husband. Helen may also symbolize wavering loyalty, as seen when she assists both sides during the Trojan War.

Helen of Troy in Art, Literature, and Everyday Life

Helen and stories about her inspired many ancient writers, including the Greek playwright Euripides and the Roman poets Virgil, Ovid, and Seneca. She also served as inspiration for later authors, including Italian poet Dante Alighieri and English playwrights William Shakespeare and Christopher Marlowe. It was Marlowe who famously wrote that Helen's was "the face which launched a thousand ships." Helen has also appeared in numerous modern

Helen of Troy was the most beautiful woman in the world, and is best known for the role she played in starting the Trojan War between the Trojans and the Greeks. © THE DE MORGAN CENTRE, LONDON/THE BRIDGEMAN ART LIBRARY.

re-tellings of the Trojan War, and was even the subject of her own television miniseries in 2003.

Read, Write, Think, Discuss

Nobody's Princess (2007) by Esther Friesner tells the story of the Trojan War from Helen's point of view. In this version, Helen is a fiercely independent young woman who cares more about her skills with a sword than her appearance. The book offers a new take on an age-old tale, and Friesner even includes a section on ancient Greek history and the original texts her tale draws upon.

SEE ALSO Agamemnon; Castor and Pollux; Greek Mythology; *Iliad, The*; Odysseus; *Odyssey, The*; Theseus

Hell

Theme Overview

Hell is a place of punishment after death or, in more abstract terms, a state of spiritual damnation. In religions and mythologies that separate the dead according to their conduct in life or the purity of their souls, the evil go to hell while the good go to **heaven**.

Although the word *hell* comes from **Hel**, the Norse goddess of death, hells appear in the beliefs and mythologies of many cultures. Common features of hells include burning heat or freezing cold, darkness (symbolizing the soul's separation from light, goodness, and truth), physical agony that represents spiritual suffering, and devils or demons who torment the damned.

Major Myths

Hindu Mythology Hinduism is based on the belief that each soul lives many, many lives. A soul may spend time in any of twenty-one hells to pay for wrong actions during a lifetime, but eventually that soul will be reborn in the world. In the Jain religion, which is related to Hinduism, sinners go to a hell called *bhumis*, where demons torment them until they have paid for whatever evil they committed in life.

Buddhist Mythology There are numerous versions of Buddhism with various ideas of hell. The strictest form of Buddhism does not include a hell, but some Buddhists still follow the traditional belief of up to 136 hells. The hell to which a dead soul goes for punishment depends on the person's actions in life. Some Buddhist doctrines speak of the *karmavacara*, the realm of physical and sensory perceptions, as a series of hells.

Chinese Mythology The Chinese belief that souls are punished after death to pay for sins or errors committed during life combines some Buddhist ideas with elements of traditional Taoist **Chinese mythology**. Sinners descend to the base of the sacred mountain, Meru, to undergo a set period of punishment in one hell or in a series of hells. When they have paid for their sins and are ready for rebirth in a new life, they drink a brew that makes them forget their past lives. In some accounts, a wheel of rebirth lifts them to their next life, while in others they are thrown from a bridge of pain into a river that carries them onward.

Pre-Christian European Mythology Before Christianity gave its own meanings to the concepts of heaven and hell, the pre-Christian peoples of Europe imagined the dark side of the **afterlife**. The Norse pictured Hel, the corpselike goddess of death, as queen of a grim underground realm populated by those who had died of sickness and old age. This view of hell involves a dread of death and a horror of the cold, dark, decaying grave, but it does not suggest a place of punishment.

The Greek **underworld** was divided into three regions: **Hades** (pronounced HAY-deez), Tartarus (pronounced TAR-tur-uhs), and Elysium (pronounced eh-LEE-zee-um). Most of the dead went to the kingdom of the god Hades. In the deepest part of the underworld, a terrible dark place known as Tartarus, the very wicked suffered eternal punishment at the hands of the **Furies**. The third region, Elysium or the Elysian Fields, was where exceptionally good and righteous people went after death.

Persian Mythology The image of hell as a place of torment for sinners emerged fully in the **Persian mythology** based on the faith founded in the 500s BCE by Zoroaster (pronounced ZOR-oh-as-tur). According to Zoroastrian belief, souls are judged after death at a bridge where their lives are weighed. If the outcome is good, the bridge widens and carries them to heaven. If they are judged to have been evil, the bridge narrows and pitches them down into a dreadful hell. Those whose lives were an equal mix of good and evil go to a realm called *hamestagan*, in which they experience both heat and cold.

Jewish Mythology The early Hebrews called their afterworld Sheol (pronounced SHEE-ohl) and pictured it as a quiet, sad place where all the dead went. By around 200 BCE, under the influence of Zoroastrianism and other belief systems, the Jews had adopted the idea of judgment for the dead. The afterworld became a heaven for the good and a hell for the wicked.

A river of **fire** known as Gehenna (pronounced geh-HEN-na) ran through hell, and sometimes the whole region was called Gehenna. Scores of demons dwelled there and so did the gods and goddesses of the Greeks, Romans, Celts, and other peoples who had also been turned into demons. Some interpretations described hell as a series of ever-smaller levels or rings, like a downward-pointing, seven-tiered mountain. Half the year the sinners being punished in hell endured the torments of fire. For the rest of the time they suffered the even worse misery of bitter cold.

Christian Mythology Christian belief built upon the Jewish notion of hell as a place of punishment for the wicked and the home of **Satan**, the chief devil, and all of his evil demons, or fallen **angels**. Most often hell was pictured as an inferno, a place of flames and cruel heat. Many early Christian writings emphasized the agonies that sinners suffered in hell when demons boiled them in kettles or stabbed them with pitchforks. In such interpretations of hell the punishments were often tailored to fit specific sins.

During the Middle Ages, Christians sometimes pictured hell as a fiery dragon's mouth swallowing up sinners. In *The Divine Comedy*, a poem about the soul's journey written in the early 1300s, Italian poet Dante Alighieri drew upon many mythological traditions. He portrayed hell as an inferno of punishment, descending through many levels where sinners of different categories received punishment. Dante also described another realm that Christians had devised called purgatory, a state between hell and heaven. Christian belief included the possibility that a soul could, after punishment in purgatory and true repentance, work its way toward heaven and salvation.

Islamic Mythology The Muslims inherited their vision of hell, like many other elements of their faith, from the Jews and the Christians. The Islamic hell is called Jahannam (pronounced JAH-hah-nahm), or sometimes Gehenna. Jahannam can be portrayed as a devouring, fire-breathing monster or a multilayered, pitlike realm below the earth whose chief characteristic is fire. As in Persian mythology, the souls of the dead are required to cross a bridge of judgment, "sharper than a sword and finer than a hair," that stretches over Jahannam to paradise. Sinners and unbelievers slip and fall into hell. The kind of punishment that each sinner receives matches his or her sins.

Central American Mythology According to the Maya, the souls of most of the dead went to an underworld known as Xibalba (pronounced shi-BAHL-buh). Only individuals who died in violent circumstances went directly to one of the heavens. In the Mayan legend of the Hero Twins, told in the **Popol Vuh**, Xibalba is divided into houses filled with terrifying objects such as knives, jaguars, and bats. The **twins** undergo a series of trials in these houses and eventually defeat the lords of Xibalba. The Aztecs believed that the souls of ordinary people went to an under-world called Mictlan (pronounced MEEKT-lahn). Each soul wandered through the layers of Mictlan until it reached the deepest level.

Hell in Context

Hell is related to the concept of the underworld. In the myths of many ancient cultures, the underworld was the mysterious and often gloomy realm of the dead. Although usually imagined as a dark underground kingdom associated with caves and holes in the earth, hell was not always a place of punishment and suffering. Later belief systems introduced the idea of an afterlife in which the wicked received punishment, and hell was where that punishment occurred.

Though a belief in some form of afterlife is found in almost every culture in the world, there are fewer examples of the afterlife as a place of punishment for those who performed evil deeds while alive. To some, it would seem to be a natural extension of a belief in heaven; if people are rewarded for their good deeds while alive, why would others not be

No Exit

Existentialist philosopher and author Jean-Paul Sartre created an unusual version of hell in his 1944 play *No Exit*. While most people have traditionally imagined hell as a fiery place of physical torture, Sartre imagined a subtler, psychological hell specially designed to torment each particular damned soul. In his play, three people are shut in a room with no windows and only one door, which remains shut throughout most of the play. The characters realize they are in hell, and expect that their physical punishment will soon begin. It never does. Instead, they begin to "torture" each other, playing on each other's fears and insecurities. In the end, it becomes clear that this is their hell. These three people are perfectly designed to madden each other for eternity, leading one of them to conclude, in a famous line: "Hell is other people."

punished for their bad deeds? However, this argument only holds true for cultures that tend to view the world as being in constant struggle between opposing forces—usually referred to as good and evil.

Hell may also be viewed as a tool for enforcing traditions and rules in a culture, particularly those rules which might be difficult to enforce through other means. For example, stealing is a crime that might be easily avoided by locking up or guarding valuables. Lying and cheating, however, are much harder to combat; by suggesting that performing some negative actions—or failing to perform actions such as observing religious days—may result in a person going to hell, cultural groups can enjoy a consistent level of "moral" or accepted behavior. The notion of hell also provides an answer to those who might wonder if justice truly exists in a world where bad things often seem to happen without noticeable repercussions.

Hell in Art, Literature, and Everyday Life

Hell has appeared in many works of art and literature. The most notable written work featuring hell is Dante's *The Divine Comedy,* which offers detailed descriptions of the types of punishment inflicted on the damned in each level of hell. Arguably the most famous painted image of hell is found in the *Garden of Earthly Delights* triptych painted by Hieronymus

Bosch in the early sixteenth century. Versions of hell have also been shown in numerous films such as *What Dreams May Come* (1998) and television shows such as *The Simpsons.*

Read, Write, Think, Discuss

American author Mark Twain once quipped, "Go to heaven for the climate, hell for the company." This statement suggests that the truly interesting souls will be in hell, and that those who lived lives pure enough to earn them a place in heaven would be boring. This attitude is a uniquely modern take on the concept of hell that is virtually absent in ancient society. Why is that so, and what does that indicate about modern ideas about hell?

SEE ALSO Afterlife; Devils and Demons; Furies; Hades; Heaven; Hel; Satan; Underworld

Hephaestus

Character Overview

An ancient god of **fire** in **Greek mythology**, Hephaestus is the counterpart of the Roman god Vulcan (pronounced VUHL-kuhn), the god of fire and of metalwork and crafts. The tales about Vulcan, who is sometimes called Mulciber (the smelter), are all based on Greek myths about Hephaestus.

Major Myths

The son of **Zeus** (pronounced ZOOS) and **Hera** (pronounced HAIR-uh; or, in some versions, of Hera alone), Hephaestus was lame and deformed. Some stories say that Zeus threw him from Olympus (pronounced oh-LIM-puhs), the mountain home of the gods, for taking Hera's side in a quarrel with Zeus and that Hephaestus became lame as a result of the fall. Other myths say that Hephaestus was born lame and that Hera threw him from Olympus because she was ashamed of his deformity. He landed in the ocean and was rescued by sea **nymphs**—or

Nationality/Culture
Greek

Pronunciation
hi-FES-tuhs

Alternate Names
Vulcan (Roman)

Appears In
Hesiod's *Theogony*, Ovid's *Metamorphoses*

Lineage
Son of Zeus and Hera

female nature deities—who raised him in a cave under the sea and taught him many skills.

Hephaestus became a master craftsman. One day he gained his revenge on Hera for throwing him off Olympus by creating for her a golden throne that contained a trap. When she sat on the throne, the trap closed and imprisoned her. The other gods begged Hephaestus to release Hera, but he would not listen. Finally, the god of wine, **Dionysus** (pronounced dye-uh-NYE-suhs), made Hephaestus drunk and obtained the key to the trap.

As craftsman for the gods, Hephaestus built palaces and other beautiful and wondrous things that enabled the Olympians to live in great luxury. He also fashioned thunderbolts for Zeus, armor for the **heroes Achilles** (pronounced uh-KILL-eez) and **Aeneas** (pronounced i-NEE-uhs) that made them unable to be harmed, and a scepter for King **Agamemnon** (pronounced ag-uh-MEM-non) that gave him great power. Some legends say that Hephaestus created **Pandora** (pronounced pan-DOR-uh) so that Zeus could take revenge on **Prometheus** (pronounced pruh-MEE-thee-uhs) for giving fire to humans. Hephaestus later made the chains that bound Prometheus to a mountain.

Hephaestus often appeared as a comic figure in myths and had little luck in love. One time he took an ax and split Zeus's skull to relieve a headache, and the goddess **Athena** (pronounced uh-THEE-nuh) sprang fully grown from the head. He fell in love with Athena, but she rejected him. He also courted **Aphrodite** (pronounced af-ro-DYE-tee), who accepted his offer of marriage but then had love affairs with others, including the god **Ares** (pronounced AIR-eez). Hephaestus fashioned a fine golden net and caught his wife and Ares in it. He then called the other gods so that they could laugh at the couple, but instead they mocked Hephaestus. The gods often made fun of him because of his limp and his soot-covered face, which came from working over the fire at his craft.

Hephaestus in Context

The Greeks believed that Hephaestus had a workshop on the volcanic island of Lemnos in the Aegean Sea. There, he taught the people the arts of metalwork, for which they became famous. The Romans thought that their god Vulcan lived and worked under Mount Etna, a volcano on the island of Sicily, and had workshops on Olympus and beneath other

The Greek god Hephaestus at his forge. TIME LIFE PICTURES/MANSELL/TIME LIFE PICTURES/GETTY IMAGES.

volcanoes as well. In this way, the Greeks and Romans provided a supernatural explanation for the violent eruptions and quakes that occurred wherever volcanoes were found: the quakes were said to be the result of the pounding of the hammers of Hephaestus.

The fact that Hephaestus is mocked for his disability is a reflection of the emphasis the ancient Greeks place on physical perfection. Physical deformity or disability in a baby was seen as something a family should be ashamed of, or a mark of the gods' disfavor. In fact, throughout ancient Greece (and in many other ancient cultures), deformed newborns were killed. Generally, they were left to die of exposure, but the Spartans actually threw them off a cliff. Hephaestus must make up for his weak legs by developing especially strong arms and skilled hands.

Key Themes and Symbols

One of the main themes in the myths of Hephaestus is disability. He is wounded at a young age by a fall from Olympus and is routinely ridiculed and dismissed by the other gods for his physical flaws. The symbols typically associated with Hephaestus—the blacksmith's hammer, anvil, and tongs—all illustrate his place among the gods as a working craftsman, and a symbol of all men who must work with their hands. In this way—and in his physical imperfection—he is perhaps the most human of all the gods.

Hephaestus in Art, Literature, and Everyday Life

Although not as popular as other Greek and Roman gods, Hephaestus had his share of followers. The Greeks built a large temple to honor Hephaestus, which still stands. Each year in August, the Romans held a festival in honor of Vulcan called the Vulcanalia.

More recently, Hephaestus (under the name Vulcan) appeared as a character in the 1988 Terry Gilliam film *The Adventures of Baron Munchausen*, played by Oliver Reed. He also appeared briefly in a segment from the original Disney animated film *Fantasia* (1940); he is shown creating lightning bolts for Zeus.

As the steel industry emerged in the nineteenth century, Vulcan enjoyed new symbolic popularity. The name "Vulcan" was applied to various products and companies associated with steel production, and the image of Vulcan was popular in steel-producing cities. Birmingham, Alabama, for example, features a 55-foot-high cast iron statue of Vulcan. Vulcan has also found his way into other industries. The process of "vulcanization," or curing process that strengthens rubber by chemically treating it at very high heat, is named after Vulcan. The process was invented by Charles Goodyear, who put the new rubber to use in tire manufacturing.

Read, Write, Think, Discuss

Hephaestus is described as being deformed and physically disabled. He is also routinely the subject of ridicule and mocking by the other gods. Compare this to the situation disabled persons face in the modern world. Are people with disabilities often made fun of in modern books, movies, or television shows? Can you also find examples of disabled persons who are respected? Which of the two types is more common in the media, and what does this indicate about attitudes toward disability in modern culture?

SEE ALSO Achilles; Aeneas; Aphrodite; Athena; Fire; Greek Mythology; Hera; Pandora; Prometheus; Roman Mythology; Zeus

Hera

Character Overview

The queen of **heaven** in **Greek mythology**, Hera was the sister and wife of **Zeus** (pronounced ZOOS), the king of the gods. The Greeks worshipped her as a mother goddess and considered her a protector of marriage and childbirth and a guardian of women. Many of the myths and legends about Hera concern her terrible jealousy of and revenge against Zeus's numerous lovers and children. Hera's counterpart in **Roman mythology** was the goddess Juno (pronounced JOO-noh). Juno closely resembled Hera, and myths about her were basically the same. However, there were some differences. In Roman mythology, for example, Juno's origin is sometimes associated with an Italian mother goddess closely connected to fertility. She is often linked with the moon, and the month that the Romans named in her honor—June—was considered the most favorable time of the year for weddings.

As the wife of Zeus, Hera bore him four children: **Hephaestus** (pronounced hi-FES-tuhs), the god of **fire** and crafts; **Ares** (pronounced AIR-eez), the god of war; Ilithyia (pronounced ee-LEE-thee-uh), the goddess of childbirth; and Hebe (pronounced HEE-bee), the cupbearer of the gods. Zeus and Hera often quarreled, and their arguments sometimes became fierce enough to shake the halls of Olympus (pronounced oh-LIM-puhs), the home of the gods. Most of their arguments concerned Zeus's seduction of other women.

Major Myths

The daughter of the **Titans Cronus** (pronounced KROH-nuhs) and Rhea (pronounced REE-uh), Hera was swallowed after birth by Cronus. Her siblings **Demeter** (pronounced di-MEE-ter), **Hades** (pronounced

Nationality/Culture
Greek

Pronunciation
HAIR-uh

Alternate Names
Juno (Roman)

Appears In
Hesiod's *Theogony*, Ovid's *Metamorphoses*

Lineage
Daughter of Cronus and Rhea

HAY-deez), **Poseidon** (pronounced poh-SYE-dun), and Hestia (pronounced HESS-tee-uh) suffered the same fate. However, Rhea managed to save Zeus, the youngest brother. Later Zeus rescued his brothers and sisters by giving Cronus a potion that caused him to vomit them out. Some stories say that Hera was raised by the Titans Oceanus (pronounced oh-SEE-uh-nuhs) and Tethys (pronounced TEE-this); others claim that she grew up under the care of Temenus (pronounced TEM-uh-nuhs), who ruled the region of Arcadia (pronounced ar-KAY-dee-uh) in Greece.

When Zeus and his brothers defeated the Titans and divided the universe among themselves, they gave nothing to their sisters. Hera was furious at being left out, and this anger persisted throughout her relationship with Zeus. According to some myths, Zeus seduced Hera while disguised as a cuckoo. Other tales say that he found her on an island and carried her away to a cave. Stories place their wedding at various sites: in the Garden of the Hesperides (pronounced heh-SPER-uh-deez), at the top of Mount Ida in Anatolia (present-day Turkey), or on the island of Euboea (pronounced yoo-BEE-uh) in the Aegean (pronounced i-JEE-uhn) Sea. Festivals commemorating the marriage took place throughout Greece.

Zeus wandered the world seducing beautiful women, goddesses, and **nymphs**—often while disguised as a mortal or an animal. His unfaithfulness made Hera insanely jealous. Most of her anger was directed at Zeus's lovers and their children, whom she persecuted and punished mercilessly. One of the greatest victims of Hera's anger was **Heracles**, the son of Zeus and a mortal woman named Alcmena (pronounced alk-MEE-nuh). Hera hounded and punished Heracles throughout his life. Soon after his birth, she sent two snakes to kill him, but the infant Heracles, who would become known for his tremendous strength, strangled the snakes instead. Another time, Hera drove Heracles temporarily insane, causing him to kill his own wife and children. Once, when she raised a storm against Heracles' ship, Zeus retaliated by hanging Hera from Mount Olympus by her wrists, with anvils attached to her feet.

Another of Hera's victims was Io (pronounced EE-oh), a Greek princess with whom Zeus had an affair. Hera suspected that Zeus had a new lover and went searching for him. To save Io from his wife's jealousy, Zeus turned the girl into a white calf. When Hera found Zeus, she asked to have the calf as a gift. Not daring to refuse, he agreed. Io roamed the meadows as a calf for a long time, constantly pestered by a horsefly sent by Hera to torment her. Feeling pity for Io, Zeus often visited her in the shape of a bull. Finally, he promised Hera that he would pay no more attention to Io, and Hera agreed to transform her back into a woman.

Semele (pronounced SEM-uh-lee), a mortal woman who gave birth to Zeus's son **Dionysus** (pronounced dye-uh-NYE-suhs), was another of Hera's victims. Hera suggested to Semele that she ask her lover to appear in his full glory. Zeus, who had promised to grant Semele any wish, sadly did so and appeared with his thunderbolts, causing Semele to burn to death immediately. Athamas (pronounced ATH-uh-mas), the king of Thebes (pronounced THEEBZ), and his wife Ino (pronounced EYE-noh), who later became a sea goddess, raised Dionysus after his mother's death. Hera punished them as well by making them go mad.

Hera's vengeful nature was directed mainly at her husband's unfaithfulness, but there were other victims too. One famous story tells of a beauty contest between Hera and the goddesses **Athena** (pronounced uh-THEE-nuh) and **Aphrodite** (pronounced af-ro-DYE-tee). The judge of the contest, the Trojan prince Paris, chose Aphrodite as the most beautiful of the three. The angry Hera punished Paris by siding with the Greeks against the Trojans in the Trojan War and by acting as protector of the Greek hero **Achilles** (pronounced uh-KILL-eez).

One of the principal Roman myths of Juno concerns Minerva (pronounced mi-NUR-vuh), the Roman counterpart of the Greek goddess Athena. According to this story, Minerva was born from the head of Jupiter (pronounced JOO-pi-tur), which angered Juno. She complained to Flora (pronounced FLOR-uh), the goddess of flowers and gardens, who touched Juno with a magic herb that caused her to give birth to the god Mars. A similar myth exists in Greek mythology, but in some versions of that story, Hera gives birth to the monster Typhon (pronounced TYE-fon), who tries to defeat Zeus and take his power. While the Greek myth illustrates Hera's vengeful nature, the Roman story emphasizes fertility and motherhood.

Hera in Context

The worship of Hera appears to be older than the worship of Zeus, even though, as the king of the other gods, he has more power and importance than Hera. Archeological evidence suggests that the temples built in

First Ladies

In cultures where a male god rules over lesser gods, the wife of the leader plays an important role, and often exemplifies cultural beliefs about women and marriage.

Figure	Nationality	Wife of	Description
Frigg	Norse	Odin	Loyal wife and mother. She does not live with Odin, but keeps her own home where she is attended by young women.
Hera	Greek	Zeus	A beautiful goddess with a short temper and plenty of power. Her husband is often unfaithful to her, and she punishes his lovers severely.
Izanami	Japanese	Izanagi	Izanami and Izanagi jointly create Japan and its gods. She is burned birthing the fire god and dies, horribly disfigured. Izanagi breaks off their marriage after unsuccessfully trying to rescue her from the underworld.
Sati/Parvati	Indian	Shiva	Sati is the first wife of Shiva. She is devoted and humble. She burns herself to death because her father fails to respect Shiva sufficiently. She is reincarnated as Parvati, another humble, devoted wife.

ILLUSTRATION BY ANAXOS, INC./CENGAGE LEARNING, GALE.

Hera's honor are the oldest of any of the other Greek deities; this fact may indicate that Hera developed from a goddess of an earlier matriarchal society (a society in which women hold power) when goddesses could be more powerful than their male counterparts. In the patriarchal society (ruled by men) of the Greeks, Hera became a figure who was powerful in her own right, but not as powerful as her husband. She could not control him, and the constant fighting between the two may reflect the conflict between the older cult worship of Hera versus the newer and more powerful cult worship of Zeus.

Hera's long-lasting bond with Zeus—despite its many problems—reflects the importance of the marriage bond in Greece, and also highlights how husbands and wives were treated differently in ancient Greece. Men spent more time away from home, where their actions could not be seen by household servants; women, being in charge of the household—and with the home being considered the safest place, particularly in times of conflict—had limited contact with men other than their husbands or servants. It seems likely that Greek husbands had more opportunity to be unfaithful than their wives did. Although divorces caused by cheating spouses were not uncommon, a wife would usually have to get the permission of her family before seeking a divorce. This meant that the divorce process was more difficult for a woman than for a man, especially since divorce often meant that her children would remain with her husband. For these reasons, wives tended to remain married even if their husbands were unfaithful. However, the myths of Hera illustrate the kinds of vengeance a wife could inflict upon her husband and his lovers; these may have served as "cautionary tales" for men engaging in affairs with other women.

Key Themes and Symbols

Hera stood as a symbol of motherhood, as well as a symbol of loyalty to her husband Zeus. However, she also represented vengeance in many myths involving Zeus's lovers. The theme of jealousy is continuous in the myths of Hera. Indeed, her jealousy extends not just to those women who are involved with Zeus, but also to their children, as shown in the tales of Heracles.

Both the cow and the peacock were sacred animals to Hera. Like the Egyptian goddess **Hathor**, Hera was a cow-goddess, described often as "ox-eyed." The pomegranate fruit also represents Hera as a fertility goddess.

Hera in Art, Literature, and Everyday Life

As the wife of Zeus, Hera was one of the more honored gods among the Greeks. She was often depicted in statue form, numerous examples of which have survived to modern times. Many temples were built in her honor, and one can still be seen in the Italian city of Paestum.

Although Hera is not as readily found in art and literature from the Renaissance to present day, she has still made some notable appearances. Carolyn Kizer's poem "Hera, Hung from the Sky" (1973) offers a feminist take on Zeus's legendary punishment of his wife. Hera appears in the 1963 film *Jason and the Argonauts*, as well as the 1997 Disney animated film *Hercules*; in the latter case, however, Hera's role in the myth of Hercules was greatly reduced. A somewhat more accurate portrayal of Hera's relationship with Hercules is shown in the television series *Hercules: The Legendary Journeys*, in which the character of Hera appeared in two episodes.

Read, Write, Think, Discuss

The purpose of marriage in ancient Greece was to bear and raise children who would continue the family bloodline, so marriages often ended when this purpose could not be fulfilled for some reason—for instance, when the couple found they could not have children, or because the wife's unfaithfulness could result in her bearing another man's children. Like in the ancient Greek society, divorce is common in the United States, with half of the marriages ending in divorce. What are the primary reasons for divorce in American society? How do these reasons reflect the purposes for marriage in modern culture?

SEE ALSO Greek Mythology; Heracles; Roman Mythology; Zeus

Nationality/Culture
Greek

Pronunciation
HAIR-uh-kleez

Alternate Names
Hercules (Roman)

Appears In
Hesiod's *Theogony*, Apollodorus's *Bibliotheca*

Lineage
Son of Zeus and Alcmena

Heracles

Character Overview

The greatest of all **heroes** in **Greek mythology**, Heracles was the strongest man on earth. Besides tremendous physical strength, he had great self-confidence and considered himself equal to the gods. Heracles (called Hercules by the Romans) was not blessed with great intelligence, but his bravery made up for any lack of cunning. Easily angered, his sudden outbursts of rage often harmed innocent bystanders. When the fury passed, though, Heracles was full of sorrow and guilt for what he had done and ready to accept any punishment for his misdeeds. Only supernatural forces could defeat him, and it was magic that ended his mortal life. In Greek mythology, only two figures with half-mortal, half-god parentage—Heracles and **Dionysus** (pronounced dye-uh-NYE-suhs)—became fully immortal (able to live forever) and were worshipped as gods.

Heracles was the son of **Zeus** (pronounced ZOOS) and Alcmena (pronounced alk-MEE-nuh), the wife of Amphitryon (pronounced am-FI-tree-uhn), a distinguished Greek warrior and heir to the throne of Tiryns (pronounced TEER-ins). One night while Amphitryon was away, Zeus came to Alcmena disguised as her husband. The next day, the real Amphitryon returned and slept with his wife. Concerned that Amphitryon did not remember being with Alcmena on both nights, the couple consulted the blind prophet Tiresias (pronounced ty-REE-see-uhs), who could see the workings of the gods. He told them that Zeus had slept with Alcmena the first night and predicted that she would bear a child who would become a great hero.

Alcmena bore twin boys—Heracles, the son of Zeus, and Iphicles (pronounced IF-i-kleez), the son of Amphitryon. When the goddess **Hera** (pronounced HAIR-uh) discovered that Zeus had seduced Alcmena and fathered Heracles, she was furious. Hera was fiercely jealous of Zeus's lovers and children and pursued them mercilessly. She tried to kill the infant Heracles by having two poisonous snakes placed in his crib one night. However, the infant grabbed the snakes and strangled them. Though Hera failed to kill Heracles, she persecuted him throughout his life, causing many of the events that led to his great suffering and punishments.

Heracles' Lesson As a young boy, Heracles became aware of his extraordinary strength—and his temper. Like most Greek youths, he took music lessons. One day Linus (pronounced LYE-nuhs), his music master, was teaching Heracles to play the lyre. Heracles became frustrated, flew into a rage, and banged the lyre down on Linus's head. The blow killed Linus instantly. Heracles was shocked and very sorry. He had not meant to kill his teacher. He just did not know his own strength.

Madness and the Death of Megara While still a young man, Heracles went to fight the Minyans, a group that had been forcing the people of

Thebes to pay money to them. As a reward for conquering the Minyans, the king of Thebes gave Heracles the hand of his daughter, Megara (prounounced MEG-uh-ruh). Heracles was devoted to Megara and the three children she bore him.

One day after Heracles returned home from a journey, Hera struck him with a fit of madness during which he killed his wife and children. When he came to his senses, Heracles was horrified by what he had done. Devastated with sorrow and guilt, the hero went to the oracle at **Delphi** (pronounced DEL-fye), where humans could communicate with the gods, to ask how he could make up for his crime. The oracle told him to go to King Eurystheus (pronounced yoo-RIS-thee-uhs) of Tiryns and submit to any punishment asked of him. The oracle also announced that if Heracles completed the tasks set before him, he would become immortal.

The Twelve Labors King Eurystheus gave Heracles a series of twelve difficult and dangerous tasks. Known as the Twelve Labors of Heracles, these were his most famous feats. The hero's first task was to kill the Nemean (pronounced ni-MEE-uhn) Lion, a monstrous beast that terrorized the countryside and could not be killed by any weapon. Heracles strangled the beast with his bare hands and made its skin into a cloak that made him invulnerable, or unable to be harmed.

For his second labor, the hero had to kill the Lernaean Hydra (pronounced ler-NEE-uhn HYE-druh), a creature with nine heads that lived in a swamp. One of the beast's heads was immortal, and the others grew back when cut off. With the help of his friend Iolaus, Heracles cut off the Hydra's eight heads and burned each wound, which prevented new heads from growing back. Because he could not cut off the ninth head, he buried the creature under a great rock.

The next task was to capture the Cerynean (pronounced ser-i-NEE-uhn) Hind, a golden-horned deer that was sacred to the goddess **Artemis** (pronounced AHR-tuh-miss). After hunting the animal for a year, Heracles finally managed to capture it. As he was taking it to Tiryns, Artemis stopped him and demanded that he return the deer. The hero promised that the sacred animal would not be harmed, and she allowed him to continue on his journey.

The fourth labor of Heracles was to seize the Erymanthian (pronounced air-uh-MAN-thee-uhn) Boar, a monstrous animal that ravaged the lands around Mount Erymanthus. After forcing the animal

As one of his Twelve Labors, Heracles had to drive away the Stymphalian Birds, monstrous man-eating birds with claws, beaks, and wings of iron. © KUNSTHISTORISCHES MUSEUM, VIENNA, AUSTRIA/THE BRIDGEMAN ART LIBRARY.

from its lair, Heracles chased it until it became so exhausted that he could catch it easily.

The hero's fifth task was to clean the Augean (pronounced aw-JEE-uhn) Stables in one day. King Augeas, the son of the **sun** god Helios (pronounced HEE-lee-ohs), had great herds of cattle whose stables had not been cleaned for many years. Heracles accomplished the task by diverting rivers to run through the filthy stables and wash them clean.

The sixth task involved driving away the Stymphalian (pronounced stim-FAY-lee-uhn) Birds, a flock of birds with claws, beaks, and wings of iron that ate humans and that were terrorizing the countryside. Helped by the goddess **Athena** (pronounced uh-THEE-nuh), Heracles forced the birds from their nests and shot them with his bow and arrow.

Eurystheus next ordered Heracles to seize the Cretan (pronounced KREET-n) Bull and bring it back to Tiryns alive. This savage bull had been a gift from **Poseidon** (pronounced poh-SYE-dun) to King Minos (pronounced MYE-nuhs) of Crete. The king gave Heracles permission to catch it and take it away.

For his eighth task, Heracles was ordered to capture the Mares of Diomedes (pronounced dye-uh-MEE-deez), a herd of horses that belonged to King Diomedes of Thrace and that ate human flesh. Heracles killed Diomedes and fed him to the mares. Then the hero tamed the horses and brought them back to Eurystheus.

The ninth labor consisted of obtaining the Girdle of Hippolyta (pronounced hye-POL-i-tuh), the queen of the **Amazons**. Hippolyta greeted Heracles warmly and agreed to give him the girdle. But then Hera caused trouble, making the Amazons think that Heracles planned to kidnap their queen. They attacked, and Heracles killed Hippolyta and took the girdle.

For his tenth labor, Heracles had to capture the Cattle of Geryon (pronounced JER-ee-on), a monster with three bodies that lived in the far west on the island of Erythia (pronounced eh-RITH-ee-uh). After a difficult journey by sea and across the desert, Heracles killed Geryon, a herdsman, and an enormous guard dog. He then took the cattle and returned with them to Tiryns.

The eleventh labor involved bringing back the golden Apples of the Hesperides (pronounced heh-SPER-uh-deez), a group of **nymphs**— female nature deities—who lived in the far west. According to one account, Heracles requested help from the Hesperides' father, the giant **Atlas** (pronounced AT-luhs), who held up the sky. Heracles offered to take Atlas's place under the sky if he would fetch the apples from his daughters. Atlas agreed and obtained the apples, but then he refused to take back the sky. Heracles asked Atlas to hold the sky for just a moment while he got a pad to ease the burden on his shoulders. Atlas agreed. But as soon as Atlas took back the sky, Heracles grabbed the apples and fled. In another version of this story, Heracles obtained the apples by himself after killing a dragon that stood guard over the tree on which they grew.

Heracles' final task was one of the most difficult and dangerous. He had to descend to the kingdom of **Hades** (pronounced HAY-deez) and capture **Cerberus** (pronounced SUR-ber-uhs), the fierce three-headed dog that guarded the gates to the **underworld**. Hades said Heracles could take Cerberus if he used no weapons to overcome the beast. Heracles wrestled Cerberus into submission or gave him drugged food and carried him to Eurystheus.

Other Adventures and Later Life Heracles had many other adventures during his lifetime. He killed other beasts and monsters, engaged in numerous battles against his enemies, joined the expedition of **Jason** and the **Argonauts** (pronounced AHR-guh-nawts), and even fought the god **Apollo** (pronounced uh-POL-oh). Throughout, he faced the hatred of Hera, who continued to persecute him because he was the son of Zeus.

Later in his life, Heracles married Deianira (pronounced dee-uh-NYE-ruh), a princess whose hand he had won by fighting the river god Achelous (pronounced ay-kee-LOH-uhs). Heracles also saved Deianira from a centaur—half-human, half-horse—named Nessus, who tried to harm her. As Nessus lay dying from Heracles' arrows, he urged Deianira to take some of his blood, telling her it would act as a magic potion that could secure her husband's love forever.

Some years later, fearing that Heracles had fallen in love with another woman, Deianira took the potion and smeared it on a robe for her husband. The potion was really a terrible poison, and when Heracles put on the poisoned garment, it burned his skin, causing an agonizing pain that could not be stopped. When Deianira discovered what had happened, she killed herself.

The dying Heracles ordered his son to build a funeral pyre, a large pile of burning wood used in some cultures to cremate a dead body, and the hero lay down upon it. As the flames of the pyre grew, a great cloud appeared, a bolt of lightning struck, and the body of Heracles disappeared. Heracles, now an immortal god, had been taken to Mount Olympus to be with his father, Zeus, and the other gods. Even Hera welcomed him and allowed him to marry her daughter Hebe (pronounced HEE-bee).

Heracles in Context

The astounding popularity of Heracles throughout the ancient world has been the source of much speculation about his appeal. Some have argued that his virtuous nature, combined with his marginal intelligence and brute strength, made him a more accessible character than even many of the gods. It has also been suggested that, since he is primarily known as a

Superheroes, Super Strength

Echoes of Heracles can be detected in modern American heroes and superheroes. The comic book idol Superman, for instance, has nearly limitless strength and a strict code of honor, much like Heracles. Whereas other comic book heroes, such as Batman, defeat evil using cunning, Superman relies on sheer power. The Incredible Hulk also resembles Heracles. The Hulk can be driven into a destructive rage by anger, and can sometimes hurt those he cares about.

conqueror of beasts instead of men, people of all regions can appreciate his feats; this is in direct contrast to some heroes who are popular only within a local area, due to their battles against a particular group generally viewed as enemies. He was worshipped in temples as far away as Egypt, and the Greeks honored his death with a festival known as the *Herakleia*. Heracles was also popular because he was a man who overcame the cruel whims of the gods to earn his place as an immortal.

After the time of Alexander the Great, when kingdoms developed out of the lands conquered by Alexander, Heracles came to represent the model king, a man who lived his life in service to the people. Overlooking the violent aspects of the life of Heracles, the focus was on his good deeds in ridding the Greek countryside of dangerous beasts. His deeds were so great that the gods elevated him to the level of a deity, although the Greeks worshipped him more as a hero than as a god. In similar fashion, kings began to claim that the deceased founders of their realm had become gods, and then the kings claimed that they were gods, too. Roman leaders adopted the idea of worshipping dead emperors, but stopped short of claiming that living rulers were also gods. The connection between gods and rulers would develop later as the "divine right" of European kings; although they did not claim to be gods, kings claimed that God deliberately appointed them to rule over the people, which meant that their rule could not be questioned or overthrown.

Key Themes and Symbols

Heracles is a symbol of pure physical strength. He was often pictured in artwork holding a club, usually fighting one of the many beasts he encountered during his twelve labors. He is so strong that he can only be destroyed by trickery and magic. Heracles also demonstrates success against all odds. His twelve fabled tasks are all virtually impossible, yet he perseveres and prevails.

An important theme found in the myths of Heracles is ill-fated romantic relationships. Heracles is driven by Hera to kill his wife and children in a fit of madness; this happens because of Hera's jealousy over Zeus having a son with a human woman. In addition, Deianira accidentally poisons Heracles because she is insecure about their relationship.

Heracles in Art, Literature, and Everyday Life

In modern times, Heracles—usually called by his Roman name, Hercules—is one of the most recognized figures in all of Greek mythology. He has appeared as a character in countless books, films, and television shows. He was the focus of the long-running television series *Hercules: The Legendary Journeys*, with Kevin Sorbo starring as the hero. His myth was famously retold—with some alterations—in the 1997 Disney animated film *Hercules*.

Read, Write, Think, Discuss

Heracles was unique in Greek mythology because he was a hero who ultimately became recognized as a god. In modern times, people continue to recognize heroes as special or different from the average human. These heroes, of course, might be sports stars, political activists, or soldiers, to name a few possibilities. Can you think of a modern-day hero, living or dead, who has earned a larger-than-life status? In what way is this person treated differently than others? Is this person already the subject of any myths or legends (anything that cannot be verified historically)?

SEE ALSO Argonauts; Atlas; Centaurs; Cerberus; Greek Mythology; Hera; Heroes; Zeus

Hercules

See **Heracles.**

Hermes

Nationality/Culture
Greek

Pronunciation
HUR-meez

Alternate Names
Mercury (Roman)

Appears In
Hesiod's *Theogony*, Ovid's *Metamorphoses*, the Homeric Hymns

Lineage
Son of Zeus and Maia

Character Overview

In **Greek mythology**, Hermes was the fleet-footed messenger of the gods. His parents were **Zeus** (pronounced ZOOS), king of the gods, and Maia (pronounced MAY-uh), one of the seven sisters known as the Pleiades (pronounced PLEE-uh-deez). The Romans identified Hermes with Mercury (pronounced MUR-kyoo-ree), the god of merchants and trade, and they placed his main temple near the merchants' quarter in ancient Rome.

The Greeks looked upon Hermes as a protector of travelers, merchants, and thieves, and as a bringer of good luck. Because of his reputation as a speedy messenger, the god became popular among athletes. Many ancient sports arenas had statues of the god.

Major Myths

While still an infant, Hermes killed a tortoise and used its shell to make a stringed instrument called a lyre. Soon afterward, he stole some cattle belonging to **Apollo** (pronounced uh-POL-oh) and then returned to his cradle. When Apollo came looking for the animals, Hermes pretended to know nothing and told a cunning tale to prove his innocence. In the course of telling his tale, he stole Apollo's bow and arrows.

Zeus insisted that the cattle be returned, so Hermes brought Apollo to the place where they were hidden. There he took up his lyre and played so impressively that Apollo agreed to overlook the theft of the cattle if Hermes would give him the instrument. Hermes also handed back the bow and arrows he had stolen. Amused by the young god's antics, Apollo became his good friend and made Hermes the protector of herdsmen.

When Hermes grew up, he often came to the aid of other gods and mortals. He accompanied Zeus on many journeys and once helped him during a struggle with the monster Typhon (pronounced TYE-fon). Another time, Hermes rescued **Ares** (pronounced AIR-eez) when the god was imprisoned in a jar. He also played a role in arranging the return of **Persephone** (pronounced per-SEF-uh-nee) from the **underworld**, or land of the dead. As a protector of travelers, Hermes escorted the spirits

Hermes stole cattle from Apollo, but was then made the protector of herdsmen by the god after he charmed him with his music. In this painting he returns the stolen animals to Apollo as the gods look on. ERICH LESSING/ART RESOURCE, NY.

of dead mortals to the river Styx (pronounced STIKS). Among the living mortals he assisted were King Priam of Troy, **Aeneas** (pronounced i-NEE-uhs), and **Odysseus** (pronounced oh-DIS-ee-uhs).

Hermes had love affairs with a number of goddesses and mortal women. The goddess he loved the most was **Aphrodite** (pronounced af-ro-DYE-tee), with whom he had two children, Hermaphroditus (pronounced hur-maf-ro-DYE-tuhs) and Priapus (pronounced pry-AY-puhs). Hermes was also the father of **Pan**, the god of shepherds and flocks who was half man and half goat.

Hermes in Context

Athletics, an activity associated with Hermes, was very important to ancient Greek men, who valued physical perfection. Every Greek city contained at least one gymnasium, a private area designed for activities such as running, wrestling, and throwing the discus (a heavy, flat disc) or javelin (a spear). Gymnasium activities were reserved for young men, and were the main form of exercise in Greek society. Many of the activities popular in ancient gymnasia have continued into modern sports as events in the Olympic Games.

Hermes is an eloquent trickster, capable of talking himself out of most of the trouble his mischievous actions get him into. The fact that he is appreciated by the other gods reveals that the ancient Greeks valued cunning and eloquence.

Key Themes and Symbols

As the messenger of the gods, Hermes represents both eloquence (required when speaking on behalf of the gods) and speed (required for delivering messages and relaying communication). The theme of eloquence is illustrated in the story about the theft of Apollo's cattle; young Hermes tells a tale that captivates Apollo and removes him from suspicion, and later plays his lyre so beautifully that Apollo forgives the boy.

Hermes in Art, Literature, and Everyday Life

As the protector of people from many different backgrounds—from thieves to shepherds to poets—Hermes was one of the more popular gods in ancient Greek art. Over time, Hermes came to be depicted as a young man wearing winged sandals and a wide-brimmed hat with wings. He also carried a staff with two snakes known as a caduceus (pronounced kuh-DOO-see-uhs).

In modern times, Hermes appeared as a character in the 1997 Disney animated film *Hercules*, voiced by musician Paul Shaffer. As the Roman Mercury, the god has lent his name to—among other things—a chemical element, a brand of automobile, and the closest planet to the **sun** in our solar system.

Read, Write, Think, Discuss

In the early myths of Hermes, the infant god steals several items from Apollo. Instead of punishing the boy, Apollo is impressed by his talent. What do you think this indicates about the ancient Greek view of theft? Do you think Americans share this attitude?

SEE ALSO Apollo; Pan; Persephone; Underworld; Zeus

Hero and Leander

Character Overview

Hero and Leander were famous lovers in **Greek mythology**. Hero, who lived in the town of Sestos (pronounced SES-tohs), served as a priestess of the goddess **Aphrodite** (pronounced af-ro-DYE-tee). Leander was a youth from the nearby town of Abydos (pronounced uh-BYE-duhs), located across a narrow strip of water called the Hellespont (pronounced HEL-uh-spont), now known as the Dardanelles.

Hero and Leander met at a festival and fell in love. However, because she was a priestess of Aphrodite, Hero had to remain a virgin and was forbidden to marry. The two lovers decided to see each other secretly. Each night Hero would leave a lamp burning in a window of the tower in which she lived, and Leander would swim across the Hellespont, using the light to guide his way. One winter night, the wind blew out the flame in the lamp, causing Leander to lose his way and drown. The next morning, when Hero saw his lifeless body washed up on the shore, she killed herself by jumping out of the tower.

Hero and Leander in Context

The myth of Hero and Leander can be seen as a cautionary tale meant to enforce the rules of ancient Greek culture. In particular, the myth warns of the dangers of not obeying religious vows. In a more general sense, the tale cautions against sexual relationships outside the tradition of marriage. Myths were often used as a way to discourage certain behaviors, especially those that would be hard to control through government means.

Nationality/Culture
Greek

Pronunciation
HEER-oh and lee-AN-dur

Alternate Names
Hero and Lymander

Appears In
Ovid's *Heroides*

Lineage
Unknown

A Mythic Feat

English poet Lord Byron was so inspired by Leander's swimming prowess that he undertook the swim across the Hellespont himself. After nearly drowning on his first attempt, Byron successfully followed in Leander's wake on May 3, 1810—supposedly making him the first person since Leander himself to complete the swim.

Key Themes and Symbols

One of the main themes of the tale of Hero and Leander is forbidden love. Hero, as a priestess of Aphrodite, was sworn to remain a virgin; therefore, a love affair was a violation of her vows and the rules of the temple. Another related theme is the wrath of the gods. Because Hero and Leander violated the rules of the gods, they were both doomed to die tragically.

In the myth, summer is a symbol of flourishing love, as shown by the fact that the lovers' affair begins in the warm summer months. By contrast, winter symbolizes the stormy fate of their doomed relationship, and a winter wind blows out the candle that guides Leander across the sea.

Hero and Leander in Art, Literature, and Everyday Life

Although well known in ancient Greece, Ovid preserved and popularized the tale of Hero and Leander in his *Heroides*. In 1598 the English author Christopher Marlowe used the story as the basis of his poem *Hero and Leander*. Lord Byron, John Keats, and Lord Tennyson were other well-known poets who wrote of the lovers. The tale also inspired paintings by Rubens, Turner, and Rossetti. The myth of Hero and Leander was referenced in several of William Shakespeare's plays, most notably *As You Like It* and *Two Gentlemen of Verona*.

Read, Write, Think, Discuss

The myth of Hero and Leander could be classified as a tale of "star-crossed lovers," much like the tale of Romeo and Juliet. Both tales center on two young lovers who are fated to be kept apart. Find another example of this kind of tale in literature, television, or film, and describe it. How does it differ from the myth of Hero and Leander?

SEE ALSO Aphrodite; Greek Mythology

Heroes

Theme Overview

At the heart of many of the world's most enduring myths and legends is a hero, a man or woman who triumphs over obstacles. Heroes are generally not all-powerful and immortal beings, able to live forever. Instead they represent the best of what it means to be human, demonstrating great strength, courage, wisdom, cleverness, or devotion. Some heroes of myth and legend are wholly fictional. Others are historical figures who have risen to the level of legendary heroes or who have been given such status by writers or by the public.

In studying myths and legends from around the world, scholars have identified a pattern that appears over and over again: the story of the universal hero. Mythology scholar Joseph Campbell has shown that these stories generally end with the hero gaining new knowledge or abilities. Often an element of miracle or mystery surrounds the birth of such heroes. Their true identity may be unknown; they may be the child of a virgin; or they may possess special powers or be demigods (half-human, half-god).

Many hero myths focus on a quest—a difficult task or journey that must be undertaken to achieve a goal or earn a reward such as the hand of a loved one. Leaving the everyday world, the hero follows a path filled with challenges and adventures, perhaps involving magic or the supernatural. A hero may even enter the **underworld**, or land of the dead, and confront death itself.

Heroes must use their strength and wits to defeat enemies, monsters, or demons, although some are aided by luck or by a protector in the form of a god or magician. Sometimes heroes have to give up something precious to move forward in the quest. In the end, the hero returns home enriched with powers, wisdom, treasure, or perhaps a mate won in the course of the quest.

The hero's quest may be seen as a symbol of the journey of self-discovery that anyone can make, the quest to overcome inner monsters and achieve self-understanding. But though quests form the basis of many myths and legends, not all heroes follow the quest pattern exactly as described. There are almost as many kinds of heroes as there are human qualities and experiences.

Major Myths

Questing or Journeying Heroes The hero on a quest or journey appears in dozens of myths, epics, legends, and fairy tales. **Greek mythology** has many questing heroes, including **Odysseus** (pronounced oh-DIS-ee-uhs), **Orpheus** (pronounced OR-fee-uhs), **Jason**, and **Heracles** (pronounced HAIR-uh-kleez; known as Hercules by the Romans). Odysseus just wants to return home after the Trojan War, but his adventure-filled voyage takes ten years. The musician Orpheus descends into the underworld in his quest to bring his beloved **Eurydice** (pronounced yoo-RID-uh-see) back from death. Jason sails to distant lands in search of the **Golden Fleece**. The trials of the mighty Heracles are organized into Twelve Labors or quests.

Questing heroes appear in the mythology of many other cultures. **Gilgamesh** (pronounced GIL-guh-mesh), the hero of an epic from ancient Mesopotamia, travels in search of immortality. The Polynesian hero Rupe changes into a bird to search for his lost sister and bring her home. In Britain's **Arthurian legends** the knight **Lancelot** and his son **Galahad** (pronounced GAL-uh-had) seek the **Holy Grail**, and in a myth of the Tewa of North America, Water Jar Boy searches for his father—a symbol of the search for identity.

Warriors and Kings A number of individuals rise to the level of heroes with their outstanding skills in combat. In myths about the Trojan War, the warriors Ajax (pronounced AY-jaks) and **Achilles** (pronounced uh-KILL-eez) fight valiantly, and the Amazon (AM-uh-zon) queen Penthesilea (pronounced pen-thess-uh-LEE-uh) leads a troop of her soldiers against the Greek forces. **Beowulf** (pronounced BAY-uh-woolf) is the monster-slaying hero of an early English epic. Chinese myths tell of Yi (pronounced YEE), an archer so skilled that he was able to shoot down extra suns in the sky. Rama (pronounced RAH-muh), hero of the Hindu epic the *Ramayana*, defeats fearsome demons called Rakshasas (pronounced RAHK-shah-sahs) in a series of duels. The Celtic hero **Finn** leads a band of warriors against animal, human, and supernatural foes. Various Native American legends feature pairs of warriors—such as the Navajo warrior **twins** and the Zuni Ahayuuta (pronounced ah-hah-YOO-tuh) brothers—who perform heroic tasks to help their people.

Some figures in mythology earned their hero status as legendary rulers. Britain's King **Arthur**, for example, may have begun as a historical figure but was transformed into a hero of great stature. Africa has a strong tradition of kingly heroes. Shaka, a leader of the Zulu people of southern Africa, gathered a huge army and established a great empire in the early 1800s. Osai Tutu (pronounced oh-SYE TOO-too), a ruler of the Ashanti people in the 1700s, succeeded in freeing the Ashanti from domination by a neighboring people with the help of a magical golden stool. Tibetans and Mongolians tell tales about the warrior-king Gesar (pronounced GAY-sahr), a god who reluctantly agreed to be born as a human in order to fight demons on earth.

National and Culture Heroes A national hero is a mythological—or even historical—hero who is considered to be the founder of a city or nation or the source of identity for a people. In ancient Greece, heroes became the object of religious worship, and local cults developed to show devotion to particular local heroes. The Romans made **Aeneas** (pronounced i-NEE-uhs) their national hero. In North America, Iroquois legends say that the hero Hiawatha (pronounced hye-uh-WOTH-uh) persuaded five tribes to come together as one group, thus giving the Iroquois greater power and a stronger identity.

Another type of ancestral hero is the culture hero who brings the gifts of civilization to a people. The Kayapo (pronounced KAH-yuh-poh) Indians of Brazil have a myth about a boy named Botoque, who stole **fire** from a jaguar and brought it to his people so they could cook food for the first time. In Greek mythology it is the Titan **Prometheus** (pronounced pruh-MEE-thee-uhs) who steals fire for the benefit of humankind. The Daribi people of Papua New Guinea, a large island in the eastern Pacific, have myths about Souw, a wandering culture hero. Souw brought death, warfare, and black magic, but he also gave humans the first livestock and crops, allowing them to shift from hunting to agriculture.

Clever Heroes and Tricksters In many myths heroes accomplish great tasks by outwitting evil or more powerful enemies. In the West African

---

Born Under a Hero's Star

Unusual circumstances often mark the birth of a mythic hero. The hero may be the result of a mixed union—Heracles was the son of the god Zeus (pronounced ZOOS) and of a mortal woman. Some heroes do not even need two parents. Kutoyis (pronounced koo-TOH-yis), a hero of the Native American Blackfoot people, was born as a clot of blood dropped by a buffalo. Karna, a hero of the Hindu epic *Mahabharata*, is born to a woman who is a virgin—a theme that occurs in many myths. The African Bantu people tell of Litulone, the child of an old woman who produced him without a man's help. Like Heracles, the Irish hero Cuchulain (pronounced koo-KUL-in), and many others, Litulone had great strength and fighting skill when barely out of infancy.

---

legend of **Sunjata**, the female character Nana Triban tricks the evil king Sumanguru Kante into telling her the source of his great strength. Nana Triban uses this knowledge to help her brother Sunjata triumph over Sumanguru. In Greek mythology, **Penelope** (pronounced puh-NEL-uh-pee), the wife of Odysseus, outwits the many suitors pressing to marry her during her husband's long absence. Claiming that she must weave a shroud for her father-in-law before she can remarry, she weaves by day and unravels the cloth by night. In the Persian tale *One Thousand and One Nights*, Sheherazade (pronounced shuh-HAIR-uh-zahd) prevents the sultan from carrying out a plan to kill her. Capturing his attention with fascinating stories, she withholds the endings, promising to continue the following evening.

Some culture heroes are **tricksters**—human or animal characters whose mischievous pranks and tricks can benefit humans. Raven and Coyote fill the trickster role in many American Indian myths. The Polynesians of the Pacific islands have myths about **Maui** (pronounced MOU-ee), a trickster whose actions have bad results as often as good ones. He loses immortality for humans, for example, but acquires fire for them. Tricksters in African myth are generally small and weak creatures, such as the hare and the spider, who outwit the strong, rich, and powerful. The African trickster hare is the distant ancestor of **Brer Rabbit**, a clever hero in African American mythology.

Folk Heroes Some heroes are ordinary individuals who have special skills. They may take up the causes of common people against tyrants and bullies or may be blessed with remarkable good fortune. Such heroes often become known through popular songs or folk tales, but they may also appear in various forms of literature.

Folk heroes include **Robin Hood**, an English adventurer who fought and robbed the rich in order to help the poor, and John Henry, an African American laborer who performed a humble job with exceptional—and fatal—strength and determination.

Defiant and Doomed Heroes The hero's story does not always have a happy ending. Some heroes knowingly defy the limits placed on them by society or the gods. Even if they face destruction, they are determined to be true to their beliefs—or perhaps to perish in a blaze of glory. Others are simply the victims of their own failings or of bad luck.

Yamato-takeru (pronounced YAH-mah-toh-tah-kay-roo), a legendary warrior hero of Japan, brings about his own end when he kills two gods who have taken the form of a white deer and a white boar. **Antigone** (pronounced an-TIG-uh-nee), a Greek princess, defies the law in order to bury her brother, knowing that the penalty will be death. The most gruesomely doomed of all heroes may be Antigone's father, **Oedipus** (pronounced ED-uh-puhs), who outrages the gods by unwittingly killing his father and marrying his mother. When he discovers what he has done, he gouges out his own eyes in shame. His heroism lies not in quests, adventures, or triumphs but in facing his tragic fate.

In Aztec myths, the culture hero **Quetzalcoatl** (pronounced keht-sahl-koh-AHT-l) was tricked by his enemy **Tezcatlipoca** (pronounced tehs-cah-tlee-POH-cah) into leaving his kingdom. After getting Quetzalcoatl drunk, Tezcatlipoca showed him a mirror with Tezcatlipoca's frightening image. Believing that the mirror reflected his own face, Quetzalcoatl went away to purify himself, promising to return to his people at the end of a fifty-two-year cycle.

Heroes in Context

Through the ages cultures have produced heroes that reflect cultural values on a larger-than-life scale. The male-dominated civilization of ancient Greece, for example, admired strong warrior heroes. By contrast, in the mythology of ancient Egypt, where religion played a central role at

Yamato-takeru, a legendary warrior hero of Japan, fought battles against people and gods. Stories about his adventures appear in the **Kojiki** *and the* **Nihongi,** *two books of Japanese myths and legends.* FITZWILLIAM MUSEUM, UNIVERSITY OF CAMBRIDGE, UK/THE BRIDGEMAN ART LIBRARY.

all levels of society, the heroes were often priest-magicians. In many cultures women became heroes by using their intelligence or forceful personalities to outwit a foe.

Heroes in many cultures function as a bridge between the divine gods and normal humans. This explains the presence of so many demigods as heroes, with one parent a god and the other a human. Indeed, the ancient Greek term "hero" was used by later Greeks to refer specifically to demigods or dead men believed to have influence in both the living world and the **afterlife.** Such figures were often worshipped by ancient Greeks just as the gods themselves were, and their powers were believed to be very real, if not as potent as the gods.

Heroes in Art, Literature, and Everyday Life

As a group, heroes are the mythological characters that have stood the test of time over all others. For example, while many modern readers may not know the characters of **Odin** or **Athena** beyond their names, the stories of Hercules and **Aladdin** are quite familiar and popular. Their stories have been adapted and retold countless times. Successful film versions have been made of many of the heroic tales mentioned here, including tales of Aladdin (the 1992 animated film *Aladdin*, among others), Hercules (the 1997 animated film *Hercules*, among others), Jason (the 1963 film *Jason and the Argonauts*), **Perseus** (the 1981 film *Clash of the Titans*), and Robin Hood (the 1938 film *The Adventures of Robin Hood*, among many others).

The concept of humans with special abilities has also been a cornerstone of the comic book industry, with many of the most popular characters—including Spider-Man and Batman—resembling the traditional mythological role of a hero.

Read, Write, Think, Discuss

The word "hero" is often used to describe people in the modern world who perform important, difficult, or dangerous jobs. What occupations, if any, do you think should earn someone the label of hero? Why?

SEE ALSO Achilles; Aeneas; Aladdin; Antigone; Arthur, King; *Beowulf*; Brer Rabbit; Cuchulain; Finn; Galahad; George, St.; Gilgamesh; Hector; Heracles; Hunahpú and Xbalanqúe; Jason; Lancelot; Maui; Odysseus; Oedipus; Orpheus; Penelope; Perseus; Prometheus; Quetzalcoatl; Robin Hood; Sigurd; Sunjata; Theseus; Tricksters

Hinduism and Mythology

Hindu Mythology in Context

Hinduism, which has millions of followers in India and around the world today, is one of the world's oldest religions. For well over three thousand years, it has been accumulating the sacred stories and heroic epics that make up the mythology of Hinduism. Nothing in this complex and colorful mythology is fixed and firm. Pulsing with creation, destruction, love, and war, it shifts and changes. Most myths occur in several different versions, and many characters have multiple roles, identities, and histories. This seeming confusion reflects the richness of a mythology that has expanded and taken on new meanings over the centuries.

Around 1700 BCE, peoples from the area to the northwest of India began migrating to India. Called Aryans or Indo-Europeans, they brought a mythic tradition that became the basis of an early form of Hinduism. Over the years, as the Aryans mingled with the peoples and cultures of the Indian subcontinent, the mythology grew increasingly complex.

Hinduism has gone through various stages, which can be linked to the most important texts surviving from each period. The earliest stage is associated with the Vedas, the oldest Indian documents. One of them, the *Rig-Veda*, is a collection of 1,028 hymns of praise and prayers to the gods with references to myths. The Vedas are based on ancient Aryan traditions that were long communicated only in oral form.

The next group of texts, the *Brahmanas*, date from 900 to 700 BCE. Though concerned mainly with the rituals of Hinduism, the *Brahmanas* contain many myths. The *Upanishads*, written around 700 BCE and after, focus on ideas communicated through myths. The two great Hindu epics, the **Mahabharata** and the **Ramayana**, written down sometime between 300 BCE and 300 CE, contain stories about a number of major Hindu deities or gods. After that time, the chief expression of Hindu mythology and religion was in texts called *Puranas*, "stories of the old days." Most of the stories are devoted to one god or another. The *Puranas* often retell earlier myths, sometimes in the voices of the gods themselves.

Core Deities and Characters

Hindu mythology is populated by an enormous cast of deities, demons, demigods (half-human, half-god), humans, and animals. Some had a central role in one era but remain in the background in later periods, while others have risen from obscurity to prominence. The attributes and histories of many mythological characters have changed considerably over the many centuries that Hinduism has existed.

Brahma (pronounced BRAH-muh), the creator of life on earth, is one of the Trimurti (pronounced tri-MOOR-tee), the three gods at the

Major Hindu Deities

Brahma: creator god.

Devi: wife of Shiva, goddess who takes many forms—both kind and fierce.

Ganesha: god of good fortune and wisdom.

Indra: god of storms and rain.

Shiva: avenging and destroying god.

Varuna: originally a creator god and ruler of the sky, later became god of water.

Vishnu: preserver god and protector of life.

center of the Hindu pantheon, or collection of recognized gods. In the early Vedic texts, the creator god was Prajapati (pronounced pruh-JAH-puht-ee), but over time Brahma took the older god's place in many myths about the creation of the universe.

Vishnu (pronounced VISH-noo), the second member of the Trimurti, is the preserver or protector of life. His attributes are mercy and goodness. Some Hindus regard Vishnu as the supreme being and Brahma and **Shiva** (pronounced SHEE-vuh) as aspects of him. Shiva, descended from the old Vedic storm god Rudra (pronounced ROOD-ruh), is the third member of the Trimurti. He is the avenging and destroying god, but his destruction allows new creation to begin. Sometimes Shiva is portrayed as a dancer who directs the movements of the universe.

Devi (pronounced DAY-vee), "the goddess," is one of the most ancient deities of the pantheon. Under her name are grouped various female deities, who represent different aspects of Devi. Among them are Parvati (pronounced PAR-vuh-tee), the wife of Shiva; Durga (pronounced DOOR-gah), the warrior goddess and fighter of demons; and the even more ferocious Kali (pronounced KAH-lee), "the dark one," who also fights demons but sometimes becomes intoxicated with blood and destruction.

The popular elephant-headed, four-handed god **Ganesha** (pronounced guh-NAYSH) is Parvati's son. One of the most popular gods in

Hinduism today, he is associated with good luck and wisdom. **Indra** (pronounced IN-druh), god of storm and rain, was one of the most important deities of the *Rig-Veda* and may have represented the warrior chieftains of the ancestral Aryan peoples. Vedic hymns suggest that Indra replaced Varuna (pronounced VUR-oo-nuh), the guardian of justice and order, as the king of the gods. As the mythology of Hinduism developed, however, Indra in turn moved to secondary status below the Trimurti. **Krishna** (pronounced KRISH-nuh) is one of the incarnations, or forms, of Vishnu. He appears in the *Mahabharata* and the *Puranas*. Many stories about him focus on his prankish, playful nature and on his many love affairs.

Manu (pronounced MAN-oo), sometimes described as a son of Brahma, is both a god and the first man, ancestor of the human race. According to one myth, a small fish warns Manu that the earth will soon be destroyed by a great flood. Manu takes care of the fish, which is really an incarnation of Vishnu, and when it is grown, it saves him from the flood so that he can repopulate the earth. The heroine Savitri, whose story is told in the *Mahabharata*, symbolizes love that defeats even death. She persuades Yama (pronounced YUHM-uh), the lord of death, to release her husband from death.

This sandstone stele shows Vishnu in the form of the fish Matsya carrying the first man Manu and the sacred Vedas on its back to save them from the flood. © BRITISH MUSEUM/ART RESOURCE, NY.

Major Myths

Hindu mythology includes a huge number of stories. Some have proved to be especially enduring and central to an understanding of Hinduism. Among these are the tales told in the *Mahabharata* and the *Ramayana* and those described below.

Creation Hindu mythology includes several different accounts of the beginning of things, but in each version, the act of creation is really an act of arranging, producing order from chaos. Vedic texts tell of the **sacrifice** of a primal being called Purusha (pronounced POOR-uh-shuh), whose cut-up body becomes all the elements of the universe. Another image of creation, that of fertilization and pregnancy, occurs in myths about Prajapati, the father of all humans and animals. Sometimes **heaven** and earth are described as parents whose mating produces the gods. Myths of Tvashtar, a minor Vedic god of carpentry or architecture, explain creation as an act of building.

As Hinduism developed and the Trimurti gained importance, a complex vision of the creation, destruction, and recreation of the universe emerged. Brahma brings the universe into being through his thoughts. The world then passes through a Maha Yuga, or great age, that lasts 4,320,000 years. The Maha Yuga contains four yugas, or ages. Each is shorter and more immoral than the one before, from the Krita Yuga—Brahma's golden age—through two intermediate ages under Vishnu's protection to the Kali Yuga—Shiva's dark age.

Each dark age in turn gives way to a new golden age, and the cycle of the Maha Yuga repeats a thousand times. Then Shiva destroys all life with scorching heat and drowning flood, and the earth remains empty while Vishnu sleeps. After a thousand Maha Yugas, a lotus flower emerges from Vishnu's navel, and it becomes Brahma, ready to perform his creative act anew.

The Forms of Vishnu Many myths deal with Vishnu's avatars, or the incarnations of the god on earth. The most common list of the ten avatars begins with Matsya (pronounced MAHT-see-yah), the fish that protects Manu from the flood. The second avatar is Kurma (pronounced KOOR-muh), a tortoise that holds Mount Mandara on his back so that the gods can use it as a paddle to churn the ocean and produce a drink of eternal life.

Varaha (pronounced VAH-rah-hah), a boar who appears after a demon giant pulls the earth to the bottom of the ocean, is the third incarnation. Varaha defeats the demon and raises the earth on his tusks. Narasimha (pronounced nah-rah-SIM-hah), the fourth avatar, is half man and half lion. He defeats a demon who cannot be killed by man or beast. The dwarf Vamana (pronounced vuh-MAH-nah), the fifth incarnation, triumphs over Bali, a being who had gained control of the world. When Bali grants Vamana as much land as he can cover in three strides, the dwarf becomes a giant and strides over heaven and earth. The sixth avatar, ax-wielding Parasurama (pronounced pah-ruh-soo-RAH-muh), frees the priests from the domination of the warriors.

The seventh incarnation, Rama (pronounced RAH-muh), is the hero of the *Ramayana*. The eighth is the god Krishna; and the ninth is Buddha (pronounced BOO-duh). Hindus believe that Buddha came to earth to draw people away from the proper worship of the Vedas so that the world would decline and be destroyed, as the cosmic cycle demands. The tenth avatar, Kalki (pronounced KAHL-kee), will appear at the end of the world to preside over its destruction and the creation of a new, pure world.

The Birth of Ganesha Shiva's wife, Parvati, produced Ganesha—and did so without any help from Shiva, according to many accounts. Some say that Shiva, being immortal (able to live forever), had no desire for a son, but Parvati wanted a child and produced the boy from her own body. In other versions, Shiva gave Parvati a doll that at her touch magically came to life as a baby.

According to one story, Shiva struck off the boy's head, either because Ganesha prevented him from approaching Parvati or because Shiva believed that his son was doomed to die. Parvati's grief, however, moved him to try to replace the head, and he finally succeeded in attaching an elephant's head to the boy's body.

Indra and the Serpent Legends of the slaying of a serpent or dragon appear in many cultures. In Hindu mythology, one such story centers on the god Indra and the "footless and handless" demon Vritra (pronounced VRIT-ruh), described as both snake and dragon. The tale is told in the Vedas and dates from the time when Indra was king of the gods.

Using a divine thunderbolt, Indra struck Vritra between the shoulders, slicing open the mountain on which Vritra lay. The blow separated heaven from earth and land from water. The waters that Vritra had contained flowed forth to bring life. Indra's heroic victory made him the champion of all who struggled to overcome obstacles or resistance.

Shiva and the Sacrifice The *Mahabharata* tells how Daksha, Shiva's father-in-law, held a ceremony of horse sacrifice for the gods. All the gods except Shiva had been invited. Angry at being excluded, Shiva attacked the ceremony with his servants. They threw blood on the **fire** and ate the priests. A drop of sweat from Shiva's brow fell to earth and formed Disease, an ugly figure that terrified the gods. Brahma promised that

Shiva could take part in all future sacrifices, and in return Shiva turned Disease into many small ailments to trouble animals and humans.

Key Themes and Symbols

Certain key beliefs in Hinduism form the background against which the myths unfold. One of these is the idea of **reincarnation**, sometimes called the transmigration of souls. In Hindu belief, each soul experiences many, many lives. After the death of one body, or incarnation, the soul is born again into a new living body. Even the gods can be reincarnated in human form.

Just as the individual soul is continually reborn, the universe is continually created and destroyed. Time moves in cycles of millions of years, endlessly building up and tearing down with no beginning or end.

All change and decay are part of a divinely directed cosmic dance that will eventually result in renewal. Faced with this immense pattern, each individual has the duty to follow his or her own pattern of right behavior, called the dharma (pronounced DAR-muh).

Hindu Mythology in Art, Literature, and Everyday Life

Hindu belief and mythology color every aspect of life and culture in India. They are the basis of countless works of art, from plays about Rama written in the 700s to modern Indian movies based on mythic stories. Temples and images of the deities are everywhere. Festivals—such as the ten-day autumn celebration of Rama and his wife, Sita—keep the traditional gods, **heroes**, and myths alive. Even place names have sacred associations. The city of Calcutta, for example, comes from Kalighat, the place where sacrifices to the goddess Kali once took place.

Besides inspiring generations of Indian artists and thinkers, Hindu mythology has appealed to many in the West as well. Ralph Waldo Emerson, an American writer of the 1800s, wrote *Brahma*, a poem celebrating the creator god. In the same era, English-speaking readers became familiar with the legends of Savitri through Edwin Arnold's poem *Savitri, or Love and Death*. A poem by the German writer Johann Wolfgang von Goethe called *The God and the Bayadere* (dancing girl) deals with an appearance on earth of the god Shiva.

English composer Gustav Holst wrote a chamber opera—one meant to be sung, not acted, with a small orchestra—called *Savitri*. Holst also translated many hymns from the *Rig-Veda* into English and wrote music to accompany them. These four sets of songs are grouped together under the title *Choral Hymns*. Bertram Shapleigh, an American composer, wrote *Vedic Hymn*, also based on a text from the *Rig-Veda*, and a piece of orchestral music called *Ramayana*. A 1989 film of the *Mahabharata* written by Jean-Claude Carrière and directed by Peter Brook has brought the ancient epic to modern movie audiences.

Read, Write, Think, Discuss

The idea of reincarnation is an important part of Hindu belief. By living a productive life as one creature, a person's soul can then progress to a higher level creature in the next life, and so on. Using just your imagination, come up with a list of five living things to include on your own reincarnation ladder. Which is the lowest life form on your list? Why? Which is the highest, and why?

SEE ALSO *Bhagavad Gita*; Brahma; Buddhism and Mythology; Devi; Ganesha; Indra; Krishna; *Mahabharata, The*; Manu; Nagas; *Ramayana, The*; Reincarnation; Shiva; Vishnu

Holy Grail

Myth Overview

According to medieval legend, the Holy Grail was the vessel from which Jesus Christ drank at the Last Supper, his final meal with his followers before he was crucified. Many works of literature describe the search for the Grail, which was believed to have sacred and mysterious powers.

According to legend, after the Last Supper, the Grail came into the possession of Joseph of Arimathea (pronounced ar-uh-muh-THEE-uh), who caught Christ's blood in it at the crucifixion. Joseph went to prison, but the Grail kept him alive by supplying daily nourishment. Released from prison, Joseph traveled to France and then to Glastonbury, England, carrying the Holy Grail. Soon, however, the Grail disappeared from the world because people were sinful. Hidden away in a mysterious castle, it was guarded by the descendants of Joseph's sister.

One of the best-known versions of the Grail's later history is connected with **Arthur**, the legendary king of Britain. This account says that the Grail was held somewhere in a wild and lonely part of Britain in the castle of the Fisher King, a wounded king who lay between life and death. Only if the purest of knights found his way to the castle and caught a glimpse of the Grail would the Fisher King's torment end and life be restored to his ruined domain.

To the knights who sat around King Arthur's Round Table, seeing the Holy Grail was the highest and most noble goal. They roamed the nation in search of it. **Lancelot** nearly achieved the quest, but the sin of his love for **Guinevere** (pronounced GWEN-uh-veer), Arthur's queen, kept him from seeing the Grail. A knight named Perceval (pronounced

Nationality/Culture
Romano-British/Celtic, Christian

Pronunciation
hoh-lee GRAYL

Alternate Names
Sangreal

Appears In
Medieval Christian myths, tales of King Arthur and his knights

The knights of King Arthur's Round Table believed that seeing the Holy Grail—the legendary cup that Christ drank from at the Last Supper—was the highest and most noble goal. Only Galahad, however, was pure enough to see it. HIP/ART RESOURCE, NY.

PUR-suh-vuhl) saw the Grail but did not understand what it was. Only **Galahad** (pronounced GAL-uh-had), Lancelot's son, was pure enough to see it with full understanding of its meaning. He had to travel to a distant land called Sarras to do so, for the Grail had left Britain at some point. The vision of the Grail brought such profound joy that Galahad died moments later.

The Holy Grail in Context

The Holy Grail legend fuses Christian elements with much older **Celtic mythology** and appears to be the product of storytelling over hundreds of years. The Grail itself is related to various vessels in Celtic lore, such as the drinking horn of the god Bran, which produced any food or drink the user desired. It was also associated with a magic cauldron or kettle that could restore life to any dead body placed in it.

Key Themes and Symbols

For Christian followers, the Holy Grail symbolized Jesus Christ and his final betrayal. Because the cup was believed to have been used by Christ at his last meal, and also to have caught his blood while he was crucified, it was considered to contain some of the only known earthly remnants of Christ. For Christians, the idea of a concrete object that was used by Christ enabled them to draw an immediate connection with the stories of the Holy Bible. The different depictions of the Grail, from a jeweled chalice to a simple clay cup, reflect the different ways in which people glorified Jesus. In a more general sense, the myth of the Holy Grail represents a search for spiritual fulfillment. Those who search for the Grail are attempting to satisfy their own needs to feel a connection to God or to find meaning in their own existence.

The Holy Grail in Art, Literature, and Everyday Life

The earliest known work to give a Christian significance to the magical vessel was *Perceval*, a romance of the late 1100s by the French poet Chrétien de Troyes. A few decades later, Robert de Borron wrote *Joseph of Arimathea*, which established the connection between the Grail of Perceval and the cup used by Christ and later owned by Joseph. *Parzival*, by Wolfram von Eschenbach, expanded on the mystical story of the innocent knight and the Fisher King and also introduced an order of knights charged with guarding the Grail. This version of the story became the basis for the opera *Parsifal* by the modern German composer Richard Wagner.

Over time, versions of the Grail story began to link the Holy Grail with the popular legend of King Arthur. One account made Sir Galahad the virtuous hero and the Grail a symbol of a rare and mystical union with the divine. Late in the 1400s, Sir Thomas Malory wrote *Le Morte D'Arthur* (The Death of Arthur), the version of the Arthurian legend that was to become the best known. With it he established the story of the Grail quest by the knights of Arthur's Round Table and of Galahad's ultimate success.

In modern times, several films have been made that focus on a quest to find the Holy Grail. Among the most famous are the comedy *Monty Python and the Holy Grail* (1979) and *Indiana Jones and the Last Crusade* (1989). The best-selling novel *The Da Vinci Code* (2003) by Dan Brown centers on the Holy Grail myth, and was made into a film starring Tom Hanks in 2006. The 2005 Tony Award–winning musical *Spamalot* was based on the Monty Python version of the legend.

Read, Write, Think, Discuss

Parzival: The Quest of the Grail Knight by Katherine Paterson is a 1998 novel adaptation of Wolfram von Eschenbach's thirteenth-century German poem by the same name. Paterson, best known as the author of *Bridge to Terabithia* (1977), recreates the myth of Perceval (also called Parzival) in modern language, and provides background information to assist readers unfamiliar with the legend.

SEE ALSO Arthur, King; Arthurian Legends; Galahad; Lancelot

Horus

Nationality/Culture
Egyptian

Pronunciation
HOHR-uhs

Alternate Names
Neferhor, Harsiesis

Appears In
Ancient Egyptian writings and mythology

Lineage
Son of Osiris and Isis

Character Overview

Horus was one of the earliest and most important Egyptian gods. He was originally portrayed as a hawk or falcon and worshipped as a **sun** god and creator of the sky. His right eye represented the sun, and his left eye represented the moon.

The early rulers of southern Egypt were followers of Horus. When they conquered northern Egypt and reunited the two lands (around 2200 BCE), Horus became the symbol of the newly unified country, and the pharaoh, or leader of Egypt, was considered the earthly form of Horus. In time, the worship of Horus—under his various names—spread to many places.

St. George Killing the Dragon

The most popular myth about the Christian saint George concerned his killing of a dragon that threatened a city. *See* George, St.

The Fall of the Damned into Hell
According to the Christian tradition,
Hell is a lake of fire into which sinners
fall to endure eternal torment. *See* Hell.

Hero Mourns the Death of Leander

In Greek mythology, Hero and Leander were lovers who had to meet in secret because Hero was under a religious vow that required her to remain a virgin. While coming to meet Hero one night, Leander drowned; Hero killed herself after discovering his fate. *See* Hero and Leander.

Erich Lessing/Art Resource, NY.

Aeneas and His Companions Fighting the Harpies

In the Roman epic *The Aeneid*, the Harpies tormented Aeneas and his companions by not allowing them to eat. *See* Harpies.

Erich Lessing/Art Resource, NY.

Temple of Jagannatha (Juggernaut) in Indonesia

Juggernaut is worshipped as a form of Krishna in Hindu society. During the Chariot Festival, an image of Juggernaut travels on an enormous cart; the deaths caused by people being crushed underneath the cart inspired the English word *juggernaut*, meaning a person or power that crushes anything in its path. *See* Juggernaut.

The Art Archive/Stephanie Colasanti/The Picture Desk, Inc.

King of the *Tengu* Wrestles with Yoshitsune

The *tengu* were minor Japanese deities that were part-bird and part-human. *See* Japanese Mythology.

© Asian Art & Archeology, Inc./Corbis.

美勇水滸傳

木曽駒若丸義仲

Achilles Defeating Hector
Hector was a brave warrior for the Trojan army, but he was no match for the Greek warrior Achilles, who killed him on the battlefield in revenge for Hector's killing of Achilles' friend Patroclus. *See* Hector.

Bridgeman-Giraudon/Art Resource, NY.

The Trojan War Rages as the Gods Look On
Although the Trojan War was fought between two mortal armies, the Greek gods took an interest in the war and often interfered in order to give one side an advantage over the other. *See Iliad, The*.

Scala/Art Resource, NY.

Krishna Lifts a Mountain

Even from a young age, Krishna had supernatural strength. Here he lifts a mountain to prove that he is more worthy to be worshipped than the older gods. *See* Krishna.

Job Tortured by the Devil

In the Bible, God gave the devil permission to take away Job's family, wealth, and health after the devil challenged God that Job would not remain faithful if he was deprived of those things. *See* Job.

Major Myths

Horus became a major figure in **Egyptian mythology**. Before he was born, his father **Osiris** (pronounced oh-SYE-ris) died at the hand of his own brother **Set**. When Horus grew up, he swore to avenge his father's death and fought Set many times.

In one version of this story, Set blinded Horus in his left eye, but the god **Thoth** (pronounced TOHT) healed it. Horus ended up killing Set, and the gods named Horus ruler of Egypt. The restored eye, called the *udjat* or *wedjat*, became a powerful magical symbol of protection in ancient Egypt. The Egyptians used the story of Horus's wounded eye to explain the changing phases of the moon.

In another account of the conflict between Horus and Set, the two came before a council of the gods to decide who would inherit Osiris's throne. Most of the council accepted Horus's claim, but the sun god **Ra** favored Set because he was older and more capable. As a result, Horus and Set undertook a series of contests to determine who would become the ruler.

On one occasion, both gods turned themselves into hippopotamuses to see who could stay underwater longer. During the contest, Horus's mother **Isis** (pronounced EYE-sis) had the chance to kill Set but chose not to do so. Horus was angry at his mother and fled into the desert. Set found him and put out his eyes, but the goddess **Hathor** (pronounced HATH-or) repaired them with the milk of a small antelope. In the end, the gods agreed that Horus should be the ruler. Horus then invited Set to join him and live in the sky as the god of storms.

Horus in Context

In ancient Egypt, more than most other cultures, the deities being worshipped—and the qualities represented by those deities—changed frequently with the changing rulers of the land. Because of this, many gods became absorbed or merged into other gods. Horus, for example, was originally worshipped as a sky god and later assumed the roles of sun and moon god as well. For some time his identity was combined with the sun god Ra. As another example, Horus was associated with leaders of Lower Egypt, while Set was associated with leaders of Upper Egypt. When Egypt became united after violent conflicts between the two sides, Horus—the god worshipped by the victors, the Lower Egyptians—became the mythical ruler of Egypt over Set.

Key Themes and Symbols

Horus represents the power and importance of the sun and sky in all aspects of ancient Egyptian life. He serves as provider and protector of the Egyptian people, especially the pharaohs. One of the most important symbols associated with Horus is the Eye of Horus, a symbol meant to offer the protection of the gods. The falcon's head that he is often depicted with is a symbol of both the sky and an all-seeing presence.

Horus in Art, Literature, and Everyday Life

Horus was a popular figure in ancient Egyptian art, and many examples remain to this day. He was often depicted with the head of a falcon. In modern times, the Eye of Horus symbol has been identified with bands such as Sisters of Mercy and Siouxsie and the Banshees, and is a common decorative symbol for members of the gothic subculture. Horus has also appeared as a character in the Warhammer gaming universe, though the character does not bear much resemblance to the god of Egyptian mythology.

Read, Write, Think, Discuss

The markings of the Eye of Horus are said to be modeled after similar markings found on the peregrine falcon, a bird of prey that resides along the Nile River. Using your library, the Internet, or other available resources, research the current status of the peregrine falcon. Is the bird endangered? Can it still be found in Egypt? What efforts, if any, are being made to preserve the falcon's habitat?

SEE ALSO Egyptian Mythology; Hathor; Isis; Osiris; Ra; Set; Thoth

Huang-Di
See **Yellow Emperor.**

Huitzilopochtli

Character Overview

Huitzilopochtli, the Aztec god of war, was associated with the **sun**. In some myths, the warlike Huitzilopochtli appears in contrast to his brother, the god **Quetzalcoatl** (pronounced keht-sahl-koh-AHT-l), who represented life and the gifts of civilization. Huitzilopochtli was also recognized as the founder of Tenochtitlán (pronounced teh-nowch-TEE-tlan), the capital of the Aztec empire.

Nationality/Culture
Aztec

Pronunciation
wee-tsee-loh-POCH-tlee

Alternate Names
None

Appears In
Aztec oral mythology

Lineage
Son of Coatlicue

Major Myths

According to legend, Huitzilopochtli's mother was the goddess **Coatlicue** (pronounced koh-aht-LEE-kway). One day she found a bunch of hummingbird feathers and stuffed them into her breast. She immediately became pregnant with Huitzilopochtli. However, some of her other children—a daughter named Coyolxauhqui (pronounced koh-yohl-SHAW-kee) and 400 sons—were jealous of the unborn child. They plotted to kill Coatlicue, but when they attacked her, Huitzilopochtli emerged from his mother's womb fully grown. He cut off the head of his sister and killed most of his brothers as well.

Another tale about Huitzilopochtli tells how he led the Aztecs to settle on the island where they built the great city of Tenochtitlán. Originally from the north of Mexico, the Aztecs followed Huitzilopochtli on a long journey south in search of a new home. The god told them to settle at a place where they saw an eagle perched on a cactus growing out of a rock. As predicted, they saw the sign described by the god and ended their journey. This story echoes some events in Aztec history. In 1345 the Aztecs were driven onto an island in the middle of a lake by a tribe called the Culhua. There they founded Tenochtitlán, which would later become the capital of the Aztec empire.

Huitzilopochtli in Context

The name Huitzilopochtli, which means "hummingbird of the south," came from the Aztec belief that the spirits of warriors killed in battle followed the sun through the sky for four years. After that, they were transformed into hummingbirds. In **Aztec mythology**, the south represented both the sun and paradise. Therefore, Huitzilopochtli was considered to be a warrior reborn from the paradise of the sun.

The Aztecs believed that to nourish Huitzilopochtli and keep the world in motion, they needed to feed the god human blood every day. For this reason, Aztec priests conducted human sacrifices at the Great Temple in their capital city of Tenochtitlán. During these rituals, victims were led up the steps of a pyramid, and while they were still alive, their hearts were cut out of their chests. The victims' bodies were then thrown down the steps of the pyramid onto a stone that featured a carved image of Coyolxauhqui. In this way, the sacrifices reenacted the story about the young god killing his sister.

Huitzilopochtli, the Aztec god of war. The Aztecs believed that the god needed to be nourished with the blood of human sacrifices every day. BILDARCHIV PREUSSISCHER KULTURBESITZ/ART RESOURCE, NY.

Key Themes and Symbols

In Aztec mythology, Huitzilopochtli represented the power of the sun. An important theme in the myth of Huitzilopochtli is the struggle against darkness; the sun god was always fighting to prevent the fall of eternal darkness, which would mark the end of the world according to the Aztecs. Another related theme was **sacrifice**, since the Aztecs believed that Huitzilopochtli could be strengthened if he was given human blood as a sacrifice, and could therefore hold off the darkness.

Huitzilopochtli in Art, Literature, and Everyday Life

Huitzilopochtli appears in works of art created during the height of the Aztec empire, as well as the many books created just after the conquest of the Aztecs by Spanish colonists. He is usually depicted as wearing hummingbird feathers and holding a mirror. Like many Aztec gods, in modern times he is primarily found in decorative art rather than as a mythological character in literature or film.

Read, Write, Think, Discuss

In modern times, the idea of human sacrifice is horrifying, yet the ancient Aztecs believed it was necessary to maintain order in their world. Do you think this type of human sacrifice is fundamentally different than the use of the death penalty, which is a tool used by modern American society to maintain order? Why or why not?

SEE ALSO Animals in Mythology; Aztec Mythology; Coatlicue; Quetzalcoatl; Serpents and Snakes

Hunahpú and Xbalanqúe

Character Overview

The twin gods Hunahpú and Xbalanqúe were **heroes** in the mythology of the Maya, a people of Central America. Through bravery and quick thinking, they outwitted the lords of Xibalba (pronounced shi-BAHL-buh), the **underworld** or land of the dead, and destroyed them. Their story is told in the sacred Mayan text, the *Popol Vuh*.

Major Myths

According to legend, the **twins**' father, Hun-Hunahpú, had also struggled with the gods of the underworld. The gods challenged him and his own twin brother to play a game of ball. Then they killed him and hung his head on a tree. A young woman passing by reached up to pick some fruit from the tree, and the head spat into her hand, saying "In my saliva and spittle I have given you my descendants." She soon gave birth to twin boys, Hunahpú and Xbalanqúe.

When the two brothers met the lords of Xibalba, the gods sent them through a series of frightening places in the underworld. They began in

Nationality/Culture
Mayan

Pronunciation
WAH-nuh-pwuh and shi-BAY-lan-kay

Alternate Names
None

Appears In
The *Popol Vuh*

Lineage
Sons of Hun-Hunahpú

the House of Gloom and then passed into the House of Knives, where they managed to avoid being stabbed. They built a **fire** in the House of Cold to avoid freezing and then faced the House of Jaguars, where they fed bones to the animals to escape being eaten themselves. After the next trial, the House of Fire, they entered the House of Bats, where disaster struck. One of the bats cut off Hunahpú's head. The gods hung the head up in a ball court and challenged the twins to play ball with them.

Xbalanqúe found a turtle to sit on Hunahpú's shoulders in place of his head, and they strode onto the ball court. During the game, the gods became distracted by a rabbit near the court. Xbalanqúe seized this opportunity to steal his brother's head from the wall and put it back in place. Much to the annoyance of the gods, the twins were now strong enough to tie the game.

Hunahpú and Xbalanqúe performed a series of tricks, during which they appeared to die in a stone oven and then transform themselves into traveling actors. When the lords of Xibalba asked the twins to perform for them, the two brothers refused at first. Eventually, they presented several acts, such as burning down and restoring a house and sacrificing Hunahpú and bringing him back to life. Impressed, the gods asked the twins to do the same for them. The brothers agreed, but after sacrificing the gods, they did not revive them. Having eliminated the gods of the underworld and avenged the murder of their father, Hunahpú and Xbalanqúe went into the heavens, where in some versions they became the **sun** and the moon.

Hunahpú and Xbalanqúe in Context

The myth of Hunahpú and Xbalanqúe illustrates two very important elements of Mayan life: the creation of male descendants and the Mesoamerican ball game. In the myth, the father of the twins impregnates a woman after he has already been killed and his head has been placed in a tree. This indicates how important the Maya considered male descendants to be. The ball game was the primary athletic activity for the Maya; it was played for entertainment by young children, while adult games often ended in the ritual **sacrifice** of the losing players.

Key Themes and Symbols

In the myth of Hunahpú and Xbalanqúe, the main theme is vengeance. Before they are even born, the twin boys lose their father when he is killed after losing a ball game against the gods of the underworld. Most of the myth focuses on their journey through the underworld in an attempt to defeat the gods who killed their father.

Hunahpú and Xbalanqúe in Art, Literature, and Everyday Life

Hunahpú and Xbalanqúe appear in the *Popol Vuh*, a collection of Mayan myths written in the sixteenth century. The characters, although central to Mesoamerican mythology, appear in very few works beyond this. This is likely due to the fact that **Mayan mythology** has only recently begun to receive the attention long given to the mythology of other cultures.

Read, Write, Think, Discuss

The Mesoamerican ball game was both sport and ritual for the Mayan people. Do you think modern sports such as football could also be viewed as cultural rituals? Why or why not?

SEE ALSO Mayan Mythology; Underworld

Hunters in Mythology

Theme Overview

Hunters appear in the mythologies of many different cultures. Hunting animals for food was an essential part of life in most cultures during their early development, and remains important in some regions even in modern times. Hunters in mythology are sometimes shown in conflicting ways, which reflects the act of hunting itself: to succeed as a hunter, one must understand and appreciate nature; at the same time, however, the end result of hunting involves destroying a piece of nature.

Major Myths

Myths about hunters or hunting can be divided into two basic categories: myths about hunting as a way of obtaining food or other resources, and myths about the hunting of a specific creature—usually to destroy it.

Most myths in the second category involve very little actual hunting because the location of the creature is already known, and the "hunters" are generally **heroes** on a quest; for this reason, the myths covered below focus mainly on those who hunt as a way of life.

Myths of Artemis and Her Companions The Greek goddess **Artemis** (pronounced AHR-tuh-miss), known to the Romans as Diana, is one of the best-known deities related to hunting. She was the daughter of **Zeus** (pronounced ZOOS) and twin sister of **Apollo** (pronounced uh-POL-oh); because she was born to a woman other than Zeus's wife **Hera** (pronounced HAIR-uh), Artemis was raised not on Olympus (pronounced oh-LIM-puhs), home of the other gods, but in the wilderness on an island Zeus called up from the sea. This led to her early exposure to wild animals and hunting, and she came to be known as an expert at archery, or hunting with a bow and arrow.

Many of the myths of Artemis center on her vengeance against humans, in some cases because they believe themselves to be better hunters than the goddess. The hunter Actaeon (pronounced AK-tee-uhn) was transformed into a deer by Artemis, either because he saw her nude while bathing or because he boasted that his hunting skills were superior to hers. As a deer, Actaeon was killed by his own hunting dogs. The handsome young man **Adonis** (pronounced uh-DON-is) was killed by a wild boar sent to attack him by Artemis; in some versions of the myth, Artemis sent the boar after Adonis bragged about his superior hunting abilities. The Greek leader **Agamemnon** (pronounced ag-uh-MEM-non) also boasted of his own hunting skills, though his punishment was for another hunting-related act: he killed a deer in a grove considered sacred to Artemis. Because of this, Artemis kept his Greek fleet from leaving port on its way to fight the Trojan War. In order to appease Artemis, Agamemnon had to **sacrifice** his own daughter, Iphigenia (pronounced if-uh-juh-NEYE-uh).

Another myth shows Artemis using her abilities to defeat two **giants**, both of whom were zealous hunters. The giants, brothers Otus (pronounced OH-tuhs) and Ephialtes (pronounced ef-ee-AL-teez), were jealous of the gods of Olympus and decided to attack them. They captured **Ares** (pronounced AIR-eez), the god of war, and kept him as their prisoner. The Olympians could not destroy the giants, each of which possessed strength equaled only by the other. Artemis, knowing the giants loved to hunt, transformed herself into a doe and passed directly between them. They both grabbed their spears and threw them at her, but she leapt out of the way and the giants were struck by each other's spears, killing them both.

Another hunter well known to Greeks was **Orion** (pronounced oh-RYE-uhn), a companion of Artemis. According to one account, Orion was out hunting with Artemis when he announced that he could hunt and kill any living thing on earth. The goddess **Gaia** (pronounced GAY-uh), also known as Mother Earth, objected to such a boast, and sent a giant scorpion to kill him. In another version of his demise, Apollo became jealous of Orion's close relationship with his sister Artemis. One day, while Orion was swimming in the water with just a portion of his head visible, Apollo challenged his sister to hit the small moving target with an arrow. She did, and discovered afterward that she had been tricked into killing Orion. After his death, Orion was preserved in the night sky as a constellation, or group of stars.

According to myth, Artemis was also connected to the popular Greek huntress **Atalanta** (pronounced at-uh-LAN-tuh). As a baby, Atalanta was abandoned in the forest by her father. Artemis happened upon the infant and arranged for a she-bear to suckle her until a group of hunters took her in and raised her. A favorite of Artemis, Atalanta was the first member of a large hunting party to draw blood from a giant boar sent by Artemis as vengeance against a disrespectful king. Atalanta's prize, awarded against the wishes of many of the male hunters in the party, was the skin of the beast.

The Wild Hunt The myth of the Wild Hunt was found throughout Europe in various forms. The gods associated with it vary depending upon the region, though the Norse god **Odin** (pronounced OH-din) and the Celtic god **Cernunnos** (pronounced kur-NOO-nohs) were common. Odin, leader of the gods in **Norse mythology**, was renowned as a hunter. In **Celtic mythology**, Cernunnos was the god of hunters and master of all animals. He was usually depicted with a long beard and the horns of a deer growing from his head.

In the various myths of the Wild Hunt, several elements remained the same. A hunting party made up of gods, ghosts, or even fairies appeared in the night sky, or sometimes hovering just above the ground. Their prey was not known, but they were thought to be seen just before the occurrence of a tragic event or terrible storm. Humans who witnessed the Wild Hunt either died or were taken up by the hunters to join them. The only way to avoid such a fate was to cover one's eyes as the hunting party passed.

Kokopelli Among the Pueblo people of the American Southwest, Kokopelli (pronounced koh-koh-PEL-ee) is a fertility deity who is also closely associated with wild animals and hunting. He is a *kachina* (pronounced kuh-CHEE-nuh), or nature spirit. Kokopelli oversees the mating of wild animals, and ensures there will be enough for the people to hunt. He carries a most unusual hunting instrument: a flute, which he plays to attract the sheep he hunts. Some scholars believe that his flute—visible in early drawings of the character—may have originally been a similarly shaped weapon such as a spear or blowgun.

Heimdall and the Gjallarhorn In Norse mythology, **Heimdall** (pronounced HAYM-dahl) was the guardian of the Norse gods. Although not known specifically for myths related to hunting, one of Heimdall's most important possessions was the Gjallarhorn (pronounced YAHL-lahr-horn), a hunting horn. Hunting horns were used to call other members of a hunting party when locating prey during a hunt. For Heimdall, however, the Gjallarhorn had a different purpose. Heimdall stood—indeed, still stands—as the guardian at the entrance to Asgard (pronounced AHS-gahrd), the home of the Norse gods. His job is to watch for the coming of the giants, a group of creatures led by **Loki** (pronounced LOH-kee) who are the enemies of the gods. When the giants attack Asgard, Heimdall will blow the Gjallarhorn loud and clear, a signal to all the Norse gods that their final battle is about to begin.

Myths about the Hunting of Specific Creatures There are many other myths from various cultures that deal with the hunting of a specific animal or monster. Most of these fall under the category of heroic feats or battles, but some actually involve tracking or hunting.

The Greek hero **Heracles** (pronounced HAIR-uh-kleez), as punishment for accidentally killing his wife and children during a fit of madness, was tasked with performing twelve labors. The majority of these tasks were centered on capturing or killing certain mythical animals. The Cerynean (pronounced ser-i-NEE-uhn) Hind, for example, was a sacred deer that was so swift it could outrun a hunter's arrow. Heracles had to capture it but not kill it, which would bring the wrath of Artemis upon him. He tracked the animal on foot for a year, finally capturing it when it at last grew tired or when it stopped to drink. His next task involved capturing the Erymanthian (pronounced air-uh-MAN-thee-uhn) Boar, a giant beast that wandered the wilderness of Arcadia. Heracles, after seeking the advice of a centaur (a half-man, half-horse creature) on how to capture it, drove the boar into deep snow so it could not run away. Heracles later had to hunt and kill the Stymphalian (stim-FAY-lee-uhn) Birds, vicious creatures with sharp bronze feathers that they could use to cut their enemies. The birds hid in a dark forest where Heracles could not see them; **Hephaestus** (pronounced hi-FES-tuhs), the god of black-smiths, created for Heracles a set of *crotala*, or bronze clappers that rang out loudly when clanged together. Heracles used these clappers to scare the birds out of their roost, and he shot them down with arrows as they flew.

Another myth related to hunting a specific creature is found in the legends of King **Arthur**. The Questing Beast was described in two dramatically different ways: in one version, it was a ferocious creature with the head of a serpent, the body of a leopard, the rear legs of a lion, and the feet of a deer; in another version, it was a small white creature whose beauty contrasted with the horrid barking sound that came from within it. It was sought by the knights Perceval (pronounced PUR-suh-vuhl) and Palamedes (pronounced pal-uh-MEE-deez), as well as King Pellinore (pronounced PEL-uh-nor). According to legend, Pellinore spent much of his life searching for the beast, without success. Palamedes then took up the search, and was unsuccessful until he joined Perceval on his quest for the **Holy Grail**. The two came across the beast and were able to slay it after driving it into a lake, where it could not escape.

Mythological Hunters in Context

Myths related to hunters and hunting can reflect a culture's views about the relationship between human beings and the natural world. The myths of the Greeks focus on the goddess Artemis (pronounced AHR-tuh-miss), whose relationship with animals is marked by respect and knowledge of their sacred nature. In many myths, Artemis punishes those who kill needlessly or who kill animals considered sacred. Similarly, many American Indian cultures focus on hunting as a part of the cycle of life, performed only as necessary and always with respect for the animals killed, since they are giving up their lives to provide continued life and comfort for their hunters. In cultures where hunting is approached with reverence or respect for nature, female mythical characters such as Artemis are often present.

By contrast, in the tales of the Norse and other northern Europeans, hunts are often waged like wars; the relationship between humans and nature is less harmonious, and more like the clash of enemies. Similar tales can be found in Greek myths—such as the tales of the labors of Heracles—but the hunts in these cases are generally for unnatural beasts or monsters, creatures clearly not meant to represent a part of the natural order. In tales where the hunt is treated as a battle, male characters are usually the focus.

Mythological Hunters in Art, Literature, and Everyday Life

The act of hunting as part of a quest is common in art and literature. Tales of the Questing Beast, for example, appear in many versions of Arthurian legend, including Thomas Malory's *Le Morte D'Arthur* and T. H. White's *The Once and Future King*. A famous painting of the Wild Hunt, titled *Asgardsreien*, was made by Norwegian artist Peter Nicolai Arbo in 1872.

Mythological hunters still make appearances in modern culture. Herne the Hunter, a specifically English version of Cernunnos, appears at the climax of the fantasy novel *The Dark Is Rising* by Susan Cooper. Artemis and Atalanta appeared as characters on the television show *Xena: Warrior Princess*, while Cernunnos appeared on *Hercules: The Legendary Journeys* and in the PlayStation 3 video game *Folklore*. A silhouetted image of Kokopelli has become a popular symbol of the Pueblo people and of the American Southwest as a whole, and is one of the most popular decorations on souvenir items from the region.

Read, Write, Think, Discuss

For many centuries, hunting was an essential part of human survival. In modern times, however, the domestication of livestock and other animals for food has eliminated the need for hunting in many cultures. In these societies, some view hunting as an unnecessary and cruel act, of killing simply for the sake of killing. Others see it as a way of getting back to nature and connecting with the roots of their culture. Which view do you support, and why? Do you think the rise in domesticated meat animals has caused a shift in the way modern society as a whole views hunting? If so, how?

SEE ALSO Artemis; Atalanta; Cernunnos; Orion

Hypnos

Nationality/Culture
Greek

Pronunciation
HIP-nohs

Alternate Names
Somnus (Roman)

Appears In
Hesiod's *Theogony*, Ovid's *Metamorphoses*, Homer's *Iliad*

Lineage
Son of Nyx

Character Overview

The ancient Greeks said that Hypnos, the god of sleep, visited people during the dark of night to ease them into a state of rest. Hypnos hid from the sunlight during the day. According to Greek myth, he was the son of Nyx (pronounced NIKS), the goddess of night, and his brother was Thanatos (pronounced THAN-uh-tohs), the god of death.

Major Myths

Some writers claimed that Hypnos lived in the **underworld**, or land of the dead, but others said that he dwelled in a cave on the Greek island of Lemnos (pronounced LEM-nohs). **Lethe** (pronounced LEE-thee), the river of forgetfulness, rippled through his dim, foggy cave. The Dreams, some of his many sons, lived with him. The most important ones were Morpheus (pronounced MOR-fee-uhs), who caused sleepers to dream about people; Icelus (pronounced EYE-suh-luhs), also known as Phobetor (pronounced foh-BEE-tor), who delivered dreams about animals or monsters; and Phantasos (pronounced FAN-tuh-sohs), who brought dreams about lifeless objects.

In the *Iliad*, Homer tells a story about the goddess **Hera** (pronounced HAIR-uh), the queen of the gods, requesting help from Hypnos during the Trojan War. She asked him to put the king of the gods, **Zeus** (pronounced ZOOS), to sleep to prevent him from interfering on behalf of Troy. At first, Hypnos hesitated, fearful of Zeus's anger. However, Hera convinced him to help by promising him Pasithea (pronounced puh-SITH-ee-uh), one of the **Graces**, as his bride.

Hypnos in Context

The ancient Greeks drew direct connections between sleep and death. Hypnos, the god of peaceful sleep, and Thanatos, the god of peaceful death, were twin brothers. Hypnos was also said to live in the underworld. The ancient Greeks clearly noticed the crude similarities between a sleeping person and a dead person, and viewed sleep itself as a product of the underworld, a sort of shadow of death.

Key Themes and Symbols

In **Greek mythology**, Hypnos symbolizes the peace of sleep without dreams. He is associated with both night or darkness and forgetfulness, both of which may be considered elements of sleep. He was also often associated with poppies, which were the source of the sleep-inducing drug known as opium.

Hypnos in Art, Literature, and Everyday Life

In ancient art, Hypnos was often depicted with wings growing from his head or shoulders. He was typically shown holding poppies or a container with opium, which brought on sleep. He was sometimes shown holding an upside-down torch. In modern times, Hypnos has appeared in the Japanese comic and animated series *Saint Seiya*, as well as several video games. Hypnos was featured as the villain in the 2001 film *Monkeybone*, though his appearance was drastically different than what is shown in traditional art.

Read, Write, Think, Discuss

Sleep is one of the most important and least understood functions of the body. It has long been believed that sleep was needed to provide physical rest for a person's body and brain; however, modern research indicates not only that dreams keep the brain very active during sleep, but also that a person burns more calories while sleeping than while watching television. What do you think is the purpose of sleep? Using your library and the Internet, find evidence that would support or disprove your idea.

SEE ALSO Graces; Hera; Lethe; Zeus

Character

Deity

Myth

Theme

Culture

Idun

Character Overview

In **Norse mythology**, Idun was the goddess of spring and rebirth. She and her husband, **Bragi** (pronounced BRAH-gee), the god of music and poetry, lived in Asgard (pronounced AHS-gahrd), the home of the gods. Idun took care of the magic apples the gods ate to remain immortal, or able to live forever.

Major Myths

The *Prose Edda*, a book of Norse legends written in the 1220s, contains a story about Idun and the magic apples. One day **Loki** (pronounced LOH-kee), the Norse trickster god, was captured by a giant named Thiassi (pronounced THYAH-tzee). The giant refused to free Loki until he agreed to bring Idun and the apples to Thiassi's home. Loki gave his word and sped off to Asgard.

He invited Idun to bring her apples and walk into the forest, where he knew of some even more precious apples. Eager to compare her special fruit with that mentioned by Loki, Idun joined the trickster. But as soon as they reached the forest, Thiassi, in the form of an eagle, dove from the sky and seized the goddess and her apples.

Without Idun's apples, the gods in Asgard began to age. They became bent and feeble and demanded that Loki rescue Idun from Thiassi. Loki flew to the giant's home disguised as a falcon. He changed

Nationality/Culture
Norse

Pronunciation
EE-thoon

Alternate Names
None

Appears In
The Eddas

Lineage
Unknown

Idun, the Norse goddess of the spring and rebirth, was the keeper of magic apples that kept the gods immortal. © MARY EVANS PICTURE LIBRARY/THE IMAGE WORKS.

Idun into a nut and hid her in his claws. As Loki flew back to Asgard, Thiassi became an eagle again and followed him. However, as soon as Loki and Idun were inside Asgard, the gods lit a **fire** on the fortress walls. Thiassi's wings caught fire as he crossed the flames, and he dropped to the ground, where the gods killed him.

Idun in Context

In the myth of Idun, the golden apples provide immortality to the gods. In Norse culture, apples were an important food item that was locally available and flourished in the relatively cold weather of northern Europe. Apples were one of the first trees cultivated by humans, and throughout Europe, apples remain an important crop today.

Key Themes and Symbols

In Norse mythology, Idun represented the energy of spring and the immortality of the gods. The golden apples tended by her symbolized

Golden Apples

Golden apples appear in myths from around the world. In Greek mythology, Atalanta, famed for her refusal to marry any man who could not beat her in a foot race, was finally defeated by Hippomenes (pronounced hi-POM-uh-neez), who left golden apples along the side of their course to distract her. The Trojan War was sparked by a dispute over a golden apple. The Greek goddess Hera's (pronounced HAIR-uh) orchard had a grove of golden apple trees whose fruit gave eternal life to those who ate them. It was one of the twelve tasks of Greek hero Heracles (pronounced HAIR-uh-kleez) to steal these golden apples. In European folktales, golden apples are often featured as precious or magical objects stolen from kings.

youth and life; when they were taken away, the gods became old. The gold color of the apples symbolized their magical nature.

Idun in Art, Literature, and Everyday Life

Although well known as the custodian of the golden apples of the gods, Idun is seldom mentioned in the tales of Norse mythology. The scene of her abduction, and the subsequent aging of the gods, is a popular one, however; it has been illustrated by many artists, including Arthur Rackham, John Bauer, and J. Doyle Penrose. A well-known image of Idun and her husband Bragi was painted in the nineteenth century by Nils Blommér.

Read, Write, Think, Discuss

It is said that "an apple a day keeps the doctor away." Indeed, the Norse gods ate apples in order to live forever. Using your library and the Internet, find out more about the health benefits of apples and the various claims made for diets involving apples or apple products (such as apple cider vinegar). Write a short summary of your findings.

SEE ALSO Atalanta; Bragi; Fruit in Mythology; Heracles; *Iliad, The*; Loki; Norse Mythology

Ile-Ife

Myth Overview

According to Yoruba mythology, the world was originally a marshy, watery wasteland. In the sky above lived many gods, including the supreme god **Olorun** (pronounced oh-loh-RUN), the Owner of the Sky. These gods sometimes descended from the sky on spiderwebs and played in the marshy waters, but there was no land or human being there.

One day Olorun called Orisha Nla (pronounced or-EE-shuh nn-lah), the Great God, and told him to create solid land in the marshy waters below. He gave Orisha a pigeon, a hen, and the shell of a snail containing some loose earth. Orisha descended to the waters and threw the loose earth into a small space. He then set loose the pigeon and hen, which began to scratch the earth and move it around. Soon the birds had covered a large area of the marshy waters and created solid ground.

Orisha reported back to Olorun, who sent a chameleon to see what had been accomplished. The chameleon found that the earth was wide but not very dry. After a while, Olorun sent the creature to inspect the work again. This time the chameleon discovered a wide, dry land, which was called Ife (meaning "wide") and Ile (meaning "house"). All other earthly dwellings later sprang from Ile-Ife, and it was revered forever after as a sacred spot. It remains the home of the *Ooni*, the spiritual leader of the Yoruba.

Ile-Ife in Context

Ile-Ife (pronounced EE-lay EE-fay), also known as Ife or Ife-Lodun, is the holy city of the Yoruba (pronounced YAWR-uh-buh) people who live in Nigeria in West Africa. Ile-Ife appears in myths as the birthplace of creation and the location where the first humans took form.

Key Themes and Symbols

For the Yoruba people, Ile-Ife is a symbol of creation and life. In their mythology, it is the oldest and most sacred land. The birds of the myth represent the natural forces that shaped the land.

Nationality/Culture
West African/Yoruba

Pronunciation
EE-lay EE-fay

Alternate Names
Ife or Ife-Lodun

Appears In
Yoruba creation mythology

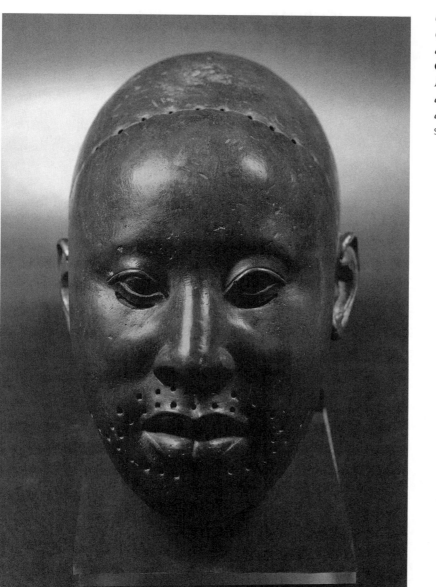

Ile-Ife in Art, Literature, and Everyday Life

Ile-Ife has been symbolized in art as a palm tree with sixteen branches, which represent the main families of the first Yoruba states. The creation myth of Ile-Ife is celebrated in the city during the Itapa festival. The city has traditionally been a center of art and agriculture, and remains so in modern times.

Read, Write, Think, Discuss

The city of Ile-Ife is believed to be over 2000 years old. In the United States, the oldest continuously settled city is less than 500 years old. Do you think that, given time, the oldest cities in the United States will develop myths similar to those found in places like Ile-Ife? Why or why not?

SEE ALSO African Mythology; Animals in Mythology; Creation Stories; Olorun

Iliad, The

Myth Overview

Nationality/Culture
Greek

Pronunciation
IL-ee-uhd

Alternate Names
None

Appears In
The *Iliad*

One of the greatest epics of ancient Greece, the *Iliad* tells of events during the final year of the Trojan War. *Iliad* means "poem of Ilios," one of the names given to the city of Troy in Asia Minor (modern-day Turkey). The Greek poet Homer is credited with creating the *Iliad*. Some scholars, however, doubt that Homer ever existed and suggest that the poem was woven together by generations of storytellers. In any case, the *Iliad* had a tremendous impact on Greek culture and holds an important place in world literature.

Contrary to popular belief, the *Iliad* does not tell the story of the entire Trojan War. Long before the events described in the *Iliad*, the Greeks had been drawn into a war with Troy because of the beautiful **Helen** of Troy. Helen was actually Greek, the wife of King Menelaus (pronounced men-uh-LAY-uhs) of Sparta. She lived happily with Menelaus until Prince Paris (pronounced PAIR-iss) of Troy—promised the most beautiful woman in the world by the goddess **Aphrodite** (pronounced af-ro-DYE-tee)—came to Greece in search of the famous beauty. Paris took Helen back to Troy. Honoring a pledge to Menelaus, the kings and princes of Greece joined together to rescue Helen and set sail for Troy with their armies to wage war.

The Wrath of Achilles As the *Iliad* opens, a dispute between two Greek leaders—the hero **Achilles** (pronounced uh-KILL-eez) and King

Agamemnon (pronounced ag-uh-MEM-non) of Mycenae, commander of the Greek armies—sets in motion events that shape the course of the war. The trouble begins when Agamemnon receives a young woman, the daughter of a priest of **Apollo** (pronounced uh-POL-oh), as a prize of war. The priest appeals to Apollo, who sends a plague to the Greek camp. When the Greeks learn the cause of the sickness, they force Agamemnon to give up his prize.

To make up for his loss, Agamemnon demands the woman who was awarded to Achilles. Furious, Achilles puts down his weapons and refuses to fight any longer, thus depriving the Greeks of their most powerful warrior. Meanwhile, the sea goddess Thetis (pronounced THEE-tis), Achilles' mother, persuades the king of the gods, **Zeus** (pronounced ZOOS), to let the Greeks suffer losses in combat to show how crucial her son is to their victory.

Without Achilles, the Greeks begin to lose ground to the Trojans. During the course of battle, Paris and Menelaus fight each other, but neither can claim victory. At one point, **Hector**, leader of the Trojan forces, leaves the battlefield and enters Troy. Telling the Trojan women to pray for help from the gods, he bids farewell to his wife, Andromache (pronounced an-DROM-uh-kee), and his young son. He knows that he will die soon and that the Greeks will destroy the city and its people.

After suffering significant losses, several Greek leaders, including **Odysseus** (pronounced oh-DIS-ee-uhs), go to Achilles and ask him to rejoin them. Even Agamemnon sends a number of gifts and promises to reward Achilles when the war is over. But Achilles refuses to reconsider his decision.

The Death of Patroclus Soon after, Achilles' beloved friend Patroclus (pronounced pa-TROH-kluhs) convinces the hero to let him wear his armor so that the Trojans will think that Achilles is fighting again. The sight of the warrior in Achilles' armor worries the Trojans, and the Greeks are able to push them back. But the god Apollo lets Hector see that another warrior is wearing Achilles' armor, and Hector kills Patroclus and takes the armor.

When Achilles learns that his beloved friend has been killed, he is overwhelmed with grief and determined to avenge his friend's death. Wearing new armor from his mother, Achilles reenters the battle and slaughters many Trojans while searching for Hector. When the two warriors finally meet, Hector flees and Achilles chases him around the walls of Troy.

The goddess **Athena** (pronounced uh-THEE-nuh) tricks Hector by appearing as his younger brother and telling him to stand and fight. When Hector does so, Achilles kills him. Achilles removes his old armor from Hector's body and then drags the corpse behind his chariot.

The Ransoming of Hector Meanwhile the Trojans, angry because Achilles will not return Hector's corpse for proper funeral ceremonies, mourn the death of their hero. Again the gods intervene, forcing Achilles to accept a ransom of gifts from Hector's father, King Priam, and return the body of his son.

The story in the *Iliad* ends as the Trojans hold a funeral for their fallen hero. But the Trojan War continues. Tales of the deaths of Paris and Achilles, the Greeks' cunning use of the Trojan horse to get inside the city walls, and the defeat and destruction of Troy are told in other works.

The *Iliad* in Context

The *Iliad* is more than just a story about ancient **heroes**, gods, and goddesses. For the Greeks of later centuries, the poem was a history of their ancestors that also revealed moral lessons about heroism, pride, revenge, and honor. As such, it also had great value as a bedrock of Greek culture and, by extension, Western culture in general.

Modern scholars believe that certain elements of the story in the *Iliad* may be based on historical events from more than three thousand years ago. Indeed, there is archaeological evidence of the destruction of a city believed to be Troy in about 1180 BCE. Almost certainly, the poem reflects the values and ideals of Greek society at that time. Perhaps more importantly, as a work of literature, the *Iliad* illustrates various universal themes and provides a realistic view of the human condition. Its major characters, though part of a distant past, exhibit personality flaws and strengths that are as real for people today as when the work first appeared.

Key Themes and Symbols

The *Iliad* lays tremendous stress on the power of the gods to determine the course of events. The benefits of divine favor and the perils of divine displeasure are the major themes of the work. Honor and duty are also prominent themes. The Greeks come to Troy out of a sense of duty to Menelaus and to protect the honor of Greece. The Trojans refuse to surrender Helen because of their own sense of honor. Many of the heroes of *Iliad*—Ajax and Hector, for example—embody the ideals of military skill and honorable conduct.

Perhaps the most interesting character in the epic is Achilles, the great warrior whose sulky absence from combat nearly costs Greece the war. Achilles symbolizes the ideal of the Greek warrior, but he is flawed by pride, a quick temper, and hunger for revenge after the death of Patroclus. He serves as a warning that even the mightiest can be undone by wrath.

The *Iliad* in Art, Literature, and Everyday Life

The *Iliad* is one of the best-known works of literature in the world. It has been retold in many forms, including plays, films, and comic books. William Shakespeare used the *Iliad* as inspiration for his comedy *Troilus and Cressida*, which offers a different take on the Trojan War through the eyes of two relatively minor characters. The Broadway musical *The Golden Apple* (1954) was an updated retelling of both the *Iliad* and the **Odyssey**.

Black Ships Before Troy: The Story of the Iliad by Rosemary Sutcliff is a retelling of Homer's epic poem in modern and accessible language. The book, first published in 1993, offers a focused and powerful version of the most important elements of the *Iliad*, while also expanding the story to include the events leading up to the epic as well as the events that took place afterward.

Read, Write, Think, Discuss

Archaeologists continue to excavate and study the site of what is believed to be Troy in northwestern Turkey. Using your library and the Internet, find out more about the discovery of this archaeological site and the recent progress made there. Write a short summary of what you learn in which you answer the question: "Was there a real Troy as described in the *Iliad*?"

SEE ALSO Achilles; Agamemnon; Greek Mythology; Hector; Helen of Troy; Odysseus; *Odyssey, The*

Inanna

See **Ishtar.**

Inca Mythology

Inca Mythology in Context

The Inca civilization flourished in the Andes mountains of South America during the 1400s and early 1500s CE. At the center of Inca religion and mythology was the worship of the **sun**, believed to be the ancestral father of the Inca people. For this reason, sun worship was closely linked to ancestor worship, and many of the myths of the Incas focus on their origins. The Incas tailored their mythology to glorify their own culture and to reinforce the idea that they were a superior people destined to rule others.

Based in the city of Cuzco (pronounced KOOZ-koh) in what is now Peru, the Incas were one of many small groups who lived in the Andes (pronounced AN-deez) mountains in the 1300s. Gradually, the Incas expanded and absorbed the surrounding peoples, peacefully at first and later by conquest. In 1438 a strong leader named Pachacuti (pronounced pah-chah-KOO-tee) became their king. He and his descendants made the Inca state into a vast empire that stretched from southern Colombia south into Chile and covered much of modern Bolivia and part of Argentina. Throughout this great empire the Incas built a network of roads as well as temples, fortresses, and other public buildings.

As the empire grew, the Incas absorbed the myths and legends of the cultures they conquered. They often reworked the old stories of others to give them a new, pro-Inca twist. Although they allowed their subjects to continue to worship their own gods, they expected everyone in the empire to participate in the state religion and to worship the Inca deities or gods. The Incas had no written language so they did not record their myths in writing. Instead, a class of professional storytellers and performers recited the official state history, which contained both fact and myth.

In 1531 the Incas came under attack by Spanish conquistadors. The following year their empire fell. The Spanish began converting the Indians to Christianity and wiping out non-Christian traditions and practices. However, some Spanish military and religious personnel recorded what they learned about Inca mythology, as did a few of the

Macchu Picchu, located high in the Andes mountains in Peru, was a holy city of the Incas. The site contains the ruins of a temple where the Incas worshiped their sun god. JORGE PROVENZA/ART RESOURCE, NY.

newly Christianized and educated Incas. Though somewhat colored by European and Christian views and values, these accounts offer a glimpse into the mythology of the Incas' mountain empire. Much of what we know about Inca mythology comes from the writings of Inca Garcilaso de la Vega (1539–1616), the son of a Spanish conquistador and an Inca princess. He learned the Inca legends from his uncles, who were members of the nobility. Moving to Spain as an adult, Garcilaso turned his early notes on Inca history and culture into *The Royal Commentaries of the Inca.*

Core Deities and Characters

Most of the principal deities of the Inca pantheon, or collection of recognized gods and goddesses, represented forces of nature that operate in the sky. The state religion focused on the worship of a few major figures.

The creator god, **Viracocha** (pronounced vee-ruh-KOH-chuh), had many titles, such as Old Man of the Sky and Lord Instructor of the World. Viracocha was believed to have had a special bond with the Inca king Pachacuti, who dreamed that the god helped his people gain victory in a war they were fighting. After winning the war, Pachacuti built a great temple to Viracocha at Cuzco. The temple contained a large solid gold statue of the god as a bearded man. According to Inca tradition, Viracocha had white skin, which explains why some of the Indians at first thought that the bearded, pale-skinned Spanish soldiers were representatives of their creator god.

Viracocha, a rather remote and impersonal god, figured less prominently in the daily life of the Incas than did some other deities. Most important of all was Inti (pronounced IN-tee), the sun god, regarded as the ancestor of the Incas. He was associated with gold, called "the sweat of the sun," and the Incas honored him with magnificent golden artworks. The Coricancha (pronounced koh-ree-KAHN-chuh), or Sun Temple, at Cuzco housed a golden image of Inti that looked like the sun. Facing the image stood the preserved remains of dead emperors, and the walls of the chamber were covered with gold.

Inti's wife, the mother of the Incas, was the moon goddess Mama Kilya (pronounced mah-muh KEEL-yuh). Her shrine in the Coricancha had walls of silver, a metal that was sacred to her because it was believed to be her tears. The Incas marked the passage of time with the phases of the moon. Mama Kilya was thus the driving force of the calendar the Incas used to schedule their rituals and festivals.

Illapu (pronounced EEL-ah-poo), the god of weather who gave the rain, had an important place in a culture that depended on agriculture. The Incas saw the Milky Way, the band of stars that arc across the sky, as a heavenly river. Illapu's sister stored the river's water in a jug until it was needed on the earth. When Illapu struck the jug with a bolt of lightning from his slingshot, making the sound of thunder, he broke the jug and released the rain. Other deities included Cuichu (pronounced koo-EE-choo), the rainbow; Paca Mama (pronounced PAH-chuh mah-muh), the earth mother; and Mama Qoca (pronounced mah-muh KOH-chuh), the sea mother.

Sacred Ceremonies Inca religious life was administered by a large organized priesthood and centered on honoring ancestors—especially royal ones—as well as the gods. The bodies of dead kings and queens

Major Incan Deities

Cuichu: god of the rainbow.

Illapu: god of weather.

Inti: sun god and supreme god.

Mama Kilya: moon goddess.

Mama Qoca: sea mother.

Paca Mama: earth mother.

Viracocha: creator god.

were mummified, or preserved through drying. They were dressed and cared for, and thought to have special powers. Young women called Acllas (pronounced ah-KEE-ahs), "chosen women" or Virgins of the Sun, served both Inti and the king, tending the god's sacred fires and serving as the king's sexual partners.

Priests relied on divination or supernatural signs to resolve all sorts of matters, from identifying illnesses to determining guilt or innocence to deciding what kind of **sacrifice** to make to which god. They had many ways of asking for supernatural guidance, including studying the movements of spiders or the patterns made by leaves. The chief method of divination, though, was the use of oracles, or places to communicate with the gods, which involved making frequent sacrifices to the gods. Inti, for example, received sacrifices of **corn** every day. Besides offering food and drink to the gods, the Incas also made animal and human sacrifices. White llamas were often used for animal sacrifices, and young children were particularly prized as human sacrifices. Often they were left to die on high mountaintops, sacred places remote from human life but close to the sky gods.

Major Myths

Many Inca myths dealt with the origin of the Inca people. These myths helped support the idea that the gods intended the Incas to be rulers. Other myths dealt with the creation of the world and the arrival of a great flood.

Creation According to one myth, Viracocha's first creation was a dark world inhabited by **giants** that he had fashioned from stone. These creatures proved disobedient, however, and Viracocha destroyed them. He may have turned them back to stone, or he may have swept them away in a great flood. Once they were gone, Viracocha made a second race, this time forming people from clay. He equipped them with the clothes, languages, songs, skills, and crops of different nations. Before the people spread out and populated the world, Viracocha ordered them to sink into the earth and to reappear on the surface again from lakes, caves, and hilltops. They did so, and each group of people built a shrine at the spot where they emerged.

Inca Civilization According to a legend recorded by Inca Garcilaso de la Vega, long ago people were ignorant and brutal, living like wild animals, without clothes or houses. The god Inti, known as Our Father the Sun, felt sorry for them and sent one of his sons and one of his daughters to earth to teach them how to live properly. The son was **Manco Capac** (pronounced MAHN-koh kah-PAHK), whom Inti made the ruler of all the races of people around Lake Titicaca (pronounced tee-tee-KAH-kah) in Bolivia. "I want you to rule these peoples as a father rules his children," Inti told Manco Capac.

The god gave his son and daughter instructions about how to find the best place for their court. Starting at Lake Titicaca, they were to visit the villages and look for a place where they could drive a gold stake into the ground with one blow. The site became the location of Cuzco, the capital of the Inca empire.

On reaching the earth, Manco Capac and his sister-wife, Mama Ocllo (pronounced MAH-muh oh-KEE-oh), taught the people the arts of farming and weaving. Manco Capac also showed his people how to make and use weapons so that they could enlarge their kingdom. In this way, the sun god himself set the Inca empire on its road to glory. Later generations honored Manco Capac as the legendary first Inca.

The myth establishes some of the rights and customs of the Inca royal class, such as the practice of brothers marrying sisters. It also paints a picture of the ancestral Incas as superior to other people and firmly identifies them as descendants of the sun god.

Great Flood Like many peoples, the Incas had a story about a great flood that wiped out a race of wicked and unruly people. The flood myth says that during ancient times people were cruel and greedy and failed to pay proper attention to the gods. Only in the highlands of the Andes mountains were the people not given over to evil. One day, two worthy shepherd brothers there noticed that their llamas were sad and acting strange. The llamas told the brothers that a great flood was coming. The brothers took their families and herds to high caves, and then rain fell for months, drowning the world below. Finally, the sun god Inti appeared again, and the warmth of his smile dried the waters. The families descended to repopulate the world. Legend says that although people now live everywhere on earth, llamas remember the flood and live only in the highlands.

Key Themes and Symbols

An important theme in Inca mythology is the divine right of the Inca people, or the belief that they were granted a special status by the gods. This is shown in their stories of Manco Capac, how he taught people to behave in a civilized way, and how the sun god Inti helped the Incas to expand their empire by conquering surrounding peoples. This is also shown in the belief that the Inca rulers are directly descended from the gods.

Another important theme in Inca mythology is the sky. Most Incan gods are connected to the sky in some way; the main gods are represented by the sun, the moon, and the rain, while the creator god is called the Old Man of the Sky. The sky was important to the Incas at least in part because they lived in mountainous regions at high altitudes. The Incas lived in a realm as close to the heavens, both literally and figuratively, as they possibly could.

Inca Mythology in Art, Literature, and Everyday Life

Although the Spanish destroyed the Inca empire, they did not wipe out the Inca people. Their descendants live in the Andean highlands today. Many of them speak Quechua (pronounced KECH-wah), the Inca language.

Andean peoples still believe, as the Incas did, that high mountain peaks are sacred places, and they make pilgrimages to them to ensure good crops and productive herds. In the same way, people have continued the Inca practice of making offerings to local gods at shrines

A sculpture of Viracocha, the creator god of the Incas. Viracocha was an impersonal god who was not prominent in the daily life of the Incas. WERNER FORMAN/ART RESOURCE, NY.

and holy places scattered across the land that once made up the Inca empire.

The Incas left larger monuments in stone as well. Walls from their temples can still be seen in the city of Cuzco. Elsewhere in the former empire stand forts and temples. One of the best-known Inca monuments is the mountaintop complex called Machu Picchu (pronounced MAH-choo PEEK-choo), where the Incas once worshipped their sun god. American explorer Hiram Bingham discovered the ruins of this vast temple and brought them to the notice of the outside world in 1912. Today Machu Picchu is one of Peru's main tourist attractions.

The culture and mythology of the Incas was used as the inspiration for the 2000 Disney animated film *The Emperor's New Groove*, which featured voice acting by David Spade, John Goodman, and Patrick Warburton.

Read, Write, Think, Discuss

Evil Star (2006) is the second novel in Anthony Horowitz's *Gatekeepers* series. The series centers on five young people who possess special powers that can stop an evil group known as the Old Ones from taking over the world. In *Evil Star*, fourteen-year-old Matt Freeman is sent to Peru to fight the Old Ones with a little help from some ancient Inca warriors. Horowitz is best known as the author of the popular *Alex Rider Adventure* series of novels.

SEE ALSO Manco Capac

Indra

Character Overview

Indra was the ruler of the gods in early Hinduism. The son of the sky and the earth, he is a warrior god who protects people and animals and provides rain to water the land. In later Hindu texts Indra loses some of his power and his warrior characteristics. Other gods, such as **Vishnu**, take his place as defender of gods and humans, while Indra continues to serve as the god of rain.

Major Myths

Indra appears as a central figure in the *Rig-Veda*, an ancient Indian religious text, and its many stories involve Indra's fights with demons. In a famous myth, he faces a demon named Vritra (pronounced VRIT-ruh), sometimes described as a dragon or serpent. Vritra had taken all the waters of the earth and placed them in a mountain where he remained on

Nationality/Culture
Hindu

Pronunciation
IN-druh

Alternate Names
Sakra

Appears In
The Vedas

Lineage
Son of the sky and earth

guard. In the devastating drought that followed, the people suffered greatly from thirst and famine.

Indra decided to fight Vritra and rescue the waters from captivity. To prepare for battle, Indra drank a large quantity of an intoxicating beverage called soma (pronounced SOH-muh) that gave him enormous strength. Then he stormed the mountain and delivered a deadly wound to the demon with his thunderbolt. Vritra's death released the waters, which flowed down from the mountain to revive the people and the countryside. Some sources suggest that Indra's defeat of Vritra takes place again whenever strong winds and rains, such as those associated with a monsoon, arrive after a seasonal drought.

Indra in Context

As the god of rain, Indra was considered an important force in the lives of Indian people. The subcontinent of India experiences one of the most significant rainfall seasons of any location on the planet. This season, known as the monsoon season, is critical to farmers that grow crops dependent on moisture, such as rice. However, monsoon rains also cause frequent and dangerous flooding across large areas, especially near rivers. Rain, like the god Indra, is seen as a force of great benefit, but also a force of potential destruction.

Indra, a warrior god and the ruler of the gods in early Hindu myths, later became known as the god of storms and rain. © NATIONAL MUSEUM OF INDIA, NEW DELHI, INDIA/THE BRIDGEMAN ART LIBRARY.

Key Themes and Symbols

In Hindu mythology, Indra is primarily associated with rain and clouds. In the tale of Vritra, he is seen as the provider of water when he slays the demon with his thunderbolt. Water symbolizes life, since it is necessary for most plants and animals to survive. Indra's thunderbolt represents the destructive power of storms. Legends about Indra describe him as riding either in a golden chariot pulled by two horses or mounted on a white elephant. In addition to rainfall, a rainbow or the sound of a gathering storm indicates that he is present.

Indra in Art, Literature, and Everyday Life

Indra is the subject of more hymns than any other Hindu god, and is a popular character in *yakshagana* (pronounced yahk-shuh-GAH-nuh), an Indian performance art form similar to opera. However, Indra is seldom worshipped by modern Hindus and is now considered a minor god in Hindu mythology.

Read, Write, Think, Discuss

Global climate change—not Indra—is often cited as a reason for increasingly violent storms and rainy seasons in many places around the world. Using your library, the Internet, or other available resources, research how rainfall levels have changed in India in the past century. Is India getting the same amount of rain as a hundred years ago? What impact does the rain have on the people of India? Write a paper summarizing your findings.

SEE ALSO Hinduism and Mythology; Vishnu

Ishtar

Character Overview

In the ancient Near East, Ishtar was an important and widely worshipped mother goddess for many Semitic peoples. The Sumerians called her Inanna (pronounced ee-NAH-nah), and other groups of the Near East referred to her as Astarte (pronounced a-STAR-tee).

A complex figure, Ishtar combined the characteristics—both good and evil—of many different goddesses. As a mother figure, she was considered the mother of gods and humans, as well as the creator of all earthly blessings. In this role, she grieved over human sorrows and served as a protector of marriage and motherhood. People also worshipped Ishtar as the goddess of sexual love and fertility. The more destructive side of Ishtar's nature emerged primarily in connection with war and storms. As a warrior goddess, she could make even the gods tremble in fear. As a storm goddess, she could bring rain and thunder.

Nationality/Culture
Babylonian

Pronunciation
ISH-tahr

Alternate Names
Inanna, Astarte

Appears In
Ancient Semitic myths

Lineage
Daughter of Sin and Shamash

Major Myths

Some myths say that Ishtar was the daughter of the moon god Sin (pronounced SEEN) and sister of the **sun** god **Shamash** (pronounced shah-MAHSH). Others mention the sky god Anu (pronounced AH-noo), the moon god Nanna (pronounced NAH-nah), the water god Ea (pronounced AY-ah), or the god Enlil (pronounced EN-lil), lord of the earth and the air, as her father.

Ishtar appears in many myths, but two are especially important. The first, part of the Babylonian *Epic of Gilgamesh*, tells how Ishtar offered to marry the hero-king **Gilgamesh** (pronounced GIL-guh-mesh) because she was impressed by his courage and exploits. According to the epic, Gilgamesh refused her offer and insulted Ishtar, reminding the goddess

Weeping for Tammuz

The biblical book of Ezekiel mentions, with great disapproval, an ancient Near Eastern ritual associated with the death of Ishtar's husband Tammuz. As recorded in the Bible, God points Ezekiel toward a temple: "Then He brought me to the entrance of the gate of the Lord's house which was toward the north; and behold, women were sitting there weeping for Tammuz." This is described in the Bible as an "abomination"—an all-female ritual in which the priestesses mourned the death of Tammuz for forty days.

Interestingly, some historians have suggested that the Christian practice of observing Lent—a period of forty days of prayer and penitence before Easter—stems from the ancient forty-day mourning period for Tammuz. Both Lent and the mourning for Tammuz precede a resurrection.

of all the previous lovers she had harmed. Enraged, Ishtar sent the fierce Bull of Heaven to kill Gilgamesh, but he and his friend Enkidu (pronounced EN-kee-doo) killed the beast instead.

The other well-known myth of Ishtar concerns her descent to the **underworld** (land of the dead) and the **sacrifice** of her husband Tammuz (pronounced TAH-mooz, also known as Dumuzi). In this story, Ishtar decided to visit the underworld, which was ruled by her sister Ereshkigal (pronounced ay-RESH-kee-gahl), perhaps to seize power there. Before departing, she instructed her follower Ninshubur (pronounced neen-SHOO-boor) to seek the help of the gods if she did not return.

To reach the underworld, Ishtar had to pass through seven gates and remove a symbol of her power—such as an article of clothing or a piece of jewelry—at each one. At the last gate, the goddess, naked and deprived of all her powers, met her sister Ereshkigal, who announced that Ishtar must die. She died immediately, and her corpse was hung on a stake.

Meanwhile, the god Enki (pronounced EN-kee) learned from Ninshubur that Ishtar was missing and sent two messengers who restored her to life. However, in order to leave the underworld, Ishtar had to substitute another body for her own. The goddess offered her young husband, Tammuz, to take her place. This tale of death and rebirth was associated with fertility and linked to the seasons and agricultural cycles, much like the story of **Persephone** (pronounced per-SEF-uh-nee) in **Greek mythology**. In another version of the story, Ishtar travels to the underworld to rescue Tammuz, who has died, and manages to bring him back—but only for part of each year. Thus the death and rebirth of Tammuz is also linked to fertility and agricultural cycles.

Ishtar in Context

Ishtar and the myths about her provide interesting insight into ancient Near Eastern views on the roles of men and women in society. For example, Ishtar is said to have had many relationships with men, gods, and animals. During those relationships, the males are almost always said to have suffered because they were distracted or weakened by Ishtar's power over them. This suggests that ancient Babylonians respected and revered women's reproductive power. The respect given this powerful female goddess translated into respect for women in Babylonian society. Though Near Eastern rulers were usually men, women were able to hold powerful and prestigious religious and political positions. This changed as the male-dominated Judeo-Christian faiths arose in the Near East, and female-dominated rituals and practices associated with the worship of Ishtar were branded as evil. As the worship of Ishtar faded, women gradually lost their religious, political, legal, and domestic power.

Key Themes and Symbols

Ishtar was believed to be the representation of the planet Venus, and the eight-pointed star is a symbol commonly associated with her. As an extension of her role as the goddess of sexual love, Ishtar was also the protector of prostitutes and alehouses. Prostitution was an important part of her cult, and her holy city Erech was known as the town of the sacred courtesans (prostitutes).

Ishtar in Art, Literature, and Everyday Life

In modern times, Ishtar has benefited from renewed interest in ancient mythologies of the Near East. The 1987 film *Ishtar*, starring Warren Beatty and Dustin Hoffman and often cited as one of the biggest box-office failures in cinematic history, is not connected with the Babylonian goddess other than by name. The name Ishtar has also been used for characters in numerous video games and Japanese comics, though most do not draw heavily from the mythology of the original goddess.

Read, Write, Think, Discuss

In the *Epic of Gilgamesh*, the hero insults Ishtar by mentioning her many loves and the sad fates they met. Do you think modern females who have a number of romantic relationships are viewed in a similarly negative way today? Do you think this same view applies to males who have several romantic relationships? Why or why not?

SEE ALSO Gilgamesh; Semitic Mythology; Shamash; Underworld

Isis

Character Overview

The great mother goddess of ancient Egypt, Isis was the sister and wife of the god **Osiris** (pronounced oh-SYE-ris). Together these two deities played a major role in many stories in **Egyptian mythology**, particularly in myths about rebirth. The worship of Isis became very popular in Egypt and eventually spread to other parts of the Mediterranean world, including ancient Greece and Rome.

According to Egyptian mythology, Isis was the daughter of the earth god Geb (pronounced GEB) and the sky goddess **Nut** (pronounced NOOT). Her sister and brothers were Nephthys (pronounced NEF-this), **Set** (pronounced SET), and Osiris. These six deities—Geb, Nut, Isis, Osiris, Set, and Nephthys—belonged to an important group of nine Egyptian gods called the Great Ennead (pronounced EN-ee-ad) of Heliopolis (pronounced hee-lee-OP-uh-luhs).

Major Myths

One famous myth about Isis tells how she discovered the secret name of the **sun** god **Ra** and increased her power. According to the story, Isis found Ra asleep one day, snoring loudly and saliva dripping from his mouth. She collected the saliva and mixed it with earth to form a

Nationality/Culture
Egyptian

Pronunciation
EYE-sis

Alternate Names
None

Appears In
Ancient Egyptian writings and mythology

Lineage
Daughter of Geb and Nut

Statue of the Egyptian goddess Isis, holding her child Horus. Isis protected Horus during his childhood so he could grow up to avenge his father's death.
THE BROOKLYN MUSEUM OF ART, 37.938E, THE CHARLES EDWIN WILBOUR FUND. REPRODUCED BY PERMISSION.

poisonous serpent. Then she placed the serpent on a path that Ra took every day.

When Ra awoke and started on his way, the serpent bit him, causing terrible pain. He called to the other gods for help, but all were helpless except Isis, who promised to cure him if he revealed his secret name. At first Ra refused, but eventually the pain became unbearable. He told Isis the name, and she gained new powers. This story was associated with a major aspect of Isis's character: her skill in magical arts.

One of the most important myths associated with Isis was the story of Osiris's death and resurrection (rebirth). According to this tale, the god Set became jealous of his brother Osiris, who ruled as king of Egypt. One day Set tricked Osiris and sealed him inside a box. Set then placed the box adrift on the Nile River, which carried it to the distant land of Byblos (pronounced BIB-luhs).

Isis searched for and found the box and then brought it back to Egypt, where she concealed it. However, Set discovered the hiding place and cut Osiris's body into many pieces and scattered them throughout Egypt. After recovering the pieces, Isis used her magical powers to restore life to Osiris, who then went to live in the **underworld** or land of the dead.

Sometime before this happened, Osiris and Isis had had a son named **Horus**. Isis kept the child hidden from Set so that he could grow up and avenge his father's death. She protected Horus against all dangers, even restoring him to life once after he was bitten by a scorpion. When Horus became a young man, he fought his uncle Set. But Isis took pity on Set and allowed him to escape. Angry at his mother, Horus cut off her head. **Thoth** (pronounced TOHT), the god of magic and wisdom, changed the severed head into a cow's head and reattached it to Isis's body. Some ancient statues and paintings of the goddess show her with a cow's head, and she is often linked to the goddess **Hathor** (pronounced HATH-or). Eventually, Isis went to live with Osiris in the underworld.

Isis in Context

The ancient Egyptians regarded Isis as a perfect mother, and she was worshipped as a protector goddess because of the way she sheltered Horus from danger. In the roles of mother and magician, she also cured the sick and restored the dead to life. As the mother of Horus, who took his father's place on the throne of Egypt, Isis also was thought to play a key role in the succession of Egyptian kings.

Many temples were built in honor of Isis, and her popularity extended to the ancient Greek and Roman cultures. These other cultures are an important source of information about Isis and her myths. During the Middle Ages and Renaissance, Isis, like other Egyptian deities, fell out of favor with the Christians that dominated Europe.

The story of Isis and Osiris is one of many myths of death and rebirth from around the world. The Near Eastern myth of the death of Tammuz, as well as the ancient Greek myths about **Persephone** (pronounced per-SEF-uh-nee) and **Adonis**, tell similar stories of those who dwell part of the time in the underworld and part of the time in the land of the living.

Key Themes and Symbols

For the ancient Egyptians, Isis was a symbol of motherhood and protection. She also represented the special nature of rulers, who often believed themselves to be directly related to the goddess. The cow, an animal commonly associated with Isis, was considered to be a symbol of life since it provided milk, just like a human mother.

Isis in Art, Literature, and Everyday Life

In the past century or so, renewed interest in Egyptian culture has led to a new popularity for Isis in Western culture. The television series *The Secrets of Isis* (1975) starred Joanna Cameron as an archaeologist who discovers an amulet that transforms her into the goddess and grants her supernatural powers. Isis has also appeared in comic book series from several publishers—most notably Marvel Comics, where the character remained at least somewhat similar to her Egyptian roots. Recent years have seen a renewed interest in ancient Egyptian beliefs, especially in Isis, among those seeking alternative spiritual studies and practices. The goddess even continues to be worshipped by members of the Fellowship of Isis, a modern religious group.

Read, Write, Think, Discuss

The *Sisters of Isis* series by Lynne Ewing is about a group of three high school girls—Sudi, Meri, and Delila—who discover that they are the descendants of ancient Egyptian pharaohs. The three girls must learn to use their magical powers to stop the evil Cult of **Anubis**, while at the same time trying to carry on normal teenage lives. The first book, *Sisters of Isis: The Summoning* (2007) focuses on Sudi's discovery of her true identity and powers. Ewing has also written two other popular series of novels, *Daughters of the Moon* and *Sons of the Dark*.

SEE ALSO Adonis; Afterlife; Demeter; Egyptian Mythology; Horus; Ishtar; Osiris; Ra; Set; Underworld

Itzamná

Character Overview

Itzamná was one of the most important gods of **Mayan mythology**. The ruler of the heavens and of day and night, he was often shown in Mayan art as a pleasant, toothless old man with a large nose. He was also identified as the son of the creator god Hunab Ku (pronounced hoo-NAHB-koo).

Itzamná is sometimes linked with the **sun** god Kinich Ahau (pronounced kee-nich AH-wah) and the moon goddess Ixchel (pronounced eesh-CHEL). The goddess may have been Itzamná's wife or a female form of his deity. Like Itzamná, she gave people many useful skills, such as weaving. However, Ixchel had a destructive nature and could cause **floods** and other violent events, while Itzamná was always kind and protective toward humans.

Major Myths

In various myths, Itzamná appears as a culture hero who gave the Maya the foundations of civilization. According to legend, he taught them to grow **corn**, to write, to use calendars, and to practice medicine. He also introduced a system for dividing up the land, and he established rituals for religious worship.

Itzamná in Context

According to legend, one of Itzamná's greatest teachings to the Maya people was how to create calendars. The Maya used several different calendars, including a basic 260-day calendar, a 365-day calendar similar to the Gregorian calendar popular in the world today, and even a calendar that combined both into an enormous 52-year cycle. The Maya used calendars to determine the ideal days for performing all important

Nationality/Culture
Mayan

Pronunciation
eet-SAHM-nah

Alternate Names
None

Appears In
Mayan creation myths

Lineage
Son of Hunab Ku

actions, from the agricultural to the religious. The most significant cultural documents produced by the Maya were calendars, which included information on daily practices as well as gods and goddesses.

Key Themes and Symbols

Itzamná represents wisdom and the transfer of knowledge. His wisdom is symbolized by his typical depiction as an old man. Unlike many Mayan gods, Itzamná also represented happiness, illustrated by his toothless smile. One important theme that runs through the tales of Itzamná is creation and invention; the god creates processes and systems that can only be described as logical, methodical, and in some cases, scientific.

Itzamná in Art, Literature, and Everyday Life

Itzamná appears in many of the Mayan documents created during and after the fall of the Mayan civilization, and also appears as a decorative figure on many Mayan structures. At the Maya archeological site of Palenque, for example, Itzamná appears on one of the existing temple platforms. Although not well known outside Mayan mythology, Itzamná remains an important part of Mayan and Mexican culture.

Read, Write, Think, Discuss

The Captive by Scott O'Dell (1979) is a historical novel set during the time of the Maya. The book centers on a young Spanish priest who works to end the enslavement of Central American tribes such as the Maya by Spanish explorers. O'Dell is also the author of the Newbery Medal–winning novel *Island of the Blue Dolphins*, first published in 1960.

SEE ALSO Mayan Mythology

Izanagi and Izanami

Character Overview

In Japanese Shinto mythology the two gods Izanagi (The Male Who Invites) and Izanami (The Female Who Invites) are the creators of Japan

Nationality/Culture
Japanese/Shinto

Pronunciation
ee-zuh-NAH-gee and ee-zuh-NAH-mee

Alternate Names
None

Appears In
The *Kojiki*, the *Nihongi*

Lineage
None

and its other gods. Stories about Izanagi and Izanami are told in two works from the 700s CE, the *Kojiki* (pronounced koh-JEE-kee) and the *Nihongi* (pronounced nee-HOHN-gee).

Major Myths

According to legend, the first gods ordered the divine beings Izanagi and Izanami to create the islands of Japan. The two stood on the floating bridge of **heaven** and stirred the ancient ocean with a jeweled spear. When they lifted the spear, the drops that fell back into the water formed the first solid land, an island called Onogoro (pronounced oh-NOH-goh-roh). Izanagi and Izanami descended to the island and became husband and wife. Their first child was deformed, and the other gods said it was because Izanami spoke before her husband at their marriage ceremony.

The couple performed another wedding ceremony, this time correctly. Izanami soon gave birth to eight lovely children, who became the islands of Japan. Izanagi and Izanami then created many gods and goddesses to represent the mountains, valleys, waterfalls, streams, winds, and other natural features of Japan. However, during the birth of Kagutsuchi (pronounced kah-guh-TSOO-chee), the **fire** god, Izanami was badly burned. As she lay dying, she continued to create gods and goddesses, and still other deities emerged from the tears of the grief-stricken Izanagi.

When Izanami died, she went to Yomi (pronounced YOH-mee), the **underworld** or land of the dead. Izanagi decided to go there and bring his beloved back from the land of darkness and death. Izanami greeted Izanagi from the shadows as he approached the entrance to Yomi. She warned him not to look at her and said that she would try to arrange for her release from the gods of Yomi. Full of desire for his wife, Izanagi lit a torch and looked into Yomi. Horrified to see that Izanami was a rotting corpse, Izanagi fled.

Angry that Izanagi had not respected her wishes, Izanami sent hideous female spirits, eight thunder gods, and an army of fierce warriors to chase him. Izanagi managed to escape and blocked the pass between Yomi and the land of the living with a huge boulder. Izanami met him there and, unable to get past the boulder, vowed to take revenge by strangling 1,000 people a day. Izanagi responded by saying he would cause the birth of 1,500 people a day. They broke off their marriage.

Izanagi felt unclean because of his contact with the dead, and he took a bath to purify himself. A number of gods and goddesses, both good and evil, emerged from his discarded clothing as Izanagi bathed. As he washed his face, the **sun** goddess **Amaterasu** (pronounced ah-mah-te-RAH-soo) appeared from his left eye, the moon god Tsuki-yomi (pronounced TSOO-kee-yoh-mee) appeared from his right eye, and Susano-ô (pronounced soo-sah-noh-OH) came from his nose. Proud of these three noble children, Izanagi divided his kingdom among them.

Izanagi and Izanami in Context

The tale of Izanami's death and Izanagi's journey to the underworld offers some insight into traditional Japanese ideas about men and women. Izanami is shown to be a creature closely tied to nature and natural processes; she gives birth much like any woman would, and when she dies, her body rots just like a human body. Izanagi, on the other hand, creates children through more supernatural means: through his own tears, and through purified parts of his body while cleansing. This suggests a traditional Japanese view of women as creators of the natural or organic, and men as creators of the supernatural or cultural.

Izanami's error in speaking before her husband during their wedding ceremony was a violation of social order, and resulted in the birth of an unnatural baby. This detail suggests a belief in the ancient Japanese culture that women should defer to men, and that their failure to do so can have bad consequences.

Key Themes and Symbols

Stories in which one-half of a romantic couple dies young and the other half attempts to retrieve the beloved from the underworld appear in several cultures. As in the case with Izanagi and Izanami, the attempt is usually either unsuccessful or only partially successful, indicating cultural beliefs regarding the impossibility of cheating death. Even love cannot conquer death. The transformation of Izanami from a creative force to a destructive one after her separation from Izanagi is an important theme, and mirrors female deities in other cultures who both give and take life.

Izanagi and Izanami in Art, Literature, and Everyday Life

Izanagi and Izanami appear in both of the main works of **Japanese mythology**, the *Kojiki* and the *Nihongi*. In art, they are usually depicted together, standing in the clouds and stirring the ancient sea with a spear.

Read, Write, Think, Discuss

Compare the story of Izanagi's journey to the underworld with the Greek myth of **Orpheus** and **Eurydice**. How are the two stories similar? How are they different? Do you think the similarities are coincidental, or could they represent themes common in many cultures?

SEE ALSO Amaterasu; Japanese Mythology; Underworld

J

Character

Deity

Myth

Theme

Culture

Jade Emperor

Character Overview

The Jade Emperor, also known as Yu Huang, was viewed by Taoists as the ultimate ruler of **heaven**, earth, and the land of the dead. According to legend, the Jade Emperor was once a prince who looked after the needy in his kingdom. He became immortal—or able to live forever—and after over two hundred million years of existence, he was selected by a panel of sages to become the single ruler of all things.

Major Myths

When Yu Huang was born, he gave off light that filled the kingdom where he lived. When he grew older, he retreated and went into meditation (a state of focused thought) and eventually became immortal. Yu Huang was concerned mostly with helping to improve the living conditions of people, and after spending much time working on this issue, he resumed his meditation—which involved passing mental "trials" in order to become more powerful—so that he might find even better ways to help.

When he emerged from his meditation, which had lasted many millions of years, he discovered that a demon had amassed an army of monsters and was attempting to take over control of heaven. Although Yu Huang was not a god, he traveled to heaven to see what was

Nationality/Culture
Chinese/Taoist

Alternate Names
Yu Huang, Heavenly Grandfather

Appears In
Early Taoist creation myths

Lineage
Son of the King of Pure Felicity and Majestic Heavenly Lights and Ornaments

Yu Huang, the Jade Emperor, was the ruler of first heaven in Taoist mythology. He was considered a part of the Taoist Triad—the founding fathers of Taoism—along with Tao Chun, ruler of second heaven, and Lao Tzu, ruler of third heaven. © PRIVATE COLLECTION/THE BRIDGEMAN ART LIBRARY.

happening. When he found that the gods were not powerful enough to stop the demon, he stepped forward and battled the demon himself. The two beings fought not with their fists or weapons, but with the power of their minds. In the end, Yu Huang was victorious. The gods were so grateful that they, along with other immortals and humans, chose to elect Yu Huang as their ruler and gave him the title of Jade Emperor.

Jade Emperor in Context

For those outside Chinese culture, the reference to jade in Yu Huang's title may not seem significant. However, jade has been one of the most culturally important stones throughout the history of China. As early as 3000 BCE, jade—which is a hard stone that resists wear—was used to create some tools, but its beauty meant that it was often saved for the creation of decorative and ceremonial items. The stone was regarded in much the same way gold has been viewed in other parts of the world, and jade items were indicators of wealth or royal connections. Nobles during the Han dynasty, roughly between 200 BCE and 200 CE, were often buried in suits made of intricately sewn jade tiles; they believed the jade had special qualities that would preserve human remains.

Key Themes and Symbols

The main theme of the myths of the Jade Emperor is the superior power of the mind over the physical realm. Yu Huang becomes immortal by meditating until he reaches a higher state of being. He continues to meditate for millions of years in order to increase his powers. When he fights the demon who is attempting to overtake heaven, the battle is waged through their minds instead of through weapons. Yu Huang's association with jade represents his connection to other Chinese rulers and to all that is sacred and beautiful in nature.

Jade Emperor in Art, Literature, and Everyday Life

Though he originally sprang from Taoist beliefs, the Jade Emperor has become one of the most significant mythical figures in Chinese culture as a whole. In modern times, the Jade Emperor still serves as a mythical judge of a person's good deeds; on the eve of the Chinese New Year, families burn a paper depiction of a god that relays the household activities of the past year, good and bad, to the Jade Emperor. Outside China, the Jade Emperor has appeared as a character in the Japanese comic and animated series *Fushigi Yugi* (1992) by Yuu Watase, and in the American science fiction television series *Stargate SG-1.*

Read, Write, Think, Discuss

The Jade Emperor is unique as a leader of the deities in the Chinese pantheon, or collection of recognized gods and goddesses. Compare him to leaders of the pantheons of other cultures, such as **Zeus** (Greek) or **Odin** (Norse). How is he different from these gods? How do you think this reflects different attitudes among the people of the Chinese, ancient Greek, and Norse cultures?

SEE ALSO Chinese Mythology; Xian; Yellow Emperor

Jagannatha

See **Juggernaut.**

Janus

Nationality/Culture
Roman

Pronunciation
JAY-nuhs

Alternate Names
None

Appears In
Ovid's *Fasti*

Lineage
Unknown

Character Overview

Janus was the Roman god of gates and doorways. Like a doorway that can be entered from two directions, Janus was usually pictured with two faces, one looking forward and one looking back. Janus was also associated with beginnings and endings, and the first month of the year is called January after him. The Romans mentioned Janus first when including a list of gods in their prayers, and they named the Janiculum (pronounced juh-NIK-yuh-luhm), one of the seven hills of Rome, in his honor.

Major Myths

Janus appears in one myth as the defender of an important Roman gateway. When the city was under attack by a tribe known as the Sabines (pronounced SAY-bines), Janus flooded the gate with a hot spring to

prevent the invaders from entering the city. In another story, Janus used his two faces while pursuing a lover. The goddess Cardea (pronounced kar-DEE-uh) was known for leading her admirers to a cave and then running away. When Janus accompanied her to the cave, he saw with the face in the back of his head that she was turning to leave and caught hold of her before she could escape.

Janus in Context

As the god who could see both the past and the future, Janus was especially important to the Romans because of their strong beliefs in both their heritage and technological progress. These were the two driving forces of the Roman Empire. Their desire for a rich heritage led the Romans to produce many examples of great art based on classical Greek models in sculpture, literature, and architecture. Their fondness for efficiency and technological advances led to great success in agriculture, politics, and military conquest.

Key Themes and Symbols

For the ancient Romans, Janus represented change or transition, just as doors, gates, and hallways represent a change or transition from one place to another. Janus also symbolized transitions such as births, marriages, and other significant life events. This also explains why Janus was recognized at the beginning of the new year and why he was also seen as a symbol of time. The two faces of Janus were sometimes said to represent the **sun** and the moon, together forming a complete daily cycle.

Janus in Art, Literature, and Everyday Life

The temple to Janus in the Roman Forum had two sets of doors facing east and west. These doors were open during a war and closed in periods of peace. The two-faced figure of Janus was common on Roman coins, and has remained a popular image even in modern times.

The international film distributor Janus Films, responsible for bringing world cinema classics such as *Seven Samurai* and many others to the United States, uses the familiar two-faced image as its logo. Janus has also lent his name to one of Saturn's moons, as well as the month of January. In addition, those who maintain hallways—the domain of Janus—were given a special title that is still used today: janitors.

Read, Write, Think, Discuss

To the ancient Romans, Janus represented change, or transition. Societies all over the world recognize social transitions, such as birth, graduation, and marriage, and celebrate them with rituals. Modern anthropologists call these rituals "rites of passage," since they ritually mark the transition of an individual or group from one social status to another. In America, for example, your eighteenth birthday is a rite of passage that acknowledges your transition from child to legal adult. Using your library, the Internet, or other available resources, research the rites of passage in another culture. For which individuals or groups within the society are the rites meant? What transitions do the rites mark? Select one particular ceremony for more in-depth research, and write a brief essay on the "before," and "after," social status of the group or individual who takes part in the rite of passage.

Japanese Mythology

Japanese Mythology in Context

The mythology of Japan has a long history dating back more than 2,000 years. It became part of two major religious traditions: Shinto, a religion that developed in Japan, and Buddhism, which developed in India and came to Japan from China and Korea.

Japanese mythology includes a vast number of gods, goddesses, and spirits. Most of the stories concern the creation of the world, the foundation of the islands of Japan, and the activities of deities (gods), humans, animals, spirits, and magical creatures. Some myths describe characters and events associated with particular places in Japan. Others are set in legendary locations, such as the heavens or the **underworld** (the land of the dead).

For many centuries myths were transmitted orally in Japan. In 712 CE, a written version of the mythology, the *Kojiki* (pronounced koh-JEE-kee), was compiled for the court of the Emperor of Japan. The tales in the *Kojiki* tell of the creation of the world, the origin of the gods, and the ancestry of the Japanese emperors, who claimed descent from the **sun** goddess **Amaterasu** (pronounced ah-mah-te-RAH-soo).

Another early source of Japanese mythology is the *Nihongi* (pronounced nee-HOHN-gee), also known as the *Nihonshoki* (Chronicles of Japan). Completed in 720 CE, this work also includes various myths and legends, and it helps establish the genealogy of the imperial family. The *Nihongi* was greatly influenced by Chinese and Korean history and mythology. Both the *Kojiki* and the *Nihongi* contain elements of Taoism, a Chinese religious movement that was introduced to Japan by the 600s.

Core Deities and Characters

In Japanese mythology, everything in nature has a *kami* (pronounced KAH-mee)—a deity or spirit. As a result, the Japanese pantheon, or collection of recognized gods, is enormous, with some sources claiming that there are millions of different spirits and deities. Throughout Japan, local myths and legends tell about the *kami* of a particular place, such as a rock, a pair of trees, or a mountain. However, several major

Major Japanese Deities

Amaterasu: goddess of the sun and fertility who brings light to the world.

Hachiman: god of warriors, known for his military skill.

Inari: god associated with rice and merchants.

Izanagi: creator god.

Izanami: creator goddess.

Kagutsuchi: god of fire.

Susano-ô: violent god associated with storms and the sea, Amaterasu's brother.

Tsuki-yomi: moon god, Amaterasu's brother.

deities appear in significant roles in a number of stories from different regions.

The two most important creator deities are Izanagi (pronounced ee-zuh-NAH-gee) and his sister Izanami (pronounced ee-zuh-NAH-mee). According to the myths, they made the islands of Japan as well as many of the gods and goddesses. **Izanagi and Izanami** also appear in a story about a descent to Yomi (pronounced YOH-mee), a land of darkness and death associated with the underworld.

Perhaps the best-known Japanese deity is the sun goddess Amaterasu. Said to be the ancestor of the imperial family, she brings light into the world and is responsible for fertility. Her shrine at Ise (pronounced EE-say) is considered by many to be the most important shrine in Japan.

Amaterasu has two brothers: the moon god Tsuki-yomi (pronounced TSOO-kee-yoh-mee) and Susano-ô (pronounced soo-sah-noh-OH), a powerful and violent god often associated with storms. Of the two, Susano-ô plays a more important role in mythology, appearing in a number of major legends, including several with Amaterasu.

Ôkuninushi (pronounced aw-KOO-nee-NOO-shee), a descendant of Susano-ô (possibly his son), is a central character in the Izumo Cycle, a series of myths set in the Izumo (pronounced ee-ZOO-moh) region of western Japan. Like the **heroes** in the legends of other cultures, Ôkuninushi has many adventures and undergoes various ordeals.

One of the most popular deities of Japanese mythology is Hachiman (pronounced HAH-chee-mahn), a protector of warriors. The character of Hachiman is based on the emperor Ôjin (pronounced OH-jeen), who lived in the 300s CE and was renowned for his military skills. According to tradition, after Ôjin died he became the god Hachiman. In the 700s, Hachiman became part of the Shinto pantheon.

The god Inari (pronounced ee-NAH-ree) appears in few myths, but he is important because of his association with the growing of rice, the major food crop in Japan. Thought to bring prosperity, Inari is the patron (protector) of merchants and sword makers.

Among the many spirits and creatures in Japanese mythology are the *tengu* (pronounced TEN-goo), minor deities that are part human and part bird. According to tradition, they live in trees in mountainous areas. The *tengu* enjoy playing tricks on humans but resent being tricked themselves. They are more mischievous than wicked.

The Oni (pronounced OH-nee), a more threatening group of spirits, may have originated in China and traveled to Japan with Buddhism. These horned demons, often of enormous size, can take human or animal shape. Sometimes invisible, the Oni have the ability to steal the souls of humans. They can be very cruel and are associated with various evil forces such as famine and disease.

Japanese mythology also includes other Buddhist deities. In addition to stories about the life of Buddha (pronounced BOO-duh), many tales concern Amida (pronounced AH-mee-duh), the ruler of a paradise called the Pure Land. Kannon (pronounced KAH-nohn), the protector of children and women in childbirth, and Jizô (pronounced jee-ZOH), who rescues souls from **hell**, are also important Buddhist figures.

A group of monkey-like creatures called *kappa* (pronounced KAHP-pah) displays both good and evil qualities in Japanese myth. Associated with water, they live in rivers, ponds, and lakes, and carry water in a hollow space on top of their heads. If the water spills, the kappa lose their magical powers. Kappa drink the blood of humans, horses, and cattle. But they also eat cucumbers, and families can avoid being attacked by throwing a cucumber bearing their names into the kappa's watery home. Among the kappa's good qualities is a tendency to be polite. When they meet someone, they bow, often spilling the water in their heads. They

also always keep their promises. In many tales, humans outwit the kappa by forcing them to make promises.

Major Myths

The most important stories in Japanese mythology deal with creation and the goddess Amaterasu. Deeply rooted in nature, they vividly describe the formation of the landscape and the origin of forces such as **fire**, wind, and light.

Creation According to the *Kojiki*, in the beginning there was only an ancient ooze, out of which **heaven** and earth were formed. Life emerged from this mud. In heaven three deities—followed by two others—appeared. These five became the Separate Heavenly Deities. They were followed by the Seven Generations of the Age of the Gods, two single deities and five male and female couples. The two single deities came out of a reedlike substance floating in the ooze.

When the youngest pair of deities—Izanagi and Izanami—were born, the other gods ordered them to make solid land out of the material drifting in the sea. Standing on the floating bridge of heaven, Izanagi and Izanami stirred the ancient ocean with a jeweled spear. When they pulled up the spear to see if any material had gathered on it, drops of salty water dripped down into the sea and formed an island called Onogoro (pronounced oh-NOH-goh-roh). Izanagi and Izanami left heaven and went to live on the island. They married and produced eight children, who became the islands of Japan.

Izanagi and Izanami then created gods and goddesses of the trees, mountains, valleys, streams, winds, and other natural features of Japan. While giving birth to the fire god Kagutsuchi (pronounced kah-guh-TSOO-chee), Izanami was badly burned. As she lay dying, she produced more gods and goddesses. Other deities emerged from the tears of her grief-stricken husband.

When Izanami died, she went to Yomi, the land of darkness and death. Izanagi followed her there and tried to bring her back. Izanami, hidden in shadow, told him that she would try to secure her release from the gods of the underworld, but that he must wait and not attempt to see her. When she did not come back for a long while, Izanagi looked for her. He discovered her rotting corpse and fled in terror. Izanami was angry that Izanagi had seen her and sent hideous spirits to chase him. Izanagi managed to escape, and he sealed off the passage to Yomi with a huge boulder. Izanami remained there and ruled over the dead.

Feeling unclean from his contact with the dead, Izanagi decided to bathe in a stream to purify himself. As he undressed, gods and goddesses emerged from his discarded clothing. Others came forth while he washed. Susano-ô came from his nose, Tsuki-yomi emerged from his right eye, and Amaterasu appeared from his left eye. Izanagi divided the world among these three gods. He gave Susano-ô control of the oceans, assigned Tsuki-yomi the realm of the night, and made Amaterasu the ruler of the sun and the heavens.

Myths of Amaterasu One famous myth tells how Susano-ô, Amaterasu's brother, was unhappy with his share of the world and caused much destruction. Banished to Yomi, he asked to go to heaven to see his sister the sun goddess one last time. Amaterasu became concerned that Susano-ô might be planning to take over her lands. The two agreed to a contest to prove their power. If Susano-ô won, he could stay in heaven forever, but if he lost, he would have to leave.

Amaterasu asked for her brother's sword, which she broke into three pieces and chewed in her mouth. When Amaterasu spit out the pieces, they turned into three goddesses. Susano-ô then took a string of five star-shaped beads that Amaterasu had given him. He put the beads in his mouth, chewed them, and spat out five gods. Susano-ô claimed victory because he had produced five gods and Amaterasu had produced only three goddesses. However, Amaterasu pointed out that he had created these gods from her possessions, which proved that her power was actually greater than his. Susano-ô refused to acknowledge defeat, and Amaterasu allowed him to remain in heaven.

While in heaven, Susano-ô began doing things that offended his sister and violated important rules. He destroyed rice fields, made loud noises, and dirtied the floors of her palace. Finally, Susano-ô killed one of the horses of heaven, skinned it, and hurled it into the hall where Amaterasu was weaving cloth. This so angered Amaterasu that she hid in a cave and refused to come out.

When the sun goddess concealed herself, the world was plunged into darkness, plants stopped growing, and all activities came to a halt. Desperate for Amaterasu's return, eight hundred gods gathered to discuss ways of getting her to leave the cave. A wise god named Omori-kane (pronounced oh-MOH-ree-KAH-nay) proposed a solution.

The gods hung a mirror on the branches of a tree outside the cave. Then had a young goddess named Ama-no-uzume (pronounced AH-muh-noh-oo-ZOO-may) dance to music while they laughed loudly. Amaterasu heard the noise and wondered what was happening. Opening the door to the cave a little, she asked why the gods were so happy. They told her that they were celebrating because they had found a goddess superior to her.

A Divine Emperor

According to Japanese myth, the goddess Amaterasu established the imperial family of Japan. She began by sending her grandson, Ninigi no Mikoto (pronounced nee-nee-gee-noh-mee-KOH-toh), to live on earth. Before Ninigi left heaven, the goddess gave him the mirror that drew her from the cave, as well as jewels and a sword belonging to the god Susano-ô. When Ninigi arrived on earth, he was accepted as the ruler of Japan, and the gifts he brought from Amaterasu became treasures of the imperial family. Ninigi married the goddess of Mount Fuji (pronounced FOO-jee), who bore him three sons. One of the sons was the father of Jimmu Tenno (pronounced JEEM-moo TEN-noh), the first historical emperor of Japan. By tradition, the Japanese imperial family traces its ancestry to Jimmu Tenno.

Curious at who this goddess might be, Amaterasu opened the door wider to look and saw her own image in the mirror. When she paused to gaze at her reflection, a god hiding nearby pulled her completely out of the cave. Another god then blocked the entrance with a magic rope. After Amaterasu emerged from the cave, her light shone once again, and life returned to normal. To punish Susano-ô for his actions, the gods banished him from heaven.

The Izumo Cycle The Izumo Cycle of myths features the god Ôkuninushi, a descendant of Susano-ô. One of the most famous stories is about Ôkuninushi and the White Rabbit.

According to this tale, Ôkuninushi had eighty brothers, each of whom wanted to marry the same beautiful princess. On a journey to see the princess, the brothers came upon a rabbit with no fur in great pain at the side of the road. They told the animal that it could get its fur back by bathing in saltwater, but this only made the pain worse. A little while later, Ôkuninushi arrived and saw the suffering rabbit. When he asked what had happened, the rabbit told him how it had lost its fur.

One day while traveling between two islands, the rabbit persuaded some crocodiles to form a bridge so it could cross the water. In return the rabbit promised to count the crocodiles to see whether they were more numerous than the creatures of the sea. As the rabbit neared the far shore, the crocodiles realized that the promise was only a trick to get the rabbit across the water. Furious, the last crocodile seized the rabbit and tore off its skin.

After hearing this story, Ôkuninushi told the rabbit to bathe in clear water and then roll in some grass pollen on the ground. The rabbit followed this plan, and new white fur soon grew on its body. The rabbit, who was actually a god, rewarded Ôkuninushi by promising that he would marry the beautiful princess. Ôkuninushi's success angered his brothers, and a number of other myths in the Izumo Cycle tell about the struggles between them.

Key Themes and Symbols

Japanese mythology features many of the same themes that are found in the mythologies of other cultures. The sun, as embodied in Amaterasu, is the most important figure in many of the tales, reflecting the importance of the sun in maintaining food and warmth to the Japanese people. As with some other cultures, the specific theme of the sun in hiding—which causes crops to wither and the earth to grow cold—is a prominent myth, if not the most prominent myth.

The act of creation is also a recurring theme in Japanese mythology. Aside from the tales of Izanagi and Izanami, who created the islands of Japan as well as the original gods and goddesses, later deities such as Amaterasu and Susano-ô are also described as creating additional gods and goddesses with little effort.

One of the most important symbols found in Japanese mythology is the mirror. The mirror is an important part of the myth of Amaterasu's hiding, since it lured the goddess from the cave and restores light to the world. The mirror represents honesty, since it reflects only what it is shown. A bronze mirror housed in the Ise (pronounced EE-say) Shrine is believed to be the mirror used to lure Amaterasu from the cave, and is one of the three sacred treasures that make up the Imperial Regalia of Japan.

Japanese Mythology in Art, Literature, and Everyday Life

Mythology plays an important role in the lives of the Japanese people today. Myths and legends are the basis of much Japanese art, drama, and literature, and people still learn and tell stories about the gods and goddesses. Traditional *kagura* (pronounced kah-GOO-rah) dances are performed to honor the deities at Shinto (the ancient religion of Japan) shrines. Legend traces the origin of this ancient art form to the dance that drew the goddess Amaterasu from her cave.

Read, Write, Think, Discuss

Compare the Shinto concept of *kami* to the Pueblo Indian entities known as **kachinas**. How are the two similar? How are they different? Do they reflect similar views of the world?

SEE ALSO Amaterasu; Buddhism and Mythology; Devils and Demons; Giants; Izanagi and Izanami; Tricksters; Underworld

Jason

Character Overview

In **Greek mythology**, Jason was the leader of a band of adventurers who set out on a long journey to find the **Golden Fleece**. Although he succeeded in this quest, he never achieved his true goal—to become king of the land of Iolcus (pronounced ee-AHL-kuhs), to which he was the rightful heir. Jason's story is one of violence and tragedy as well as adventure, partly because of his relationship with the enchantress and witch **Medea** (pronounced me-DEE-uh).

Early Life Like many Greek **heroes**, Jason was of royal blood. His father was King Aeson (pronounced EE-son) of Iolcus in northwestern Greece. The king's half brother Pelias (pronounced PEEL-ee-uhs) wanted the throne himself and overthrew Aeson while Jason was still a boy. Jason's mother feared for his safety. She sent him away to be guarded by Chiron (pronounced KYE-ron), a wise centaur—a creature that is half man and half horse—who took charge of the boy's education. Chiron taught Jason hunting, warfare, music, and medicine. Some accounts say that the centaur also gave Jason his name, which means "healer," in recognition of the boy's skill in the medical arts.

At about the age of twenty, Jason headed back to Iolcus, determined to gain the throne that rightfully belonged to him. On the way, he helped an old woman across a flooded stream and lost one of his sandals.

Nationality/Culture
Greek

Pronunciation
JAY-suhn

Alternate Names
None

Appears In
Ovid's *Metamorphoses*, Hyginus's *Fabulae*

Lineage
Son of King Aeson and Queen Alcimede of Iolcus

Unknown to him, the old woman was the goddess **Hera** (pronounced HAIR-uh) in disguise. She vowed to destroy Pelias, who had failed to worship her properly, and to help Jason.

An oracle, or person who could communicate with the gods, had warned Pelias to beware of a man wearing one sandal. When Jason arrived in Iolcus, the king confronted him. Jason identified himself and declared that he had come for his throne. Prevented by the laws of hospitality from attacking Jason openly, Pelias resorted to trickery. He said that if Jason could bring him the fabled Golden Fleece, he would make him his heir. Pelias believed that obtaining the heavily guarded fleece from the distant land of Colchis (pronounced KOL-kis) was a nearly impossible task.

The Quest for the Golden Fleece Jason assembled a band of brave adventurers—including the sons of kings and gods and some other former students of Chiron—to accompany him on his quest. They sailed in a magic ship called the *Argo* (pronounced AHR-goh) and were known as the **Argonauts** (pronounced AHR-guh-nawts). Among them were the famous musician **Orpheus** (pronounced OR-fee-uhs) and the hero **Heracles** (pronounced HAIR-uh-kleez).

The Argonauts' eventful journey to Colchis, their seizure of the Golden Fleece, and their long voyage home became the subject of many tales and works of art. They might never have succeeded without the help of Medea, the daughter of King Aeëtes (ay-EE-teez) of Colchis, who fell in love with Jason. Some versions of the story say that Hera persuaded **Aphrodite** (pronounced af-ro-DYE-tee), the goddess of love, to inspire Medea's passion. Both a clever woman and a witch with knowledge of magic, Medea would be a useful helpmate to Jason.

When Jason arrived in Colchis, Aeëtes set harsh conditions for handing over the Golden Fleece, including the accomplishment of several seemingly impossible tasks. Jason had to hook two fire-breathing bulls to a plow, sow a field with **dragons**' teeth, and then fight the armed warriors that grew from those teeth. In all these trials, Medea used her magic powers to protect and guide Jason. Then after Jason promised to marry her, she helped him steal the fleece from the serpent that guarded it.

With the fleece on board, the *Argo* sailed away from Colchis, pursued by Medea's brother Apsyrtus (pronounced ap-SUR-tuhs). Apsyrtus caught up with the ship and spoke with Jason, promising to let him keep the Golden Fleece if he would give up Medea. However,

Medea objected to this plan. When she and Jason next met Apsyrtus, Jason killed him.

Return to Iolcus After a long journey home with many adventures along the way, Jason and the Argonauts finally arrived back in Iolcus. Jason delivered the Golden Fleece to Pelias. Meanwhile, Medea decided to get rid of Pelias (accounts differ on whether Jason knew of her plan). She persuaded the king's daughters that she could make their father young again, but first they would have to cut him up and put him in a pot. This procedure led only to a messy death, and the horrified people of Iolcus drove Jason and Medea away. The couple settled in Corinth, where they lived for ten years and had several children.

Their peaceful interlude ended when Creon (pronounced KREE-ahn), the king of Corinth, offered Jason his daughter in marriage. Jason accepted and divorced Medea. Enraged at this poor treatment, Medea sent the new bride a poisoned wedding gown, which killed her when she put it on and killed Creon as he tried to save her. Some versions of this myth say that, to punish Jason still further, Medea went on to kill the children she had borne him, while other accounts say that the angry Corinthians killed them. Either way, the children perished and Medea fled to Athens.

According to some accounts, Medea killed Jason at Corinth as part of her bloodbath. Much more common, though, is the story that Jason lived out his last days at Corinth, alone and broken by tragedy. One day as he sat near the *Argo*, which was rotting away, a piece of wood broke off from the ship and fell on him, killing the one-time hero of the Golden Fleece.

Jason in Context

The story of Jason centers on the passing of royal power from one generation to the next. These myths pre-date government rule by elected officials and represent an older system of rule still common in many regions during the height of the Greek empire. Historical records suggest that plots and overthrows of rulers were all too common in ancient Greece and Rome. The story of Jason helps to encourage the tradition of passing of power from a king to his son; this is done by showing Jason to be a sympathetic hero, prompting the audience to root for his success.

The seeds of Jason's downfall are sown when he accepts help from Medea, a witch with few scruples. In the end, Jason's desire for power

Jason was able to capture the Golden Fleece with the help of Medea. Using her magic, she put the dragon that guarded the fleece to sleep. © NATIONAL GALLERY COLLECTION; BY KIND PERMISSION OF THE TRUSTEES OF THE NATIONAL GALLERY, LONDON/ CORBIS.

leads to the deaths of Medea's brother, Pelias, Creon, Creon's daughter, and his own children. The myth warns that not all paths to power are worth taking.

Key Themes and Symbols

In the myth of Jason and the Argonauts, the Golden Fleece is a symbol of that which is unattainable or cannot be gotten. Pelias only gives Jason the task because he believes it cannot be completed. Even after arriving in Colchis, the fleece seems impossible to take. And once Jason returns to Iolcus with the fleece, he is still unable to attain his rightful place as king. The Golden Fleece can also be seen as a symbol of rightful heirs to royal power, as Jason possessed the fleece and was the rightful heir to his father's throne.

Jason himself represents justice, as the heir who returns in an attempt to claim the throne that, according to tradition, rightfully belonged to him. He may also represent a method of leadership that was growing increasingly unpopular in the face of more democratic forms of government; in the end, Jason does not reclaim his kingdom for himself, and dies in a way not at all befitting a hero or rightful king.

Jason in Art, Literature, and Everyday Life

Many writers have been inspired by the subject of Jason's quest for the Golden Fleece. Among the ancient Greek works concerning the subject are Pindar's *Pythian Ode,* Apollonius Rhodius's *Argonautica,* and Euripides' play *Medea.* In the Middle Ages, English writer Geoffrey Chaucer retold the story in the *Legend of Good Women,* and in the 1800s, William Morris wrote the long narrative poem *Life and Death of Jason* which centered on the quest. Robert Graves's novel *The Golden Fleece* was published in 1944, and John Gardner's *Jason and Medeia* was published in 1973. The story of the search for the Golden Fleece has also been adapted to film, most notably the 1963 movie *Jason and the Argonauts.*

Read, Write, Think, Discuss

Voyage with Jason by Ken Catran (2000) is a re-telling of Jason's adventures during his search for the Golden Fleece. The tale focuses on Pylos, a young apprentice shipbuilder who is taken aboard the *Argo* as the only crew member who is not a hero. The novel, first published in New Zealand, was named Book of the Year at the 2001 New Zealand Post Children's Book Awards.

SEE ALSO Argonauts; Golden Fleece; Greek Mythology; Medea

Job

Character Overview

Job is the name of a book in the Hebrew Bible and the name of the book's main character. Many scholars consider the Book of Job to be one

Nationality/Culture
Judeo-Christian

Pronunciation
JOHB

Alternate Names
Ayyub (Islamic)

Appears In
The Book of Job

Lineage
Unknown

of the finest works of literature ever written. It focuses on the question of why the innocent suffer.

Job, a wealthy man, blessed with a loving wife and family, is known for his goodness and devotion to the will of Yahweh (pronounced YAH-way), the Hebrew god. The Bible indicates that Job's prosperity and general good fortune are a reward for his goodness and belief in Yahweh. However, in a meeting between Yahweh and his heavenly advisors, **Satan** questions Job's faith, claiming that he is faithful only because of the many blessings he enjoys. If Job were to suffer misfortune, suggests Satan, he would curse Yahweh as readily as he now praises him. Satan challenges Yahweh to test Job's faith, and Yahweh accepts the challenge.

Yahweh allows Satan to inflict a number of terrible misfortunes on Job. He kills Job's children and causes him to lose all his wealth, but Job's belief in the goodness of Yahweh remains unshaken. This show of faith does not convince Satan, however, who says that physical pain and suffering would cause Job to abandon his belief. So Yahweh allows Job to be afflicted with painful boils all over his body, and still his faith remains firm.

At this point three friends visit Job, supposedly to comfort him by explaining why Yahweh is causing him to suffer. They suggest that Job must be guilty of some sin, because Yahweh only punishes the wicked. Knowing that he is a righteous man, Job refuses to accept their arguments. Finally Job pleads with Yahweh to end his suffering and asks him to explain why he is being tormented. Yahweh appears to Job in all his glory, overwhelming him with his magnificence. He proceeds to question Job about the mysteries of the universe. When Job cannot answer, Yahweh asks him how he could possibly hope to understand the will of the almighty if he cannot explain the workings of nature. Job accepts this answer and renews his faith in Yahweh, who rewards him by restoring his health and prosperity.

Job in Context

The tale of Job was intended to address the question of why a god would allow bad things to happen to good people. The god of the Near East referred to here as Yahweh was fundamentally different from many earlier gods; in this case, there was only one god in charge of everything, and this god was described as being an all-powerful protector and provider. Yahweh was not prone to the very human emotions, like jealousy, shown by ancient Greek and Roman gods. This essential goodness of Yahweh was an important point in the adoption of monotheistic (meaning "one god") religions in the Near East. This also meant that there had to be a reason why Yahweh, if he was indeed all-powerful, would not always provide for and protect his followers.

In the end, the story offers no answer to the question of why the innocent must suffer. Instead, the Book of Job delivers the message that one must believe in the goodness of Yahweh, even in the face of seemingly unjust punishment, because such issues are beyond human understanding.

Key Themes and Symbols

The two most important themes in the tale of Job are faith and suffering. The whole point of Yahweh's trial of Job is to test his faith, to see whether or not he is willing to accept Yahweh's actions even when he does not understand them. He does this by causing Job to suffer in every way imaginable: by taking away his children, by taking away his riches, and even by causing boils on his skin. Still, Job remains faithful.

Job in Art, Literature, and Everyday Life

The original tale of Job has proven to be one of the most popular stories of the Bible, and is known to Christians, Jews, and Muslims around the world. Events of the tale were commonly depicted in illuminated manuscripts, and artist William Blake created a famous series of illustrations for the Book of Job. More recently, the 1984 novel *Job: A Comedy of Justice* by Robert A. Heinlein offers a science fiction version of the account of Job, with a main character that is sent bouncing through parallel universes and spends time in both **heaven** and **hell**. The 2003 comedy film *Bruce Almighty*, starring Jim Carrey, includes many elements of the account of Job. In modern times, the phrase "the patience of Job" is often used to describe someone who can endure a great deal of hardship or suffering without having a negative attitude.

Read, Write, Think, Discuss

The account of Job suggests that suffering exists for reasons beyond the grasp of humans and should be endured to demonstrate faith in God. If enduring difficult times is a way of showing devotion, what would be the consequences of a world without suffering? Is suffering, in some ways, good?

Jove

See **Zeus.**

Juggernaut

Nationality/Culture
Hindu

Pronunciation
JUG-er-nawt

Alternate Names
Jagannatha

Appears In
The Vedas

Lineage
Unknown

Character Overview

Juggernaut (Jagannatha) is a form of the Hindu god **Vishnu**'s (pronounced VISH-noo) incarnation, or embodiment, known as **Krishna** (pronounced KRISH-nuh). Although Juggernaut does not appear in many myths, he is an important part of one of the largest annual festivals in India.

Major Myths

Juggernaut is worshipped at the religious city of Puri (pronounced POOR-ee) in India. A temple to Juggernaut there dates from the 1100s. According to one legend, a priest chose the site for the temple when he saw a crow dive into the nearby Bay of Bengal. Inside the temple is a wooden image of Juggernaut with a black face, large eyes, a wide smile, and no arms or legs. According to myth, Krishna was walking along and overheard a group of cow-herding girls who were talking about how much they loved him. He was so overwhelmed by their talk that his eyes grew huge, his limbs shrank, and his mouth stretched into a gaping smile.

Juggernaut in Context

Juggernaut is a rather minor form of Krishna in Hindu mythology, with very few references or myths. It is interesting to note that the fourteenth-century book *The Travels of Sir John Mandeville* popularized the notion in Europe that Juggernaut caused such a frenzy among devotees in Puri that they threw themselves under the wheels of his festival cart as human sacrifices. The book is filled with many such dubious claims, and is now viewed largely as a work of fiction. However, this description of Juggernaut was commonly used by European Christians as a way of illustrating the supposed backwardness of Hindus who had not accepted Christianity.

Key Themes and Symbols

Juggernaut is a symbol of happiness and mercy to those familiar with Hindu mythology, and is also associated with Krishna's homecoming to Vrindavan. To others, however, Juggernaut represents something much more sinister and destructive. It is important to note that Hindus do not view Juggernaut as a destructive deity like **Shiva**, and that this is a misinterpretation by outside observers.

Juggernaut in Art, Literature, and Everyday Life

Several festivals are held at the temple in Puri each year, the most important being the Chariot Festival in midsummer. On this occasion, the image of Juggernaut is placed on an enormous cart—at least forty-five feet tall—built especially for the occasion and pulled through the town by hundreds of people. Early Western visitors reported that worshippers would throw themselves beneath the wheels of the cart to be crushed as a **sacrifice** to Juggernaut. Later anthropologists have questioned these accounts, but acknowledge that the huge, unwieldy vehicles have caused death either due to accidents or carelessness. This gave rise to the English word "juggernaut," meaning a person or power that crushes anything in its path.

Read, Write, Think, Discuss

Early descriptions of Juggernaut by European writers seem largely unconnected to the true nature of the god in Hindu mythology. This often happens when an outside observer describes elements of a culture with which they are not familiar. This inevitably causes bias, or an opinion of the culture's worth based on the observer's own beliefs. Do you think it is possible for someone to observe another culture and describe it without exhibiting some level of bias? Why or why not?

SEE ALSO Hinduism and Mythology; Krishna

Juno
See **Hera.**

K

Character

Deity

Myth

Theme

Culture

Kachinas

Character Overview

Spirits known as kachinas are central to the religion and mythology of the Pueblo Indians of the American Southwest, in particular the Hopi who live in Arizona. These groups believe that kachinas are divine spirits present in features of the natural world such as clouds, winds, thunder, and rain. They are also ancestral spirits that help connect humans with the spirit world.

Each Pueblo tribe and village has its own distinct kachinas. There may be more than five hundred in total, and all are equally important. The Pueblos hold the kachinas sacred and look to them for help, especially in bringing rain to water, **corn**, and other crops.

The kachinas dwell in sacred mountains and other sacred places. However, they spend half of each year living near Pueblo villages. During this time, the men of kachina cults perform traditional ceremonies linked with the presence of the spirits. They wear costumes and elaborate masks and perform songs and dances associated with specific kachinas. The Pueblos say that during these rituals each dancer is temporarily transformed into the spirit being represented.

Kokopelli Kokopelli (pronounced koh-koh-PEL-ee) is one of the most important kachinas among the Pueblo. A complex character, he plays various roles, and is regarded as a fertility spirit, a trickster, and a hunter.

Nationality/Culture
American Indian/Pueblo

Pronunciation
kuh-CHEE-nuhz

Alternate Names
Qatsinas

Appears In
Pueblo Indian oral mythology

Lineage
Varies

The Hopi have several fertility kachinas connected with Kokopelli. In some Hopi tales, Kokopelli's bag contains gifts that he uses to attract women. In others, he carries a baby on his back and leaves it with a young woman. The Hopi also have a female kachina called Kokopell' Mana. During ceremonial dances, a performer dressed as Kokopell' Mana challenges Hopi men to race with her. If she catches her opponent, she knocks him down and pretends to mate with him.

Kokopelli is identified with various insects. Kuwaan Kokopelli, or the Robber Fly Kachina, is named after a humpbacked fly that is always mating. Like Kokopell' Mana, this kachina represents fertility. In a tale about how Kokopelli guided the Hopi to a new land, Kokopelli is either a locust or a grasshopper. When an eagle dares him to pass an arrow through his body, he cleverly slips the arrow under one of his wings.

Kokopelli's flute is similar to the flutes used in American Indian religious rituals. As a hunter, Kokopelli may play the flute to attract the mountain sheep he is hunting. The Zuni call him a rain priest and connect him and his music with the gift of rain. According to the Hopi, Kokopelli warmed the land and the winds by playing his flute as he led them to their homeland.

Kachinas in Context

Kachinas reflect the unique worldview of the Pueblo people. They do not limit the presence of spirits to people and animals. Instead, they view spirits in all parts of the natural world, such as clouds and soil. This reflects a basic belief in the interconnection of every part of nature.

Key Themes and Symbols

To the Pueblo people, different kachinas symbolize different aspects of the natural world. In all cases, they represent a way for people to connect to the world. This is shown in Pueblo dance ceremonies where the dancers are believed to become possessed by various kachinas as they perform.

Kachinas in Art, Literature, and Everyday Life

Kachinas are typically portrayed in elaborately carved wooden dolls adorned with the costumes and masks that identify them. The Hopi and other Pueblo peoples use these dolls to teach their children about the hundreds of different kachinas.

The Hopi and other Pueblo peoples use kachina dolls to teach their children about divine and ancestral spirits. These wooden figures are often elaborately carved and adorned. ROBERT F. SISSON/NATIONAL GEOGRAPHIC/GETTY IMAGES.

Images of Kokopelli are among the oldest that survive in ancient rock art in the Southwest. He is also a popular figure on painted pottery. Usually depicted as a humpbacked figure playing a flute, he often carries a large bag on his back and has antennae like an insect. A silhouette design of Kokopelli is popular on many modern decorative pieces from the American Southwest.

Read, Write, Think, Discuss

The creation of kachina dolls and other traditional Pueblo artifacts specifically for tourists to buy is an important part of the modern Pueblo economy. These objects usually differ in some way from similar objects created specifically for tribal use, so they can be easily identified as souvenirs by knowledgeable Pueblos. However, some Pueblos still believe that selling copies of cultural artifacts should not be allowed. Do you think this type of business hurts or helps the Pueblo people? Why?

SEE ALSO Corn; Native American Mythology

Kali

See **Devi.**

Krishna

Nationality/Culture
Hindu

Pronunciation
KRISH-nuh

Alternate Names
Hari, Juggernaut, Ishvara

Appears In
The Vedas, the *Mahabharata*

Lineage
Son of Vasudeva and Devaki

Character Overview

Krishna, one of the most popular Hindu gods, is revered as a supreme deity (god) and the eighth embodiment of the god **Vishnu** (pronounced VISH-noo). In Hindu mythology, Krishna came to be when Vishnu plucked two of his hairs—one black and one light. Krishna became the black hair; in fact, his name means "Dark One," and artistic works usually show him with dark skin.

Major Myths

According to myth, Vishnu desired to punish the wicked King Kamsa (pronounced KUHM-suh) of Mathura (pronounced MUHT-oo-ruh), and so sent Krishna to do so as the son of Vasudeva (pronounced VAH-soo-dev) and Kamsa's sister Devaki (pronounced DEE-vuh-kee). Kamsa heard through a prophecy—or prediction—that he would be killed by the eighth child of Devaki. As a result, Kamsa vowed to kill the child. However, when Devaki gave birth to Krishna, her eighth child, the god Vishnu helped switch him with the newborn child of a cowherd and his wife. This couple raised Krishna as their own son.

After the evil Kamsa discovered that Krishna was alive, he sent demons to destroy the child. Krishna managed to overcome them all. He put an end to the ogress Putana (pronounced poo-TAH-nah) by sucking the life out of her and caused a cart to crush the monstrous flying demon named Saktasura (pronounced sahk-tuh-SOO-ruh). He also destroyed

Trinavarta (pronounced tree-nuh-VAR-tuh), a whirlwind demon, by smashing it against a rock.

Krishna grew up as a cowherd, and often amused himself by playing pranks on people. He also enjoyed teasing the daughters of the other cowherds and had many romantic adventures. A popular myth describes how he stole the clothes of cowgirls who were bathing in a river, and he refused to return them until each girl came out of the river with their hands clasped in prayer. The cowgirls liked Krishna just as much; Krishna multiplied his hands when he danced with them so each girl would be able to hold his hand. A girl named Radha was his particular favorite, although he had many lovers.

Several myths reveal the supernatural strength of Krishna. In one popular story, Krishna persuades a group of cowherds from worshipping the god **Indra** by explaining that they should instead worship the mountain that provides them and their herds with food and drink. He then declared himself to be the mountain, which angered Indra. Indra sent a week-long rainstorm as punishment, but Krishna held the mountain over his head to prevent the storm from doing any damage to the people.

Krishna became a hero renowned for ridding the area of monsters and demons, including the evil snake Kaliya. King Kamsa continued his attempts to kill Krishna by luring him and his brother Balarama (pronounced bah-luh-RAH-mah) to Mathura to a wrestling contest. As the brothers entered the city, Kamsa released a wild elephant to trample them. Krishna killed the beast. Next Kamsa sent his champion wrestlers to fight the brothers, but Krishna and Balarama defeated them all. Finally, Kamsa ordered his demons to kill Krishna's real parents, Vasudeva and Devaki. Before this could take place, however, Krishna killed Kamsa, thus fulfilling the prophecy made years before.

After killing Kamsa, Krishna led his tribe, the Yadavas (pronounced YAH-duh-vuhz), to the fortress city of Dvaraka (pronounced DWAR-kuh). He settled there and married a beautiful princess named Rukmini (pronounced ruk-MIN-ee). He later took other wives as well.

The climax of Krishna's long struggle against the forces of evil came with the great war called the Kurukshetra. The war was between two families: the noble Pandavas (pronounced PAHN-duh-vuhz) and their evil cousins the Kauravas (pronounced KOW-ruh-vuhz). Krishna served as the charioteer of Arjuna (pronounced AHR-juh-nuh), one of the Pandava leaders. Although he took no part in the fighting, Krishna gave advice to Arjuna, and the Pandavas eventually defeated the Kauravas and rid the world of much evil. The conversations between Krishna and Arjuna are found in a section of the *Mahabharata* called the *Bhagavad Gita*.

After the war, Krishna returned to Dvaraka. One day while he sat in the forest, a hunter mistook him for a deer and shot an arrow at him. The arrow pierced Krishna's heel, his only vulnerable spot. After Krishna died, his spirit ascended to Goloka, a heavenly paradise, and his sacred city of Dvaraka sank beneath the ocean.

Krishna in Context

Krishna was considered the greatest of the representations of the god Vishnu, and actually became more popular than Vishnu himself with Hindus. Krishna's exploits reveal his popularity over other gods. His victories over the god Indra and snake Kaliya (who represents snake gods) show that Krishna is more worthy to be worshipped than older gods. In both stories, Krishna is a figure who brings order from chaos, and creates a safe place for his worshippers. In addition to this role, he is worshipped as the figure who best represents divine love in two forms: the first as a mischievous child (family love), and the second as a lover who is both passionate and yet also unattainable. Though Krishna loved many women, he did not limit his affections to just one; even his favorite Radha was sad that she could never hold on to his love.

Some modern rituals for Krishna involve worshipping him in a series of eight daily "viewings" in which the god allows himself to be seen as an image. His worshippers may change the image's clothing, jewelry, other decorations, and food offerings during the course of the day, or sing devotional songs as they observe a ritual related to Krishna's cowherding.

Key Themes and Symbols

One of the key themes of the myths of Krishna is protection. The god serves as a protector to his people, leading them to the safety of Dvaraka and helping them overcome the Kauravas. Another theme common in tales of Krishna is playfulness; he is often shown having fun, dancing, or enjoying romance. This also reflects Krishna's associations with youth and vigor. In Hindu art, Krishna is usually depicted as a young prince or a cow-herder playing a flute. The popular image of Krishna playing his flute for the cowgirls is symbolic of the divine call for humans to leave

Hare Krishna

Krishna came to widespread Western attention in the late 1960s with the founding of the International Society for Krishna Consciousness (ISKCON)—a group that was soon referred to as the "Hare Krishnas." The Hare Krishnas were a prominent manifestation of the countercultural movement in the United States. Many young people at the time rejected traditional Western values and sought meaning in Eastern traditions. ISKCON based its teaching on the *Bhagavad Gita*, and tried to spread its philosophy by singing and chanting the Hare Krishna mantra (a short poem or phrase with mystical properties) in public places, such as airports and shopping centers. The Hare Krishnas recognized Krishna as the supreme deity. By the late 1970s, the group's popularity had faded amid allegations of brainwashing and child abuse at ISKCON schools.

their everyday activities in order to worship. He is nearly always shown with blue or black skin, a color traditionally associated with divinity and the universe itself.

Krishna in Art, Literature, and Everyday Life

The most important source of stories about Krishna is the *Mahabharata*, the great Hindu epic written between 400 BCE and 200 CE, and the *Bhagavatam*, written later. Krishna is shown more frequently in Indian art, dance, and music than any other god. Drama, in particular, is very important in the modern-day worship of Krishna; in some areas of India, festival seasons to honor Krishna include dramas about his life in which child actors are said to represent and even become Krishna. These plays usually begin with a ceremonial dance that represents the dances Krishna performed with the cowgirls.

Read, Write, Think, Discuss

Compare the story of Krishna to the ancient Greek myth of **Achilles**. How are the two stories similar? In what ways are the characters different? Do you think both characters qualify as **heroes**? Explain your answer.

SEE ALSO *Bhagavad Gita*; Devils and Demons; Hinduism and Mythology; Indra; *Mahabharata, The*; Shiva; Vishnu

Character

Deity

Myth

Theme

Culture

Nationality/Culture
Romano-British/Celtic

Alternate Names
Viviane, Nimuë

Appears In
Tales of King Arthur

Lineage
Unknown

Lady of the Lake

Character Overview

The Lady of the Lake, an enchantress also known as Viviane (pronounced VIV-ee-uhn) or Nimuë (pronounced neem-OO-ay), appears in many of the tales of King **Arthur**. She is remembered best for her relationships with the knight **Lancelot** and the magician **Merlin**.

According to legend, the Lady of the Lake lived in a castle beneath a lake surrounding the mystical island of Avalon (pronounced AV-uh-lahn). She raised Lancelot after his father died, and gave Arthur the magical sword Excalibur, which he treasured. When Arthur was near death, she saved him by taking him to Avalon to await a time when his people would once again need his leadership.

Arthur's magician Merlin fell in love with the Lady of the Lake, but she did not return his affection. However, she did persuade him to teach her some of his magic. While the two were traveling together, the Lady of the Lake used the spells she learned from Merlin to imprison him in a tower with invisible walls. (In some versions of the story she traps him in a tree or cave instead.)

The Lady of the Lake was also associated with Pelleas (pronounced peh-lay-AHS), one of the knights of the Round Table. When Pelleas was rejected by Ettard (pronounced ay-TAHR)—the woman he loved—the Lady of the Lake took care of him. She and Pelleas fell in love and were married.

The Lady of the Lake in Context

The British Isles are soggy places surrounded by water and covered with lakes, ponds, rivers, and springs. Naturally, water featured prominently in the mythology of the early inhabitants of England and Ireland.

The Lady of the Lake, though later adopted by French authors of Arthurian legend, appears to be based on older Celtic goddesses associated with water. There are many Celtic water spirits and goddesses, most of them women. Ceridwen (pronounced kuh-RID-wen) was a Celtic goddess who possessed a magic cauldron or kettle. She made a brew with herbs and water that would grant wisdom to whoever drank it. Even more notably, Brigid (pronounced BREED) was a goddess who kept watch over a well (or many wells) from which a prospective king had to drink in order to earn his place on the throne.

Key Themes and Symbols

One of the main symbols of the Lady of the Lake is water. Because she lives underwater, she exists in a realm almost completely unknown to readers, which adds to her depiction as a symbol of mystery and magic. Water was also often used as a symbol of healing, which is illustrated in her treatment of Arthur after he falls on the battlefield.

The Lady of the Lake in Art, Literature, and Everyday Life

The Lady of the Lake, for being a rather minor character in Arthurian legend, has inspired many artists in various media over the centuries. Most notably, the 1810 poem *The Lady of the Lake* by Sir Walter Scott offered a re-telling of her myth set in a Scottish lake; this poem was the basis of a later opera by Italian composer Gioachino Rossini. The tale also loosely inspired the 1944 Raymond Chandler detective novel *The Lady in the Lake*, which was made into a film in 1947. The Lady of the Lake also makes a brief appearance in the 1981 John Boorman film *Excalibur*, as an arm that reaches up from the water to reclaim Excalibur when Arthur dies.

Read, Write, Think, Discuss

Viviane, the Lady of the Lake, is a main character in Marion Zimmer Bradley's 1979 fantasy novel *The Mists of Avalon*, which tells the tales of

Arthurian legend from the point of view of several female characters. The novel also explores the clash between Christian and pre-Christian beliefs in medieval England. The novel, which remains a popular title nearly thirty years after its publication, spawned an additional series of novels written by Bradley and, after her death, fantasy author Diana L. Paxson.

SEE ALSO Arthur, King; Lancelot; Merlin

Lancelot

Character Overview

In the medieval legends about King **Arthur** of Britain and his knights, Lancelot is the greatest knight of all. In time, however, Lancelot's love for **Guinevere** (pronounced GWEN-uh-veer), the king's wife, leads him to betray his king and sets in motion the fatal events that end Arthur's rule.

Like many **heroes** of myth and legend, Lancelot enjoyed a royal birth and an unusual upbringing. He was the son of King Ban of Benoic (BEN-uh-wik) in western France, but he was raised by a mysterious figure known as the **Lady of the Lake**, who appears in various roles in the Arthurian tales. For this reason, he is sometimes called Lancelot of the Lake.

The Lady of the Lake prepared the youth to excel in all the knightly virtues and pastimes and then presented him to King Arthur's court. There Lancelot became the foremost knight, the model of noble behavior, and the good friend of the king. However, Lancelot fell in love with Queen Guinevere—an event that would ultimately destroy Arthur's kingdom.

Some of Lancelot's knightly feats had to do with Guinevere. On one occasion, he rescued her after she had been kidnapped by a rival prince, but he had to swallow his pride and ride in a lowly cart to do so. The same prince later accused Guinevere of adultery, and Lancelot fought as her champion against the accuser. His love for Guinevere was such that he resisted the charms of a maiden called Elaine of Astolat (pronounced AS-tuh-laht), who died of love for him. Another Elaine, this one the daughter of King Pelleas (pronounced peh-lay-AHS), proved more

Nationality/Culture
Romano-British/Celtic

Pronunciation
LANS-uh-lot

Alternate Names
None

Appears In
Tales of King Arthur

Lineage
Son of King Ban

enterprising. She tricked Lancelot into sleeping with her, pretending that she was Guinevere. Elaine bore Lancelot's son, **Galahad** (pronounced GAL-uh-had), who grew into a pure and sinless knight. As Christian beliefs played an increasing role in the **Arthurian legends** over time, Galahad came to replace his flawed father as the supreme knight in tales of Arthur's Round Table.

The uproar over Lancelot's affair with Guinevere tore King Arthur's court apart—as those who opposed Arthur had hoped that it would. Some of the knights followed Lancelot to France and set up another court, while others remained with Arthur. The two sides went to war until a rebellion led by Arthur's nephew **Mordred** broke out and the king had to return to Britain to suppress it. Arthur was mortally wounded fighting against the rebel army and was carried away to the island of Avalon. When Lancelot returned to Britain, Arthur's court was no more. Guinevere, in the meantime, had become a nun. Lancelot followed her example and devoted himself to religious service as a monk until he died.

Lancelot in Context

Lancelot is generally considered to be a French contribution to the Arthurian legends. He first appears in the romances of the French writer Chrétien de Troyes in the 1100s. However, some students of mythology see Lancelot as a later version of Celtic heroes or even of older images of gods associated with lightning and fertility. The myth of Lancelot and Guinevere may have served as a cautionary tale about the dangers of adultery, especially after the rise of Christianity in western Europe. However, scholars have suggested that the tale was actually requested by a woman of French royalty as an example—and, therefore a justification—of a noblewoman taking a lover who was not her husband.

Key Themes and Symbols

In many ways, Lancelot is a symbol of perfect knighthood: noble, just, and always willing to defend a woman's honor. However, he also symbolizes the human weaknesses of lust and envy, shown by his pursuit of and affair with Guinevere. Indeed, one of the most important themes of the tale of Lancelot is that no man, however he might appear, is perfect.

Lancelot in Art, Literature, and Everyday Life

Although it appears to be a later contribution to the myths of King Arthur, the tale of Lancelot and Guinevere is one of the best-known stories in Arthurian legend. It has been retold countless times in many forms. T. H. White's third volume of *The Once and Future King* (1958) is a notable version of the myth. The 1960 musical *Camelot*, based on T. H. White's books, focuses on the affair between Lancelot and Guinevere, as does the 1995 film *First Knight*, starring Richard Gere as Lancelot and Sean Connery as King Arthur. Outside traditional Arthurian legend, Lancelot was the subject of a 1950s British television series. He is also portrayed as a violent fighter by John Cleese in the 1975 comedy film *Monty Python and the Holy Grail*.

Read, Write, Think, Discuss

According to the legend, Lancelot and Guinevere are good people who struggle against their feelings of love for each other, but, in the end, are powerless to resist their attraction. Their forbidden love eventually ruins both their lives and the reign of a good and wise king. What does this story reveal about this culture's perception of the nature of love, and do we see this same attitude in modern society?

SEE ALSO Arthur, King; Arthurian Legends; Galahad; Guinevere; Holy Grail; Lady of the Lake

Laocoön

Nationality/Culture
Greek/Roman

Pronunciation
lay-OK-oh-ahn

Alternate Names
None

Appears In
Virgil's *Aeneid*, Hyginus's *Fabulae*

Lineage
Son of Acoetes

Character Overview

In Greek and **Roman mythology**, Laocoön was a seer—a person who could foretell the future—and a priest of the god **Apollo** (pronounced uh-POL-oh) in the ancient city of Troy. He played a notable role in the last days of the Trojan War and met a violent death with his twin sons, Antiphantes (pronounced an-tuh-FAN-teez) and Thymbraeus (pronounced thim-BRAY-uhs).

Toward the end of the Trojan War, the Greeks placed a large wooden horse before the gates of Troy. Laocoön hurled a spear at it and warned the Trojans not to bring the horse into the city. He said, "I fear the Greeks even when they offer gifts." Soon afterward, the Trojans ordered Laocoön to **sacrifice** a bull to the god **Poseidon** (pronounced poh-SYE-dun). While he was making the sacrifice near the sea, two great serpents emerged from the water and crushed Laocoön and his sons to death. The Trojans interpreted this event as a sign of the gods' disapproval of Laocoön's prediction, and they brought the horse into the city—an action that led to their downfall. Hiding inside the horse were Greek soldiers, who sneaked out of the horse and opened the gates of Troy at night, allowing the Greek army to enter and destroy the city.

Some stories say that the death of Laocoön and his sons was punishment from **Athena** (pronounced uh-THEE-nuh) or Poseidon for warning the Trojans against the wooden horse. This is the reason given in the *Aeneid*, an epic by the Roman poet Virgil. According to other legends, however, Apollo sent the serpents to kill Laocoön as punishment for an earlier wrong—breaking his vow to the god that he would never marry or have children.

Laocoön in Context

In ancient Greece, many people believed in the power of **seers** and oracles, because it was believed they could communicate with the gods. The tale of Laocoön may have served as a reminder that seers and oracles should be obeyed rather than ignored. This tale also affirms the special powers of those who communicate with the gods; the other citizens of Troy, who come up with their own ideas to explain why Laocoön was killed, end up not listening to Laocoön's prediction and ultimately lose the Trojan War because of it.

Key Themes and Symbols

The myth of Laocoön centers on the themes of misinterpretation and the vengeance of the gods. The Trojans misinterpret the intentions of the Greeks who offer them the horse; later, when Laocoön is killed by sea serpents, the Trojans misinterpret his death as a sign to ignore his warning about the Greeks. Laocoön is killed by one of the gods out of vengeance, either for revealing the Greeks' plan or for disrespecting the gods in another way. The death of Laocoön foreshadows, or hints at, the coming fall of Troy.

Laocoön in Art, Literature, and Everyday Life

Although a minor character in stories of the Trojan War, Laocoön and his sons were immortalized in a famous marble monument attributed to three different sculptors from the island of Rhodes. The sculpture is currently on display in the Vatican Museums in Rome. Laocoön was also the subject of a play by Sophocles, but the play—like many other Greek works—has been lost.

Read, Write, Think, Discuss

During presidential election years, opinion pollsters constantly run surveys to gauge the popularity of the various candidates. Nearly every day, the results of a new poll are released showing which candidate is ahead. These polls serve as a sort of modern prophecy of the future. But, like the prophecy of Laocoön, the polls can have unexpected consequences. Do you think opinion polls are useful to potential voters? Are they useful to candidates? Why or why not?

SEE ALSO Animals in Mythology; Greek Mythology; Roman Mythology; Seers; Serpents and Snakes

Lares and Penates

Nationality/Culture
Roman

Pronunciation
LAIR-eez and puh-NAY-teez

Alternate Names
None

Appears In
Ovid's *Fasti*

Lineage
Varies

Character Overview

In **Roman mythology**, Lares and Penates were groups of deities, or gods, who protected the family and the Roman state. Although different in origin and purpose, the Lares and Penates were often worshipped together at household shrines.

Lares were considered spirits of the dead who had become divine, and they guarded homes, crossroads, and the city. Every Roman family had its own guardian, known as the *Lar familiaris* (pronounced lar-fuh-mil-ee-YAHR-iss), to protect the household and ensure that the family line did not die out. Each morning Romans prayed and made offerings to an image of the *Lar familiaris* kept in a family shrine. Deities known as *Lares compitales* (pronounced LAIR-eez kom-puh-TAY-leez), who guarded crossroads and neighborhoods, were honored in a festival called the Compitalia. Another group of deities, the *Lares praestites* (pronounced LAIR-eez pree-STYE-teez), served as the guardians of the city of Rome.

The Romans set up altars such as the one shown here, to the Lares. The Lares were spirits of the dead that guarded homes, crossroads, and cities. THE ART ARCHIVE/GIANNI DAGLI ORTI/THE PICTURE DESK, INC.

The Penates, originally honored as gods of the pantry, eventually became guardians of the entire household. They were associated with Vesta, the goddess of the hearth or household fireplace. The main function of the Penates was to ensure the family's welfare and prosperity. The public Penates, or *Penates publici*, served as guardians of the state and the object of Roman patriotism. According to legend, they were once the household gods of **Aeneas** (pronounced i-NEE-uhs), the mythical founder of the Roman Empire.

Major Myths

Few myths exist about the Penates and Lares, and the ones that do exist concern their lineage. King Servius Tullius, for example, was supposedly the son of a lar living in the royal palace; he went on to found the lares cult in towns and villages, including the festival of the Compitalia. The Lares praestites, on the other hand, were the result of the rape of the nymph Lara by the god Mercury.

Lares and Penates in Context

Lares and Penates illustrate the importance of preserving the family line in ancient Rome. Lares were believed to be dead ancestors who tried to help living members of the household preserve the family name, mostly by having children. Lares presided over major life changes, including birth, death, disease, the freeing of slaves, and a young person's passage from childhood to adulthood. The Penates, in their original form, ensured that the household contained enough food to support the family and therefore preserve its existence. As beings that participated in both the divine world and the world of humans, they served as a link between the two worlds to harmonize them.

Key Themes and Symbols

Lares and Penates are both represented as guardians in Roman mythology. They guard members of a household and protect travelers in certain places such as at crossroads or at sea. The hearth is often associated with Lares and Penates. The Greeks pictured Lares wearing crowns and drinking wine, sometimes in the company of half-men, half-goats called **satyrs**.

Lares and Penates in Art, Literature, and Everyday Life

Lares and Penates were often represented in a household by small statues kept in a special shrine. Lares statues wore short tunics and carried dishes to hold food or drink offered to them. Shrines honoring household gods have been uncovered by archaeologists in locations such as Pompeii.

Read, Write, Think, Discuss

City: A Story of Roman Planning and Construction by David Macaulay (1974) is an illustrated look at how the Romans went about constructing cities from the ground up. In addition to technical illustrations and information about architectural structures, Macaulay also delves into household dynamics and smaller details of everyday Roman life. The author has written and illustrated several other books similar in style, including *Pyramid*, *Cathedral*, and *Ship*.

SEE ALSO Aeneas; Roman Mythology

Lear, King

Character Overview

King Lear, a legendary ruler of ancient Britain, is a tragic figure who loses his authority through his own foolishness. One of the primary sources of King Lear's legend is the *History of the Kings of Britain* by the medieval English writer Geoffrey of Monmouth.

According to myth, the aging king decides to divide his kingdom among his three daughters and asks each of them to declare their love for him. King Lear's two oldest daughters, Regan and Goneril, flatter him with grand, but insincere, expressions of devotion. By contrast, Lear's youngest daughter, Cordelia, conveys only her natural, true love for her father.

Angered by what he perceives as Cordelia's insufficient love, Lear splits the kingdom between Regan and Goneril. Their treachery, however, soon becomes clear as they strip their father of all his authority and possessions. Lear then realizes the sincerity of Cordelia's love. Fearing that she will reject him because of the way that he treated her earlier, he goes to her and finds that she welcomes him with generosity and compassion. Lear eventually regains authority over his lands after joining Cordelia and her husband, and when he dies a few years later, Cordelia inherits the throne of Britain.

King Lear in Context

Most monarchies are inherited according to the common law right of primogeniture (pronounced pri-mo-JEN-i-chur), according to which the first-born son of the monarch inherits the crown and the entire

Nationality/Culture
British

Pronunciation
KING LEER

Alternate Names
None

Appears In
Geoffrey of Monmouth's *History of the Kings of Britain*, William Shakespeare's *King Lear*

Lineage
Son of King Bladud

estate. Difficulties arise when there is no obvious male heir, and many wars have been fought between family members struggling to assert their claims to power. The story of King Lear can be seen as a reflection of early British attitudes about the importance of male heirs. The problem of dividing up Lear's kingdom arises only because he has no sons, and must therefore pass his kingdom on to his daughters and their husbands.

Key Themes and Symbols

Flattery and greed are two important themes in the myth of King Lear. The king's two oldest daughters offer insincere flattery to their father in their attempts to secure more land for themselves. Cordelia, on the other hand, symbolizes true and sincere love, which is ultimately victorious over the fake emotions of her sisters.

King Lear in Art, Literature, and Everyday Life

The legendary king is best known through William Shakespeare's play *King Lear*. In this version, Lear goes mad after he is humiliated by his two older daughters. When Cordelia learns of her father's condition, she raises an army to fight her sisters' forces. Cordelia's army is defeated, and she is imprisoned and hanged. King Lear dies soon after, heartbroken over the death of his daughter.

The story of King Lear has been retold in many forms over the centuries. Two notable modern examples are Akira Kurosawa's 1985 film *Ran*, which switches the setting to medieval Japan and changes the daughters to sons, and Jane Smiley's 1991 Pulitzer Prize–winning novel *A Thousand Acres*, which adapts the King Lear myth to modern-day Iowa.

Read, Write, Think, Discuss

The story of King Lear emphasizes the importance of having a male heir in medieval Britain. Do you think modern society still places an importance on continuing family lines through male children, or do you think modern families treat males and females equally when it comes to carrying on the family legacy? Find examples that support your position.

SEE ALSO Celtic Mythology

Leprechauns

Character Overview

A leprechaun is a tiny elf or fairy from Irish folklore who is supposed to know the whereabouts of hidden treasure—usually a pot of gold. They are always male and were believed to have been featured in Irish folklore predating the Celts. Leprechauns are cobblers and shoemakers by trade.

According to most legends, a person who catches a leprechaun and threatens him may be able to convince him to reveal the location of his treasure, sometimes said to be at the end of a rainbow. However, finding a leprechaun is not easy. The best way is to sneak up while he is mending his shoes, the only time he sits still for very long. After catching a leprechaun, a person must stay alert because leprechauns are very clever and can easily outsmart humans.

Leprechauns are great mischief makers who often play pranks on people, such as riding their sheep or dogs during the night or causing small accidents around the house. Occasionally they "adopt" a family and faithfully follow the members during their travels. However, if not treated well, a leprechaun will abandon the family after causing trouble. Some stories claim that leprechauns are the offspring of evil spirits and bad fairies. However, one legend says that the leprechaun is actually the ancient Irish god **Lug**. After the Irish people forgot the old gods, the legend goes, Lug became a fairy cobbler named Lugh Chromain, which means "little stooping Lug."

Leprechauns in Context

Leprechauns are just one example of the many races of ancient creatures that lived in Ireland, according to Celtic belief. For the Celts, leprechauns are a connection to the land's ancient roots. The leprechaun's hidden pot of gold may reflect Celtic views of the land itself as a treasure to be appreciated.

Key Themes and Symbols

A leprechaun is traditionally pictured as an old man wearing a bright red vest, an old-fashioned cocked hat, a leather apron, and heavy leather

Nationality/Culture
Irish/Celtic

Pronunciation
LEP-ruh-kawnz

Alternate Names
None

Appears In
Irish folklore

Lineage
Varies

shoes with silver buckles. Only in the twentieth century did the standard image of a leprechaun come to include primarily green clothing, a color closely associated with their Irish roots. In the tales of leprechauns, the pot of gold symbolizes great wealth that can only be achieved by performing a nearly impossible feat. The rainbow's end is a symbol of an imaginary place that can never be reached. Most tales of leprechauns center on the theme of outwitting the cunning creature.

Leprechauns in Art, Literature, and Everyday Life

Leprechauns have appeared in many films, television shows, and commercials. The 1959 Disney classic *Darby O'Gill and the Little People* features a leprechaun king matching wits with a wily Irish grounds-keeper. The best-known leprechaun in modern times is Lucky the Leprechaun, the mascot for Lucky Charms breakfast cereal; Boston's NBA team, the Celtics, also has a leprechaun mascot, as does the college of Notre Dame, whose sports teams are known as the "Fighting Irish."

Read, Write, Think, Discuss

Mythical and magical creatures are often used as mascots for products such as snack foods and breakfast cereals. Using the Internet, your own kitchen cupboards, television commercials, or any other resource you can think of, find three more product mascots that resemble creatures or beings found in myth and folklore. Why do you think advertisers use these creatures? Do you think they are effective? Why or why not?

SEE ALSO Celtic Mythology; Dwarfs and Elves; Lug

Nationality/Culture
Greek/Roman

Pronunciation
LEE-thee

Alternate Names
None

Appears In
Ovid's *Metamorphoses*,
Virgil's *Aeneid*

Lethe

Myth Overview

In Greek and **Roman mythology**, Lethe (pronounced LEE-thee) was one of five rivers in the **underworld**, or the kingdom of the dead. Drinking from Lethe (whose name means "forgetfulness") caused the souls of the dead to forget all knowledge of their previous lives.

Lethe in Context

The ancient Greeks believed in the possibility of **reincarnation**: rebirth on Earth in a different body or form. The shades of the dead were supposed to drink from Lethe to purge themselves of past memories. Some Greek religious groups taught their members not to drink from Lethe after they died, however. They believed that it was important to remember the mistakes of one's past lives so that, when reborn, one would be wiser in the next life. Members of these sects were told to drink from a spring named Mnemosyne (pronounced nee-MOSS-uh-nee, meaning "memory") that was near Lethe.

Dante drinks from the river Lethe in this sculpture from the **Divine Comedy.** *Whoever drank from its waters would forget his past life.* © ALINARI ARCHIVES/THE IMAGE WORKS.

Key Themes and Symbols

Lethe represents the peace of forgetfulness. It is generally associated with the removal of painful memories or worries as opposed to the loss of cherished memories, although both are handled the same way by the river's powerful waters.

Lethe in Art, Literature, and Everyday Life

Springs called Lethe and Mnemosyne were located at a cave near the Greek town of Lebadeia. The cave was believed to be an entrance to the underworld. The river Lethe is an important part of a story about the **afterlife** told in Plato's *Republic*.

In modern times, the myth of Lethe has remained popular enough to be referenced in many works, including poems by John Keats, Lord Byron, Charles Baudelaire, and Edgar Allan Poe. Lethe has also found its way into Dante's *Divine Comedy*, Bram Stoker's *Dracula*, and three of William Shakespeare's plays.

Read, Write, Think, Discuss

The saying "ignorance is bliss" can be applied to the idea of washing away old memories in the waters of Lethe. The saying suggests that it is impossible to worry about or fear something if you do not know it exists. Do you think this is an effective way to deal with the potential risks found in the modern world? What do you think are the consequences of living a life in ignorance?

SEE ALSO Afterlife; Hades; Underworld

Leviathan

Character Overview

Nationality/Culture
Jewish/Christian

Pronunciation
luh-VYE-uh-thuhn

Alternate Names
None

Appears In
The Old Testament, the Talmud

Lineage
None

The sea serpent Leviathan is mentioned several times in the Old Testament of the Bible. Legends about this immense and powerful creature were based on earlier stories about **Tiamat** (pronounced TYAH-maht), a dragon defeated by the god **Marduk** (pronounced MAHR-dook) in a Babylonian (pronounced bab-uh-LOH-nee-uhn) creation myth. Later, a similar tale appeared among the ancient Canaanites (pronounced KAY-nuhn-eye-ts), who claimed that the god **Baal** (pronounced BAY-uhl) slaughtered an ancient seven-headed serpent named Lotan.

In the Bible, Leviathan roamed the sea, breathing **fire** and spewing smoke from his nostrils. The book of Psalms describes how the Hebrew god Yahweh (pronounced YAH-way) struggled with the many-headed Leviathan and killed it during a battle with the waters of chaos (disorder). Yahweh then created the universe, day and night, and the four seasons. Other versions state that Leviathan was made by Yahweh on the fifth day of creation. Scriptural references to the end of time say that the flesh of Leviathan will be part of a feast served on the Day of Judgment.

Leviathan in Context

It is not known whether the ancient peoples of the Near East viewed Leviathan as a mythical sea monster, a real creature, or a symbol for another culture, such as Egyptian or Roman. Many translations of the Old Testament refer to Leviathan as an animal, such as a crocodile.

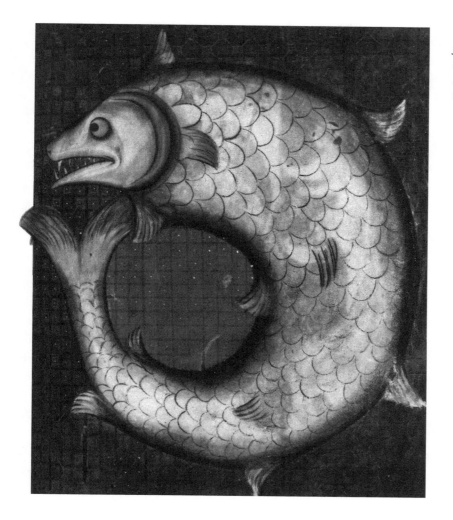

Considering the similarities to Babylonian myth and the relatively limited knowledge of sea life at the time, it seems likely that Leviathan was viewed as a very real and very powerful creation of Yahweh, unlike anything else in the sea.

Key Themes and Symbols

In ancient Jewish tradition, Leviathan represents the wild disorder that ruled the heavens before Yahweh created the universe. In this way, Leviathan did not represent evil, but instead symbolized a time before gods. The flesh of Leviathan, said to be feasted upon by the righteous on the Day of Judgment, represents a victory over godlessness. In Christian works, Leviathan is viewed more as a creature of evil.

Leviathan in Art, Literature, and Everyday Life

Although Leviathan is generally limited to appearances in religious texts, over the centuries the term has come to mean a large beast, especially one from the sea. In 1651, Thomas Hobbes used the name Leviathan in the title of a book about political philosophy to express the idea of society as a giant body ruled by a central sovereign figure. Herman Melville used the term Leviathan in his 1851 whaling novel *Moby Dick* to refer to the great white whale.

Read, Write, Think, Discuss

Ancient and modern cultures have been fascinated with the sea and its mysteries, and sea monsters have been one of the most popular animals in myths and fables. Some scholars argue that these monsters were either wholly imaginary or were real sea animals that the ancients either did not recognize or deliberately portrayed as exotic to make their stories more fantastic. So the question remains: Were sea monsters real animals that became myths; mythic figures that were eventually recognized as real animals; or entirely imaginary creatures? Select five sea monsters that have a mythic past, and using your library, the Internet, or other available resources, trace their history and their stories to see which category they best fit.

SEE ALSO Baal; Creation Stories; Dragons; Marduk; Semitic Mythology; Serpents and Snakes; Tiamat

Leza

Character Overview

Various Bantu-speaking peoples of central and southern Africa believe in a supreme deity or god called Leza. A sky god and creator spirit, Leza is believed to have once lived on earth and is the subject of several myths.

Nationality/Culture
African/Bantu

Pronunciation
LEE-zuh

Alternate Names
None

Appears In
Bantu creation myths

Lineage
None

Major Myths

According to a story told by the Basubiya people, Leza taught humans different arts as well as the proper way to worship him. When he finished, Leza climbed up a spiderweb to his home in the sky. The people tried to follow him, but the spiderweb broke and they fell to earth.

In a legend told by the Ila people, a woman who had lost all the members of her family decided to find Leza to ask him why he made her experience such sorrow. She built a ladder to the sky, but it crashed to earth. While searching for a road to the sky, she told the sad story to people she met. They explained that all people were meant to suffer, and that she was not alone in her sorrow. The woman never found Leza, and she, too, eventually died.

In yet another story, told by the Kaonde people, Leza once gave three gourds to a honeybird and instructed it to take them to humans. He told the bird that two of the gourds contained seeds and that humans could open these. The third gourd, however, should remain closed until Leza came to earth. While carrying the gourds, the bird became curious and opened all of them. Two held seeds, but the third contained death, sickness, and dangerous animals. Leza could not capture these unpleasant things, so humans were forced to build shelters to protect themselves.

Leza in Context

Leza is an example of how some African cultures viewed themselves as having a direct kinship with the gods. Leza is said to have once lived on earth as a human and to have been a very powerful chief. He later became the god of the sky and rain. This may indicate a legend about a specific tribal leader who died and became a subject of worship after he was gone.

Key Themes and Symbols

Leza is identified with the sky and rain. He is also presented in various myths as a provider and teacher. He gives seeds to the people so they can grow crops, and he teaches them about art and religious ceremonies. He is also the creator of disease and death, though he tries to protect people from these. This further shows him to be a guardian and protector of his people. In the myth of the Kaonde, the honeybird that opens the gourds symbolizes curiosity—a potentially dangerous quality that can lead to much trouble.

Leza in Art, Literature, and Everyday Life

Leza is a popular figure in Bantu-speaking cultures. In everyday Bantu expressions about weather he is credited as the bringer of rain. He is mentioned throughout Alice Werner's important 1933 work *Myths and Legends of the Bantu*, which brought many elements of Bantu mythology to the attention of the Western world.

Read, Write, Think, Discuss

Real people often become legendary characters through the re-telling of tales over the course of centuries. Imagine what kind of tale might be told about you five hundred years from now. What characteristics of yours would be remembered and emphasized? What real-life experiences of yours might be exaggerated into compelling myths? Try re-creating a real event into a myth about your legendary self.

SEE ALSO African Mythology

Lilith

Nationality/Culture
Jewish

Pronunciation
LIL-ith

Alternate Names
Lilitu

Appears In
The Talmud, *The Alphabet of Ben-Sira*, Jewish legends

Lineage
Created by God

Character Overview

In Jewish mythology Lilith was a female demon who killed newborn children in the night. She was associated with an ancient Babylonian (pronounced bab-uh-LOH-nee-uhn) demon called Lilitu, whose name often appeared in magical spells. According to a Jewish legend that appeared around the eighth century CE, Lilith was the original wife of Adam, the first man created by God. She often quarreled with Adam and eventually left him. God sent three **angels**—Senoy, Sansenoy, and Semangelof—to find Lilith and bring her back. They found her at the Red Sea, where she was giving birth daily to numerous demons. When Lilith refused to return to Adam, God punished her by causing one hundred of her children to die each day. He then created Eve to be Adam's companion.

Furious at her punishment, Lilith began to kill the newborn babies of others. Parents could protect their children from her attacks by placing near the child an amulet, or charmed object, bearing the names of the

three angels sent to find her. Through medieval times, Jewish people often kept amulets to ward off Lilith and her demon children, the *lilim*.

Lilith in Context

The myth of Lilith as Adam's first wife can be viewed as a cautionary tale to disobedient wives in ancient Jewish culture. Lilith is described as arguing with her husband and leaving him after he refuses to accept her as an equal. Lilith's negative qualities led to her giving birth to demons—a violation of all that is considered natural and right. This reflects the view that women were meant to obey their husbands, not try and function as their equals.

Key Themes and Symbols

In Jewish legend, the most well-known tale of Lilith paints her as a symbol of disobedience and conflict. She represents a violation of the

Evil, Scary Women

Female goddesses or mythological figures are sometimes associated with magic, darkness, and mysterious knowledge; rightly or wrongly, these figures are often considered evil. Other female goddesses are so ferocious and scary it is hard to imagine their good side.

Figure	Nationality	Description
Coatlicue	Mesoamerican	Both a mother goddess and goddess of death, Coatlicue is pictured with a face formed by two serpents; a skirt of writhing snakes; a necklace made of the hands, hearts, and skulls of her children; and sharp-clawed hands and feet for digging graves.
Hecate	Near Eastern/ Greek	Hecate is associated with the moon, the underworld, crossroads, and dark magic. She is eventually considered a goddess of witches.
Kali	Indian	Like Coatlicue, Kali is associated with both motherhood and death, and she is fearsome looking: she has four arms, with a sword in one hand and a demon's head in another. She is smeared with blood, has a skull necklace, and a skirt made of hands. Her skin is black, her tongue lolls out, and she is often pictured trampling Shiva.
Lilith	Jewish	Lilith was Adam's first wife. She quarreled with him a lot, and eventually left him. Afterwards, she gave birth to numerous demons. God ordered her to return to Adam, but she refused, so God began killing her children. In revenge, Lilith began killing newborns in the night.

ILLUSTRATION BY ANAXOS, INC./CENGAGE LEARNING, GALE.

natural and proper order of things, as shown by her abandonment of her husband and her delivery of demon children.

Lilith in Art, Literature, and Everyday Life

In ancient times, Lilith was depicted as a wicked creature. In modern times, however, Lilith has become something of a symbol for feminists. Her insistence on equality with Adam, once viewed negatively, is now seen by many as a trait worthy of praise. It is in this spirit that Lilith's name has been used by an award-winning Jewish feminist magazine, as well as an annual musical fair focusing on women performers, which occurred in the late 1990s.

Read, Write, Think, Discuss

In recent decades, women's rights have become an important issue in many countries. It is only within the past century that American women were granted the right to vote. How do you think this relatively recent shift affects modern views of ancient mythologies? Do you think ancient myths should be adjusted for modern readers in order to offer a more balanced image of women in ancient cultures? Why or why not?

SEE ALSO Adam and Eve; Angels; Devils and Demons; Semitic Mythology

Lir

Character Overview

Lir is the god of the sea in Irish and Welsh mythology. He was known during the time of the Tuatha Dé Danaan (pronounced TOO-uh-huh day DAH-nuhn), an ancient race of gods who conquered and ruled Ireland long before humans arrived. His most notable appearance is in *Children of Lir*, a tale from the Mythological Cycle of Irish legend.

Major Myths

The Tuatha Dé Danaan were ruled by a king named Bodb Dearg (pronounced boov DEERG), who was not liked by Lir. In an attempt to

Nationality/Culture
Irish/Welsh

Pronunciation
LEER

Alternate Names
Allod, Llyr (Welsh)

Appears In
Children of Lir

Lineage
Son of Elatha

make peace with Lir and maintain order in his kingdom, Bodb Dearg sent Lir one of his own daughters, Aoibh (pronounced EEV), to marry. Lir and Aoibh had four children, three sons and a daughter named Fionnuala (pronounced fin-NOO-lah). Unfortunately, Aoibh died, and Bodb, wanting to ease Lir's sadness, sent another one of his daughters to marry Lir and serve as the mother of his four children. This daughter, Aoife (pronounced EE-fah), was a cunning young woman well-versed in the arts of magic.

Aoife was jealous of the family bond between Lir and his children, and began plotting a way to get rid of the youngsters. After a plan to murder them failed, Aoife used her skills with magic to transform the children into swans. According to the spell, the children had to remain as swans for nine hundred years, spending three hundred years in each of three different places on or near the water. They would not change back into human form until church bells rang out in announcement of the coming of God.

When Aoife's father Bodb discovered what she had done, he turned her into a demon as punishment. The children spent three centuries at each of the required locations, and afterward were taken in at a monastery where they were chained together and protected by a monk named Mochua (pronounced MUK-oo-uh). When a local queen found out about the swans, she convinced her husband to attack the monastery and take the swans for her. After they were captured, the church bells rang out, transforming the swans back into children. Because so many centuries had passed, however, the children aged quickly and soon died. Soon after, the rest of the Tuatha Dé Danaan also died out, and a new race ruled the land.

Lir in Context

According to Irish history and legend, the island of Ireland has been ruled by many different groups over the centuries. The legendary version of this history is documented in the *Book of Invasions*, a list of the different ruling groups since the beginning of the world, as well as the battles they undertook. Many of these legendary invasions are clearly based on actual historical events; for example, the Milesians (pronounced mi-LEE-zhuhnz)—the group who, according to tradition, ruled Ireland after the Tuatha Dé Danaan—are most likely the Gaelic people, who invaded Ireland around the first century BCE.

Key Themes and Symbols

The most important theme in the tale of Lir's children is the death of old traditions and beliefs, coupled with the arrival of new beliefs. This is shown when the children are cursed to remain swans until church bells announce the coming of God; pre-Christian gods are ineffective against the curse, but the arrival of Christianity puts an end to it. The children are even baptized as Christians before they die. After they die, the Tuatha Dé Danaan—symbols of the old beliefs before Christianity—also fade away.

Lir in Art, Literature, and Everyday Life

Though he is described as a god of the sea, Lir appears in few Irish myths. However, the story of his children is one of the more popular tales from Irish legend, and Lir may have also served as the original inspiration for the later legend of **King Lear**. A park in Dublin known as the Garden of Remembrance contains a popular sculpture depicting the children of Lir; the statue is meant to compare their nine centuries of struggle with the struggles of the Irish people to gain independence from England.

Read, Write, Think, Discuss

Daughter of the Forest (2000), by Australian author Juliet Marillier, is largely a retelling of the legend of the children of Lir. In it, Sorcha is the daughter and youngest child of the warrior Lord Colum. One day her father brings home a new wife who, jealous of the children, casts a spell that turns Colum's six sons into swans. Sorcha escapes the same fate and finds that she is the only one who can save her brothers. The book is the author's first in a series of three, known collectively as the Sevenwaters Trilogy; the other two titles are *Son of the Shadows* (2001) and *Child of the Prophecy* (2002).

SEE ALSO Celtic Mythology; Dagda

Llyr

See **Lir.**

Loki

Nationality/Culture
Norse

Pronunciation
LOH-kee

Alternate Names
Sky Walker, Wizard of
Lies, Loge

Appears In
The Eddas

Lineage
Son of giants Fárbauti and
Laufey

Character Overview

In **Norse mythology**, Loki was a trickster god who caused endless trouble for the gods but who also used his cunning to help them. He lived in Asgard (pronounced AHS-gahrd), the home of the gods, and he served as a companion to the great gods **Thor** and **Odin** (pronounced OH-din). Loki enjoyed mischief and disguise and could change his form to imitate any animal. At first the gods found him amusing but eventually they became tired of his tricks and grew to dislike him.

Major Myths

Despite his mischievous nature, Loki helped the gods on many occasions. One time a giant, disguised as a builder, came to Asgard and offered to build a wall within a year and a half in exchange for **Freyja** (pronounced FRAY-uh), Odin's wife. Thinking the task was impossible, the gods agreed to the deal. The giant, however, had a powerful stallion that could perform great feats of labor. When it looked as if the giant would succeed, Loki disguised himself as a mare and lured the stallion away, preventing the wall from being completed. The mare later gave birth to an eight-legged horse, called Sleipnir (pronounced SLAYP-nir), which Loki gave as a gift to Odin.

Loki had a number of wives and children. With his second wife, the giantess Angrboda (pronounced AHNG-gur-boh-duh), he had three fearsome offspring: a supernatural being named **Hel**, a serpent named Jormungand (pronounced YAWR-moon-gahnd), and a wolf named **Fenrir** (pronounced FEN-reer). As these creatures grew larger and more terrifying, the gods decided to get rid of them. They cast Hel into the dismal realm called Niflheim (pronounced NIV-uhl-heym), where she became the goddess of the dead; they threw Jormungand into the sea; and they bound Fenrir with a magical ribbon and fastened him to a huge rock.

As time went on, Loki grew increasingly evil. Angry with the gods because they now disliked him, he arranged the death of Odin's son **Balder** (pronounced BAWL-der). Loki discovered that Balder could be harmed only by mistletoe. One day, while the gods were tossing objects at Balder in fun, Loki gave a piece of mistletoe to the blind god Höd and told him to throw it at Balder. The mistletoe struck Balder and killed him.

In honor of Balder the gods held a banquet, to which, naturally, Loki was not invited. But he showed up anyway, insulted the gods, and then fled again when they became angry. To escape detection, Loki disguised himself as a fish, but the gods knew his tricks by this time and caught him in a net.

To punish Loki, the gods captured two of his sons, Narfi and Vali. They turned Vali into a wolf and let him tear his brother Narfi to pieces. They then took Narfi's intestines and used them to tie Loki to rocks in a cave. A giantess named Skadi (pronounced SKAY-dee) hung a great snake over Loki's head, and when its venom dripped onto Loki's face it caused terrible pain. Loki would twist in agony, causing the whole world to shake. It is said that Loki will remain in that cave until **Ragnarok** (pronounced RAHG-nuh-rok), the end of the world, arrives.

Loki in Context

Loki fulfills the role of trickster in Norse mythology. As with other **tricksters**, he is often at odds with the supreme gods and is frequently viewed as an enemy. He is also seen by humans as a sometimes helpful god, as shown in a ballad that describes how Loki saved a farmer's son from a giant who was terrorizing him. Although Loki was not worshipped by the Norse people, his role in Norse mythology seems to have been an important one: he brings both entertainment and invention to the Norse gods.

Key Themes and Symbols

In Norse mythology, Loki represents many things, including wickedness, cunning, playfulness, and cowardice. He serves as an opposing force to Odin's bravery and strength. His wickedness is shown in his plot to kill Balder, while his cowardice and cunning are shown in his escapes from trouble—often through lies, promises, or a quick transformation into an animal. His playfulness is shown in his many bets with the other gods, especially Odin.

Loki in Art, Literature, and Everyday Life

Loki is a popular character in Norse mythology and appears in many illustrations of Norse myths. Artists such as Jon Bauer and Arthur

Rackham have created some of the most famous illustrations of Loki and his associates. Loki appears under the name Loge in composer Richard Wagner's 1869 opera *Das Rheingold*. More recently, Loki has appeared as a villain in the Marvel Comics' Universe. Much of the character's history and personality is carried over from the original Norse myths.

Read, Write, Think, Discuss

Mythical Detective Loki Ragnarok (2004), by Sakura Kinoshita, is a Japanese comic series that features unusual updated versions of the Norse gods and goddesses. In the first volume of the series, Loki is a teenage detective who must solve mysteries and, at the same time, figure out who is trying to kill him. The comic is written to appeal to those who are already familiar with Norse mythology. *Mythical Detective Loki Ragnarok* has also been adapted into a successful animated series.

SEE ALSO Balder; Fenrir; Freyja; Giants; Hel; Norse Mythology; Odin; Ragnarok; Thor; Tyr

Lucifer

See **Satan.**

Lug

Character Overview

An important and popular deity in **Celtic mythology**, Lug (or Lugh) was a god of the **sun** and light known for his handsome appearance and skills in arts and crafts. A protector of **heroes**, Lug appears in many Irish and Welsh legends. Lug is also the father of the famous Irish hero **Cuchulain**.

Major Myths

Lug was the son of Cian (pronounced KEE-an) and the grandson of Balor (pronounced BAH-lor), the king of the evil Fomorians (pronounced foh-MAWR-ee-uhnz), a race of violent beings who lived in darkness. Warned by a prophecy—or prediction—that he would be killed by his grandson, Balor locked his daughter, Ethlinn, in a crystal tower. In spite of his efforts, she gave birth to three children. Balor became furious and threw the infants into the ocean, but a Celtic priestess rescued one child and raised him in secret. According to some

Nationality/Culture
Irish/Celtic

Pronunciation
LOO

Alternate Names
Lámhfhada, Ildanach

Appears In
The Book of Invasions,
The Cattle Raid of Cooley,
other Celtic legends

Lineage
Son of Cian and Ethlinn

legends, Lug was raised by the blacksmith god Goibhniu (pronounced GOYV-noo), his father's brother.

When Lug reached manhood, he went to the court of Nuada (pronounced NOO-uh-duh), the ruler of the Tuatha Dé Danaan (pronounced TOO-uh-huh day DAH-nuhn), to offer his services as a warrior and master crafts worker. The Tuatha Dé Danaan, another race of supernatural beings, were the sworn enemies of the Fomorians. Lug soon became involved in the ongoing war between the two groups. Besides getting magic weapons from the craft gods Goibhniu, Luchta (pronounced LOOK-tuh), and Creidhne (pronounced KREV-nee), Lug also helped organize the military campaigns of the Tuatha Dé Danaan.

During one battle, King Nuada fell under the spell of Balor's evil eye, which had the power to destroy those who looked at it. Lug pierced the eye with a magic stone and killed Balor, thus fulfilling the prophecy and defeating the Fomorians as well. Lug became king of the Tuatha Dé Danaan, married the mortal woman Dechtire (pronounced DEK-tir-uh), and had a son named Cuchulain (pronounced koo-KUL-in), who became a great hero. In the saga *The Cattle Raid of Cooley*, Lug fought alongside Cuchulain in battle and soothed and healed him when he was wounded. Eventually defeated by invaders, the Tuatha Dé Danaan retreated underground and were gradually transformed into the fairies of Celtic folklore. Meanwhile, Lug became a fairy crafts worker known as Lugh Chromain, a name that later turned into leprechaun—the tiny sprite or goblin of Irish folklore.

Lug in Context

The legend of Lug illustrates a larger pattern of myth found in Celtic mythology that reveals much about the settlement of Ireland and surrounding areas. Celtic myths feature a recurring theme of different races battling for and gaining control over the land. This reflects a historical pattern of different waves of human settlers in Ireland. The history of Ireland is one of frequent invasion and conquest by various peoples, and it makes sense that this would be shown in the culture's mythology.

Key Themes and Symbols

In Celtic mythology Lug represents destiny and justice. After escaping from his evil grandfather's plot to kill him as an infant, Lug later joins forces with his grandfather's sworn enemies. He kills Balor on the battlefield, an act that fulfills an old prediction and exacts revenge for Balor's treatment of Lug. Lug, as a leader of the Tuatha Dé Danaan, also represents kingship.

Lug in Art, Literature, and Everyday Life

In Celtic art, Lug was usually depicted holding his two favorite weapons: a sling, which he used to kill Balor, and a magic spear that was powerful enough to fight on its own. Although not as popular as some other Celtic heroes, including his son Cuchulain, Lug remains an important part of Irish culture. Citizens in some areas of Ireland even claim to be descendants of Lug.

Read, Write, Think, Discuss

Compare the myth of Lug and Balor to the Greek story of **Cronus** and **Zeus**. How are the two tales similar? How are they different? Do you think the similarities suggest that one of the myths developed from the other, or do you think the two myths just happen to share themes that are important in many cultures?

SEE ALSO Celtic Mythology; Cuchulain; Dwarfs and Elves; Leprechauns

Where to Learn More

African

Altman, Linda Jacobs. *African Mythology.* Berkeley Heights, NJ: Enslow Publishers, 2003.

Ardagh, Philip, and Georgia Peters. *African Myths & Legends.* Chicago: World Book, 2002.

Giles, Bridget. *Myths of West Africa.* Austin, TX: Raintree Steck-Vaughn, 2002.

Husain, Shahrukh, and Bee Willey. *African Myths.* 1st ed. North Mankato, MN: Cherrytree Books, 2007.

Lilly, Melinda. *Spider and His Son Find Wisdom: An Akan Tale.* Vero Beach, FL: Rourke Press, 1998.

Lilly, Melinda. *Warrior Son of a Warrior Son: A Masai Tale.* Vero Beach, FL: Rourke Press, 1998.

Lilly, Melinda. *Zimani's Drum: A Malawian Tale.* Vero Beach, FL: Rourke Press, 1998.

Schomp, Virginia. *The Ancient Africans.* New York: Marshall Cavendish Benchmark, 2008.

Seed, Jenny. *The Bushman's Dream: African Tales of the Creation.* 1st American ed. Scarsdale, NY: Bradbury Press, 1975.

Anglo-Saxon/Celtic

Ardagh, Philip, and G. Barton Chapple. *Celtic Myths & Legends.* Chicago: World Book, 2002.

Crossley-Holland, Kevin, and Peter Malone. *The World of King Arthur and His Court: People, Places, Legend, and Lore.* New York: Dutton Children's Books, 2004.

Hicks, Penelope, and James McLean. *Beowulf.* New York: Kingfisher, 2007.

Lister, Robin, Alan Baker, and Sir Thomas Malory. *The Story of King Arthur.* Boston: Kingfisher, 2005.

Martell, Hazel Mary. *The Celts.* 1st American ed. New York: Peter Bedrick, 2001.

Morris, Gerald. *The Lioness & Her Knight.* Boston: Houghton Mifflin, 2005.

Whittock, Martyn J. *Beliefs and Myths of Viking Britain.* Oxford: Heinemann, 1996.

Williams, Marcia, ed. *Chaucer's Canterbury Tales.* London: Walker, 2008.

Asian/Pacific

Behnke, Alison. *Angkor Wat.* Minneapolis: Twenty-First Century Books, 2008.

Carpenter, Frances. *Tales of a Korean Grandmother.* Boston: Tuttle Pub., 1973.

Coburn, Jewell Reinhart. *Encircled Kingdom: Legends and Folktales of Laos.* Rev. ed. Thousand Oaks, CA: Burn, Hart, 1994.

Coulson, Kathy Morrissey, Paula Cookson Melhorn, and Hmong Women's Project (Fitchburg, MA). *Living in Two Worlds: The Hmong Women's Project.* Ashburnham, MA: K. M. Coulson and P. C. Melhorn, 2000.

Dalal, Anita. *Myths of Oceania.* Austin, TX: Raintree Steck-Vaughn, 2002.

Green, Jen. *Myths of China and Japan.* Austin, TX: New York: Raintree Steck-Vaughn Publishers, 2002.

Htin Aung, U., G. Trager, and Pau Oo Thet. *A Kingdom Lost for a Drop of Honey, and Other Burmese Folktales.* New York: Parents' Magazine Press, 1968.

Kanawa, Kiri Te. *Land of the Long White Cloud: Maori Myths, Tales, and Legends.* 1st U.S. ed. New York: Arcade Pub., 1989.

Sakairi, Masao, Shooko Kojima, and Matthew Galgani. *Vietnamese Fables of Frogs and Toads.* Berkeley, CA: Heian International, 2006.

Sakairi, Masao, Shooko Kojima, and Matthew Galgani. *Vietnamese Tales of Rabbits and Watermelons.* Berkeley, CA: Heian International, 2006.

Egyptian

Ardagh, Philip, and Danuta Mayer. *Ancient Egyptian Myths & Legends.* Chicago: World Book, 2002.

Broyles, Janell. *Egyptian Mythology.* 1st ed. New York: Rosen Pub. Group, 2006.

Cline, Eric H., and Jill Rubalcaba. *The Ancient Egyptian World.* California ed. New York: Oxford University Press, 2005.

Gleason, Katherine. *Ancient Egyptian Culture.* New York: Newbridge Educational Pub., 2006.

Kramer, Ann. *Egyptian Myth: A Treasury of Legends, Art, and History.* Armonk, NY: Sharpe Focus, 2008.

Kudalis, Eric. *The Royal Mummies: Remains from Ancient Egypt.* Mankato, MN: Capstone High-Interest Books, 2003.

McCall, Henrietta. *Gods & Goddesses in the Daily Life of the Ancient Egyptians.* Columbus, OH: Peter Bedrick Books, 2002.

Mitchnik, Helen. *Egyptian and Sudanese Folk-Tales.* New York: Oxford University Press, 1978.

Schomp, Virginia. *The Ancient Egyptians.* New York: Marshall Cavendish Benchmark, 2008.

Wyly, Michael J. *Death and the Underworld.* San Diego, CA: Lucent Books, 2002.

Greek/Roman

Bingham, Jane. *Classical Myth: A Treasury of Greek and Roman Legends, Art, and History.* Armonk, NY: M. E. Sharpe, 2008.

Hepplewhite, Peter, and Mark Bergin. *The Adventures of Perseus.* Minneapolis, MN: Picture Window Books, 2005.

Lister, Robin, Alan Baker, and Homer. *The Odyssey.* Reformatted ed. Boston: Kingfisher, 2004.

McCarty, Nick, Victor G. Ambrus, and Homer. *The Iliad.* Reformatted ed. Boston: Kingfisher, 2004.

Mellor, Ronald, and Marni McGee. *The Ancient Roman World.* New York: Oxford University Press, 2005.

Roberts, Russell. *Athena.* Hockessin, DE: Mitchell Lane Publishers, 2008.

Roberts, Russell. *Dionysus.* Hockessin, DE: Mitchell Lane Publishers, 2008.

Roberts, Russell. *Zeus.* Hockessin, DE: Mitchell Lane Publishers, 2008.

Schomp, Virginia. *The Ancient Romans.* New York: Marshall Cavendish Benchmark, 2008.

Spires, Elizabeth, and Mordicai Gerstein. *I Am Arachne: Fifteen Greek and Roman Myths.* New York: Frances Foster Books, 2001.

Whiting, Jim. *The Life and Times of Hippocrates.* Hockessin, DE: Mitchell Lane Publishers, 2007.

Hindu

Choudhury, Bani Roy, and Valmiki. *The Story of Ramayan: The Epic Tale of India.* New Delhi: Hemkunt Press; Pomona, CA: Distributed in North America by Auromere, 1970.

Dalal-Clayton, Diksha, and Marilyn Heeger. *The Adventures of Young Krishna: The Blue God of India.* New York: Oxford University Press, 1992.

Ganeri, Anita. *The* Ramayana *and Hinduism.* Mankato, MN: Smart Apple Media, 2003.

Ganeri, Anita, and Carole Gray. *Hindu Stories.* Minneapolis: Picture Window Books, 2006.

Ganeri, Anita, and Tracy Fennell. *Buddhist Stories.* Minneapolis: Picture Window Books, 2006.

Husain, Shahrukh, and Bee Willey. *Indian Myths.* London: Evans, 2007.

Kipling, Rudyard. *The Jungle Book.* New York: Sterling Pub., 2008.

Parker, Vic, and Philip Ardagh. *Traditional Tales from India.* Thameside Press; North Mankato, MN: Distributed in the United States by Smart Apple Media, 2001.

Sharma, Bulbul. *The* Ramayana *for Children.* Penguin Global, 2004.

Staples, Suzanne Fisher. *Shiva's Fire.* 1st ed. New York: Farrar Straus Giroux, 2000.

Judeo-Christian

Geras, Adele. *My Grandmother's Stories: A Collection of Jewish Folk Tales.* New York: Alfred A. Knopf, 2003.

Kimmel, Eric A., and John Winch. *Brother Wolf, Sister Sparrow: Stories about Saints and Animals.* 1st ed. New York: Holiday House, 2003.

Schwartz, Howard, and Barbara Rush. *The Diamond Tree: Jewish Tales from Around the World.* 1st Harper Trophy ed. New York: HarperTrophy, 1998.

Schwartz, Howard, and Stephen Fieser. *Invisible Kingdoms: Jewish Tales of Angels, Spirits, and Demons.* 1st ed. New York: HarperCollins Publishers, 2002.

Self, David, and Nick Harris. *Stories from the Christian World.* Englewood Cliffs, NJ: Silver Burdett Press, 1988.

Senker, Cath. *Everyday Life in the Bible Lands.* North Mankato, MN: Smart Apple Media, 2006.

Taback, Simms. *Kibitzers and Fools: Tales My Zayda (Grandfather) Told Me.* New York: Puffin, 2008.

Native American

Ardagh, Philip, and Syrah Arnold. *South American Myths & Legends.* Chicago: World Book, 2002.

Berk, Ari, and Carolyn Dunn Anderson. *Coyote Speaks: Wonders of the Native American World.* New York: Abrams Books for Young Readers, 2008.

Brown, Virginia Pounds, Laurella Owens, and Nathan H. Glick. *Southern Indian Myths and Legends.* Birmingham, AL: Beechwood Books, 1985.

Curry, Jane Louise. *The Wonderful Sky Boat and Other Native American Tales from the Southeast.* New York: Margaret K. McElderry, 2001.

Monroe, Jean Guard, and Ray A. Williamson. *They Dance in the Sky: Native American Star Myths.* Award ed. Boston: Houghton Mifflin, 1993.

Parker, Victoria. *Traditional Tales from South America.* North Mankato, MN: Thameside Press. Distributed in the United States by Smart Apple Media, 2001.

Philip, Neil. *The Great Mystery: Myths of Native America.* New York: Clarion Books, 2001.

Pijoan, Teresa. *White Wolf Woman: Native American Transformation Myths.* 1st ed. Little Rock, AR: August House Publishers, 1992.

Ramen, Fred. *Native American Mythology.* 1st ed. New York: Rosen Central, 2008.

Schomp, Virginia. *The Native Americans.* New York: Marshall Cavendish Benchmark, 2008.

Vogel, Carole G. *Weather Legends: Native American Lore and the Science of Weather.* Brookfield, CT: Millbrook Press, 2001.

Near Eastern/Islamic

Ganeri, Anita. *Islamic Stories.* 1st American ed. Minneapolis, MN: Picture Window Books, 2006.

Grimal, Pierre. *Stories from Babylon and Persia.* Cleveland, OH: World Pub, 1964.

Ibrahim, Abdullahi A. *Enuma Elish.* Austin, TX: Steck-Vaughn Co., 1994.

Jabbari, Ahmad. *Amoo Norooz and Other Persian Folk Stories.* Costa Mesa, CA: Mazda Publishers, 2000.

León, Vicki. *Outrageous Women of Ancient Times.* New York: Wiley, 1998.

Marston, Elsa. *Figs and Fate: Stories about Growing Up in the Arab World Today.* 1st ed. New York: George Braziller, 2005.

Marston, Elsa. *Santa Claus in Baghdad and Other Stories about Teens in the Arab World.* Bloomington: Indiana University Press, 2008.

McCaughrean, Geraldine. *Gilgamesh the Hero.* Oxford: Oxford University Press, 2002.

Podany, Amanda H., and Marni McGee. *The Ancient Near Eastern World.* New York: Oxford University Press, 2005.

Schomp, Virginia. *The Ancient Mesopotamians.* New York: Marshall Cavendish Benchmark, 2008.

Walker, Barbara K. *Turkish Folk-Tales.* Oxford: Oxford University Press, 1993.

Norse/Northern European

Andersen, H. C., Diana Frank, Jeffrey Frank, Vilhelm Pedersen, and Lorenz Frolich. *The Stories of Hans Christian Andersen: A New Translation from the Danish.* Durham: Duke University Press, 2005.

Ardagh, Philip, and Stephen May. *Norse Myths & Legends.* Chicago: World Book, 2002.

Branford, Henrietta, and Dave Bowyer. *The Theft of Thor's Hammer.* Crystal Lake, IL: Rigby Interactive Library, 1996.

D'Aulaire, Ingri, and Edgar Parin. *D'Aulaires' Book of Norse Myths.* New York: New York Review of Books, 2005.

Evan, Cheryl, and Anne Millard. *Usborne Illustrated Guide to Norse Myths and Legends.* London: Usborne, 2003.

Jones, Gwyn, and Joan Kiddell-Monroe. *Scandinavian Legends and Folk-Tales.* New ed. Oxford: Oxford University Press, 1992.

Osborne, Mary Pope. *Favorite Norse Myths.* New York: Scholastic, 2001.

Porterfield, Jason. *Scandinavian Mythology.* New York: Rosen Central, 2008.

Web Sites

American Folklore. http://www.americanfolklore.net/ (accessed on June 11, 2008).

The British Museum: Mesopotamia. http://www.mesopotamia.co.uk/menu.html (accessed on June 11, 2008).

The Camelot Project at the University of Rochester. http://www.lib.rochester.edu/CAMELOT/cphome.stm (accessed on June 11, 2008).

Common Elements in Creation Myths. http://www.cs.williams.edu/~lindsey/myths (accessed on June 11, 2008).

Egyptian Museum Official Site. http://www.egyptianmuseum.gov.eg/ (accessed on June 11, 2008).

Internet History Sourcebooks Project. http://www.fordham.edu/halsall/ (accessed on June 11, 2008). Last updated on December 10, 2006.

Iron Age Celts. http://www.bbc.co.uk/wales/celts/ (accessed on June 11, 2008).

Kidipede: History for Kids. http://www.historyforkids.org/ (accessed on June 11, 2008).

Mythography. http://www.loggia.com/myth/myth.html (accessed on June 11, 2008). Last updated on April 17, 2008.

National Geographic. http://www.nationalgeographic.com/ (accessed on June 11, 2008).

NOVA Online: The Vikings. http://www.pbs.org/wgbh/nova/vikings/ (accessed on June 11, 2008).

Perseus Project. http://www.perseus.tufts.edu/ (accessed on June 11, 2008).

Sanskrit Documents. http://sanskritdocuments.org/ (accessed on June 11, 2008). Last updated on February 2, 2008.

United Nations Educational, Scientific and Cultural Organization. http://portal. unesco.org/ (accessed on June 11, 2008).

World Myths & Legends in Art. http://www.artsmia.org/world-myths/artbycul-ture/index.html (accessed on June 11, 2008).

Italic type indicates volume number; **boldface** type indicates main entries and their page numbers; (ill.) indicates photos and illustrations.

H

J

M

O

P

S